THE 24 UNDENIABLE LAWS OF SUCCESS

Be All You Can Be and Bring Out The Best in Others

John C. Maxwell

Strand Publishing
Sydney

This edition issued by special arrangement with Chariot Victor Publishing, Colorado Springs, Colorado, U.S.A.

Original title: *Be All You Can Be* and *Be a People Person* by John C. Maxwell.

ISBN 187 682 560X

First one volume Strand edition 2000

Distributed in Australia by:
Family Reading Publications,
B100 Ring Road,
Ballarat, Victoria, 3352.
Phone: (03) 5334 3244.
Fax: (03) 5334 3299.
Email: enquiries@frp.com.au
Web: www.familyreading.com.au

Typeset and designed by Midland Typesetters, Maryborough, Victoria
Printed in Australia by Australian Print Group, Maryborough, Victoria

Contents

Part 1
BE ALL YOU CAN BE

1

FRUITFULNESS IS FUN!

IN JOHN 15, Jesus says that fruitfulness is fun. In fact, the theme of John 15 is that Jesus wants us to live fruitful lives. Look at verse 16: 'You did not choose Me, but I chose you, and appointed you, that you should go and bear fruit, and that your fruit should remain, that whatever you ask of the Father in My name, He may give it to you.'

Let me share with you what I consider to be fruitfulness according to the Bible. When God speaks in His Word of a fruitful life, He means active, positive attitudes. The passage of Scripture that deals with the fruit of the Spirit, Galatians 5:22–23, is the premier passage on fruitful living. 'The fruit of the Spirit is love, joy, peace, patience, kindness, goodness, faithfulness, gentleness, self-control; against such things there is no law.' Fruitfulness is exhibiting positive, active attitudes on a daily basis in our lives. When that happens, we begin to sense real joy and to see positive things happen in our lives. When we put these attitudes together, five 'PRs' appear.

First of all, there are *positive results.* When you begin to inject these attitudes into your society, you're going to see constructive results.

You're going to have *positive relationships.* You will begin to develop fruitful relationships with others.

You're going to have *positive reactions,* especially in areas that were previously tough problem areas for you. You're going to find that you receive reactions that are positive when you begin to have these active, positive attitudes.

You'll receive *positive reinforcement.* Life is like a mirror: what you show is what you see; what you put in is what you get out. When you encourage others, you'll find that they will encourage you. Attitudes are contagious.

Last, you'll have *positive rejoicing.* That's what Jesus says in John 15:11. 'These things I have spoken to you, that My joy may be in you, and that your joy may be made full.' People often tell me they're not happy; they say they're unfulfilled. They talk about not having joy in their lives. I get the impression that seeking for joy has become their purpose in life—but joy (or happiness or fulfillment) comes to us not when we seek it, but when we put the right principles into practice in our lives. It is a by-product of doing what is right.

It is when we live by the right principles that we begin to love the right principles. Most of the time, we want to *love* first. We want to fall in love with what is right and then have it happen to us. That's backward—it's when we learn what's right and live according to it that we begin to *want* to be right; then we begin to have the by-product, which is joy. You have probably seen the bumper sticker that asks, 'Are we having fun yet?' Every time I see that bumper sticker, I want to write another one: 'Are we doing right yet?' If we're doing right, we'll be having fun.

OUR POWER SOURCE

In John 15:1–10, Jesus gives us the principles of fruitful living. Let's look at them together. First, our potential for fruitful living is unlimited because of our source. Jesus starts by saying, 'I am the true vine' (v. 1). Jesus is our source. When we realize that, then we understand why Paul could say, 'I can do all things through Christ who strengthens me' (Phil. 4:13). We become fruitful when we tap into the right source.

A friend of mine was discussing the implications of Micah 6:8 with his seven-year-old grandson: 'What does the Lord require of you but to do justice, to love kindness, and to walk humbly with your God?' The little boy, who was memorizing this verse, said, 'Grandpa, it's hard to be humble if you're really walking with God.' That's great theology coming from a seven-year-old. When we begin to get a glimpse of the unlimited resources at our disposal—the power of God Himself—then and only then will we sense the assurance that we are fully equipped to do whatever it is that God calls us to do.

We might feel like the little mouse who was crossing a bridge over a very deep ravine with an elephant. As the elephant and the mouse crossed the bridge, the bridge shook. When they got to the other side, the mouse looked at his huge companion and said, 'Boy, we really shook that bridge, didn't we?'

When we walk with God, that's often how we feel—like a mouse with the strength of an elephant. After crossing life's troubled waters, we can say with the mouse, 'God, we really shook that bridge, didn't we?'

Hudson Taylor, the great missionary to China, said, 'Many Christians estimate difficulty in the light of their own resources, and thus they attempt very little, and they always fail. All giants have been weak men who did great things for God because they reckoned on His power and His presence to be with them.'

Like David, who said, 'The battle is the Lord's' (1 Sam. 17:47), we also need to understand that Jesus is our source, and we can be directly connected to Him.

THE CARE OF OUR OWNER

In this passage of Scripture, Jesus says that we have potential for fruitful living not only because of our source but because of our care. Just as Jesus is the source, the Father is the vinedresser. The vinedresser takes care of the vine; he would be a man of skill and knowledge, an expert at growing grapes. But in this passage of Scripture, He is also the owner. When you think of an owner, you think of personal interest. You think of commitment—something more than knowledge and skill. As branches we not only have our source from the vine, but we have God who oversees us, takes care of us, and prepares us to be productive and fruitful.

You've probably noticed that the person who owns something, whatever it is, has a certain pride that a mere observer never has. I remember when I was a little kid, my grandfather often walked me around his farm. As we walked and looked, he would find uniqueness and beauty in things I wouldn't have looked at twice. He would see great potential in a run-down shed on a back lot; I would see kindling. He would show me a rusty, old tractor and see a machine with possibilities; I would see a piece of rust-covered junk. Why? How could we look at the same objects and see different things? He owned them and I didn't. Ownership makes a difference. God owns us, so when He looks at our lives, He looks at them not as an observer but as an investor.

OUR PRUNING

Our potential for fruitful living is great because Jesus is our source. The fact that God is our caretaker and owner adds to that potential. One of the things God does as vinedresser is to prune us. His pruning greatly increases our potential for fruitful living. 'Every branch that bears fruit, He prunes it, that it may bear more fruit' (v. 2). God, the vinedresser, removes everything that hinders our usefulness. He knows that if He doesn't cut back the deadwood, all of our resources will go toward producing more wood and we won't be fruit producers.

I have found that productive people are continually being pruned, going through this process that God uses to make us more fruitful. And God knows exactly what to prune from our lives. He's like the professional logger, who, when there's a jam on the river, climbs a tall tree, looks over all the logs, and identifies the problem area. Then he takes a little bit of dynamite and blows that part up so the logs can continue to flow downriver. Now, that's not the way I'd do it. I would probably jump in and start knocking logs around until I finally worked my way to the problem area. But God doesn't mess around with the peripherals. He goes right in with His dynamite and blows up only the areas in our lives that aren't productive. He cuts away that 'sin which so easily entangles us' (Heb. 12:1), whatever it is that keeps us from becoming the persons we really want to become.

OUR PARTNERSHIP

Our potential for fruitfulness is also tremendous because of our partnership. In verse 4, Jesus talks about this partnership. (And in fact, you can see it throughout the passage.) 'Abide in Me, and I in you. As the branch cannot bear fruit of itself, unless it abides in the vine, so neither can you, unless you abide in Me.' Ten times in verses 4–10 we see the word *abide.* Basically He's saying, 'Connect with the vine, and everything will be fine.' When Robert Morrison was on his way to China, where he would be a missionary, the captain of the ship was skeptical of his dream and gave him a hard time. As Morrison was leaving the ship, the captain said to him, 'I suppose you think you're going to make an impression on China.' Robert Morrison replied simply, 'No, sir. I believe God will.' He was in partnership with God.

This partnership with God ought to give us the same sense of confidence as the youngster had who was selling five-cent pencils door-to-door to raise money for a 30-million-dollar hospital for the community. One day a woman opened the door, and he said, 'Ma'am, would you buy one or two pencils from me? I'm going to help build a 30-million-dollar hospital for our community.' She said, 'Sonny, that's a mighty big goal for just one kid selling pencils for a nickel.' He said, 'Oh, Ma'am, it's not me alone. See that boy across the street? He's my partner. He's helping. We're really doing it together.' This little boy had great faith in a partner who was probably his equal. Should we not have this kind of confidence in a God who is unequalled, a God who is in partnership with us to make our lives fruitful?

OUR PROMISE

We also have potential for fruitfulness because of the promise given to us in verse 7. 'If you abide in Me, and My words abide in you, ask whatever you wish, and it shall be done for you.' There are two observations I would like to make. First, the promise is conditional: *if* we abide in Him. Second, our asking needs to be according to His Word. What Jesus is really saying is that if we abide in Him, our delight will be in Him, so much so that we will ask all things according to His will. It reminds me of Psalm 37:4: 'Delight yourself in the Lord; and He will give you the desires of your heart.' Delight comes before desire. If I delight, what I delight in determines what I desire. If I delight in God, my desire will be to do things according to His will and to ask according to His will. Too often we try to make this principle work in reverse.

As a high school student, one of my chores was to do the

dinner dishes. I hated doing the dishes. I was dating Margaret at the time, and often the prospect of seeing her in the evening outweighed my sense of duty at home, so I would jump in the car and be gone before I was missed. When I got to her house, you can guess what she was doing! I would immediately pick up a towel and begin drying dishes—and have a wonderful time doing it! The person I delighted in was doing dishes, and when you really delight in someone, you enjoy doing things you normally dislike. So often we lack desire because our delight is not great enough. God promises us that if we delight in Him, we will desire things we need, and He will give them to us.

OUR LIFE'S PURPOSE

Our potential for fruitfulness is great because of the purpose in our lives. That's in verse 8: 'By this is My Father glorified, that you bear much fruit, and so prove to be My disciples.' In other words, we are created to be fruitful. That's our purpose. Look at verse 16: 'You did not choose Me, but I chose you, and appointed you.' Why? 'That you should go and bear fruit,' that you should have active, positive attitudes in your life. We have been chosen, appointed by God, for fruitful living. Those active, positive attitudes, like love, joy, peace, and long-suffering, ought to be becoming part of our lives. When they become part of us inwardly, then we begin to pass them on.

The problem so often with us Christians is that we do not show these positive attitudes that can make us salt and light in our world. The story is told that when Berlin was being divided into East Berlin, controlled by the Communists, and West Berlin, part of the free world, a group of East Berliners dumped a whole truckload of garbage on the west side. The people from West Berlin thought they'd pick up all the garbage, put it on a truck, and dump it back on the east side. Then they decided that wasn't the way to handle it. Instead they filled a dump truck with canned goods and other non-perishable food items, went over to the east side, stacked it neatly, and put a sign beside it. The sign read, 'Each gives what each has to give.' I think they were preaching, don't you? You can only give fruit to others when you are living a fruitful life inwardly.

THE FRUIT OF OBEDIENCE

Our potential for fruitfulness is tremendous because of our obedience. Jesus says in verses 7 and 10 that if we abide in Him and if we keep His commandments, we will be fruitful. I think the key word is that little *if*: I have a mug at home that says, 'If it's to be, it's up to me.' I think that's what Jesus is saying. He says if you're going to be fruitful, it's going to be up to you. Jesus assumes in John 15 that He will have a fruitful relationship with us. In verse 6 He says, 'If anyone does not abide in Me.' He doesn't say, 'If I do not abide in you.' He's going to be plugged into us. His question for us is, Are you going to be plugged into Me? He's already here; He has the power; He has the strength; He has the wisdom to implant in us; He has all the resources that we need, and He's ready to deliver. All we need to do is to plug into Him.

Why don't we always abide in Him? Pure lack of obedience. We begin to think that we can do it on our own; we begin to have an unhealthy self-confidence instead of a Christ-confidence. When we do not have active, positive attitudes, it is because we aren't plugged into the vine. Christians should not have to psych themselves up every day, as the world does, to have active, positive attitudes. It will be as natural as breathing when the relationship is right. Jesus is saying that when the relationship is right, we begin to live fruitful lives. That's when we really begin to become productive.

Everybody wants to be productive. A psychologist at Stanford University tried to show that we live for productive results, or fruit. This researcher hired a man—a logger. He said, 'I'll pay you double what you get paid in the logging camp, if you'll take the blunt end of this axe and just pound this log all day. You never have to cut one piece of wood. Just take the end that is blunt and hit it as hard as you can, just as you would if you were logging.' The man worked for half a day and he quit. The psychologist asked, 'Why did you quit?' The logger said, 'Because every time I move an axe, I have to see the chips fly. If I don't see the chips fly, it's no fun.' I'm convinced that there are many Christians who are using the wrong ends of their axes, and there are no chips flying. In other words, they are producing no fruit, and their joy is gone. Joy has been replaced by a sense of futility, uselessness, immobility. Fruitful people like to see the chips fly.

FORMULA FOR FRUITFULNESS

Jesus gives us a three-word formula for fruitfulness in John 15. These three words are the ones I want you to remember, because they are the key to fruitful living. The first word is *remain.* Throughout John 15 Jesus tells us to remain. In fact, the word *abide* in the original language can be translated 'remain.' 'Remain in Me,' Jesus says. He's talking about our willingness to take time with Him in prayer and in study of the Word. We need to let Him begin to be part of our lives and work on our lives.

The second word in the formula is *receive.* Jesus says in John 15 that if we remain in Him, we will begin to receive certain things. What we'll receive is good, fruitful living.

The third word is *reproduce.* If we remain in Him, we're going to receive what He has for us. When we receive what He has for us, then and only then will we begin to reproduce in our lives.

FRUITFUL FOLLOW-UP

Let me give you a couple of suggestions for applying these things to your life. First of all, I would encourage you to commit yourself *now* to a productive lifestyle. Climb out on the limb; that's where the fruit is. All great accomplishments have to begin with an initial decision. Make up your mind that you're going to be a fruitful Christian, that you're going to begin to reproduce for Christ.

Second, follow the formula for fruitfulness I just gave you, and follow it daily. *Remain* by spending perhaps fifteen minutes in prayer and meditation daily. *Receive* by spending thirty minutes every day in the Word of God, positive books, and teaching tapes. Feed your mind on things that will help you think right and then reproduce. Find someone—today, not tomorrow—with whom you can share maybe one of the truths you learned from this chapter. Pass it on. One of the quickest ways to grow is to tell someone else what you just learned. The more you verbalize it, the more it becomes ingrained in your life.

Third, list the seeds that you are planting in your life. What things are you doing right now that are going to help you to be fruitful? Think not only of today but also of a year from now and five years from now. What are you investing in the soil of your life that's going to come back to you tenfold, thirtyfold, or a hundredfold?

Fourth, list some positive results that are happening in your life. If you're connected to the vine, you should be seeing evidences of that relationship. Remember the five 'PRs'? They should begin to happen in your life. Look for them. Write them down and carry them with you. As you begin to put good seed into the soil of your life, you should be starting to reap some positive benefits, possibly in and through people who have previously reacted negatively. Begin to cultivate the soil; plant some positive seeds and watch the five 'PRs' come back to you. Remember the theme: 'These things I have spoken to you, that My joy may be in you, and that your joy may be made full' (John 15:11).

2

FORMULA FOR SUCCESS

I RECENTLY HEARD a story about a man who was honored as his city's leading citizen. Called on to tell the story of his life, he said, 'Friends and neighbors, when I first came here 30 years ago, I walked into your town on a muddy dirt road with only the suit on my back, the shoes on my feet, and all of my earthly possessions wrapped up in a red bandana tied to a stick, which I carried over my shoulder. Today I'm the chairman of the board of the bank. I own hotels, apartment buildings, office buildings, three companies with branches in 49 cities, and I am on the boards of all the leading clubs. Yes, friends, your city has been very good to me.'

After the banquet a youngster approached the great man and asked him, 'Sir, could you tell me what you wrapped in that red bandana when you walked into this town 30 years ago?' The man said, 'I think, son, it was about a half million dollars in cash and $900,000 in government bonds.'

For us to understand what success is, we have to first ask what's in the red bandana. If I asked you to define what success is, you would define it according to what you have wrapped up in your red bandana, the things you really need in order to live.

WHAT IS SUCCESS?

I want to approach this formula for success from two angles. First we need to define success from the world's point of view, and then we need to define success from a Christian perspective. There is a difference.

The best way to define success from the world's standpoint is that it's the power with which to acquire whatever one demands of life without violating the rights of others. In other words, it's the power to get what you want without stepping on other people: worldly success equals power. But a Christian definition of success has to include more than that. Here's my definition of success: choosing to enter into the arena of action, determined to give yourself to that cause which will better mankind and last for eternity. Success is more than just power or not violating the rights of others; it is the privilege of contributing to the betterment of others.

According to the world's definition of success, self demands of life, whereas according to the Christian definition of success, life demands of self. The world can say that I am successful as long as I meet my needs even if I do not help others. The Christian has to say that to be a success, I must contribute to the welfare of others. To put it another way, to be all I can be, I need to help you be all you can be.

The only one who can stop you from becoming the person God intends you to be is *you.* If you're not the person God had in mind when He created you, it's not His fault. He never asks us to be what He doesn't enable us to be. But too many times we stop short—we never attain success.

WHY DO PEOPLE FAIL?

I think there are three reasons why people do not become successful.

Many people just don't feel the need to succeed. These people are secure; they don't need to prove anything. They're happy, content, and they like what's happening to them. But if success means becoming all that God intends us to be, and we're satisfied with less than that, we not only fall short of God's glory ourselves but we limit what others can be for Him.

The greatest responsibility of leaders is that they not shortchange themselves, thereby shortchanging those whom they lead. If God has given a gift, we are to use it and succeed, so that we not only enhance the kingdom from our perspective but from our followers' as well.

The second reason people do not succeed is that *they are afraid of success.* What are some of the reasons people fear success? Sometimes we back off because of the commitment level required. Sometimes we are afraid because success puts pressure on us to continue to succeed. A person who gets straight A's on a report card sets a pattern of achievement and must keep achieving. Often we just don't want to be responsible, so we shrink from success.

People who have poor self-images will always shy away from success. Others don't want to be successful because they don't like to be lonely. They would rather be with the crowd; it's lonely at the top. Risk is another reason; people don't want to stick their necks out. There are many more reasons, but the main point is that some people are afraid of success.

The third reason why many people fail is that *they are suspicious of success.* It's as if they think that if you want to be successful, you certainly can't be spiritual: successful people couldn't be humble. We've almost equated humility with poverty. Yet when I look through the Word of God, one of the things that impresses me most is that the Bible is chock-full of successful people who chose to enter into the arena of action and give themselves to a cause that would better humanity. They were successful in changing lives for eternity. Think of people like Joseph, Nehemiah, the Apostle Paul, Joshua, David, and Abraham. Many of the men of the Bible were what we would consider to be successful. To fail to become all that God created you to become limits not only yourself but also those under your influence.

S—SELECT YOUR GOAL

Let's take each letter of the word *success* and make an acrostic. The first letter *S* stands for 'select your goal.' The reason most people don't succeed is simply that they really don't know what they want out of life. The Apostle Paul wrote, 'one thing I do' (Phil. 3:13). He knew what he wanted to do. I heard a fellow say one time that success is the 'progressive realization of a predetermined, worthwhile goal.' We have to know where we are going.

The goal is predetermined. Success is not an accident; it's not luck or fate. It is predetermined. *Success is worthwhile.* Nothing is successful that does not contribute in a positive way to help people. *Success is continual.* It's not an event but a journey, an ongoing process. It's not an accolade that we receive for a race won or a job well-done. Success is the positive result of steady forward movement.

Research shows that approximately 95 percent of us have never written out our goals in life, but of the 5 percent who have, 95 percent have achieved their goals. In 1953 at Yale University, 3 percent of the graduating class had specific, written goals for their lives. In 1975 researchers found that the 3 percent who wrote down their goals had accomplished more than the other 97 percent put together.

I wonder how much we don't achieve because we don't establish definite goals and put them in writing. I run into people all the time who don't set definite goals because there are too many factors in life over which they have no control. There are physical limits to what we can do. I can only throw a ball so high and so far—beyond that maximum I have no control. But within the limit of my ability I have total freedom. Determinism and free will are both a part of life, but it is far better to make the most of what we can do than to bemoan what we cannot do.

The average person's lifetime includes 20 years of sleeping, 6 years of watching television, 5 years of dressing and shaving, 3 years of waiting for others, 1 year on the telephone, and 4 months of tying shoes. To help you understand the importance of goals and to facilitate your own goal setting, let me give you six important guidelines.

Your goal must include others. No goal is worthwhile that is only for yourself. Set a goal big enough to include and help other people.

Your goal must be worthwhile. There is no such thing as a successful frivolous goal.

Your goal must be clear. If you don't know where you are headed, a map will be of no use.

Your goal must be measurable. You need a way to see if you are making any progress toward the goal.

Your goal must be expandable. Don't set your goals in concrete. If your goal is not expandable, it's expendable. As we grow, we see the picture more clearly, and we need to continually 'up' our goals. It's a sad day when we realize we have achieved our goals and have nothing else to do.

Your goals must be filled with conviction. Conviction is the unshaken confidence that the goal is worthwhile. It's the fuel that pushes us to achieve.

U—UNLOCK YOUR IMPRISONED POTENTIAL

Most people only use about 10 percent of their potential; if they use as much as 25 percent, they're called geniuses. If we can go from using 10 percent of our potential to using 20 percent, we could double our productivity and still have 80 percent of our potential untapped.

Michelangelo worked on 44 statues in his life. He only completed 14 of them. *David* and *Moses* are probably the most famous. The other ones were never finished. They're just blocks of stone, with perhaps an arm or a head. There is a museum in Italy where you can see these unfinished works, the unfulfilled potential of a great genius.

It is sad enough to realize that there are unfinished works of Michelangelo, but what is even more sad is to look every day at the people around us and realize that they are like blocks of stone that haven't yet been developed. If we as leaders could somehow, through the wisdom and the power of God, take the chisel to our people—not the ball bat, the chisel—and begin to peck away, define what they are and begin to release them from that granite block that has kept them from being what they should be, then we would be doing our people a great service.

How do you unlock your potential? Here are just a few ways to begin.

Look up. The first thing is to look up and find a model, somebody who is doing a better job than you are. Are there any people that you know who are reaching more of their potential now than ever before because they know you? Can you think of anything better as a parent, an employer, or a pastor to do for others than to help unlock their potential by being a model for them? Nothing can be more challenging than to be the person whom others look up to.

What we need is somebody a little bigger and a little better than we are, and we need to spend time with them. Let me give you an example. I play racquetball with a colleague of mine. He is a good racquetball player; in fact he is better than I am, and he always wins the first game. I'm challenged because he's better than I am, so I give it my best. If you have ever played anybody who is worse than you, you know that you start going downhill. You get lazy, and you don't keep your mind on the game. That's what happens to my colleague. By the third game, I win. When you play somebody better, you stretch; when you play somebody worse, you shrink.

So if you want to unlock your hidden potential, spend your time with people who will stretch you. Find somebody who thinks faster, runs faster, and aims higher. Those are the people who will lift you up.

Give up. To reach our potential, we must give up at any moment all that we are in order to receive what we can become. Many people don't understand this. They want to hang on to what they are and at the same time be all they can be. You have to let go.

In the Bible there are all kinds of beautiful illustrations of men of God who gave up something to rise higher. Abraham gave up his home to seek a better country. Moses gave up the riches of Egypt. David gave up security. John the Baptist gave up being first so he could be second. The Apostle Paul gave up his past and made a radical turnaround. Jesus Himself gave up His rights. And you will find that you too will have to give up something good if you want something better.

You'll never find anybody that achieves great success in life without a give-up story. Nothing comes free.

Fire up. I'm talking about what Phillips Brooks meant when he said, 'Sad is that day for any man when he becomes absolutely satisfied with the life that he is living, the thoughts he is thinking and the deeds he is doing; until there ceases to be forever beating at the door of his soul a desire to do something larger which he seeks and knows he was meant and intended to do.'

Show up. Nothing will help you reach your potential like facing the challenges of your life. Some people never become all they can be because when they see a challenge coming, they fail to show up for the match. They close the door and hide in the corner while the challenge is met by someone else. Don't be intimidated by challenges: meet them head-on.

Go up. If we *look up* to a person who is reaching his or her potential, if we *give up* anything that hinders us from being our best, if we *fire up* our desires until we are no longer satisfied, and if we *show up* to our challenges and not become fearful, then we will *go up.* We'll go up to the top of our potential—but only after we look up, give up, fire up, and show up.

C—COMMIT YOURSELF TO GOD'S PLAN

Ted Engstrom said, 'Success means a person is reaching the maximum potential available to him at any given moment.'

If success is what Ted Engstrom says it is—tapping into the available potential that we have and making the best use of it—shouldn't Christians be more successful than non-Christians? The power God gives to Spirit-filled believers ought to make a world of difference between them and nonbelievers. 'Greater is He who is in you than he who is in the world' (1 John 4:4). 'I can do all things through Him who strengthens me' (Phil. 4:13). We have all these things through the power of God's Spirit that should enable us to live on a higher plane.

How do I find God's plan for my life? How do I commit myself to God's plan? There are seven questions to ask yourself.

- *Am I consecrated to Him?* Romans 12:1–2 tells us that we have to be consecrated before we can know the plan of God.

- *Am I spending time with Him?* I find God's plan when I spend time getting to know God. The more intimate I become with God, the more knowledgeable I become about His plan for my life.
- *What are my gifts?* Most of the time the plan of God fits right in with the gifts God has given us.
- *What are my desires?* I have found that our desires and gifts also fit together. The gifts God gives us are often realized through our desires.
- *What are my Christian friends saying?* What do they say are my strengths and weaknesses?
- *What are my opportunities?* What lies before me that God may be giving to me as an open door to walk through?
- *Am I in ministry now?* It's amazing how many people who want to know God's plan for their lives are doing nothing now. If you really want to know what God's plan is for your life, do something. God works through a busy person. Commit yourself to God's plan.

C—CHART YOUR COURSE

This has to do with planning. It's better to took ahead and prepare than look back and regret.

A passenger was talking to the captain of the *Queen Mary* during an ocean cruise, and he asked the captain, 'How long would it take you before you could stop this vessel?' The captain said, 'If I shut down all the engines, it would take me a little over a mile to get this vessel completely stopped.' He added, 'A good captain thinks at least a mile ahead.'

I went through the Proverbs in the *Living Bible*, and here are the verses I pulled out that have to do with planning.

We should make plans—counting on God to direct us. (Prov. 16:9)

Plans go wrong with too few counselors; many counselors bring success. (Prov. 15:22)

It is dangerous and sinful to rush into the unknown. (Prov. 19:2)

A sensible man watches for problems and prepares to meet them. The simpleton never looks, and suffers the consequences. (Prov. 27:12)

Any enterprise is built by wise planning, becomes strong through common sense, and profits wonderfully by keeping abreast of the facts. (Prov. 24:3–4)

Plan ahead, chart your course, and if God is going to be your partner, make your plans large.

E—EXPECT PROBLEMS

Paul Harvey said, 'You can always tell when you are on the road to success; it's uphill all the way.' If you find a path that has no problems, you will find that it leads nowhere.

I've talked many times to leaders about 'sap strata.' Sap strata are those levels of living beyond which it is hard to rise. It happens in churches, organizations, and in individual lives. Have you ever felt that you just weren't making any progress, as if you were hitting your head up against the wall? We have to make an extra burst of effort to get through those strata that keep us from being what God wants us to become. There are two ways to meet our problems, two ways to get through those sap strata. One way is to *change the problem.* This is only a temporary, partial solution. We can try to make the problem more manageable, but it will get out of hand again tomorrow.

The most effective way for us to overcome our problems is to *change the person.* Adversity is not our greatest enemy. The human spirit is capable of great resiliency and resourcefulness in the face of hardship. It's not problems that mess us up. Someone said, 'Cripple [a man] and you have Sir Walter Scott; lock him in prison and you have John Bunyan; bury him in the snows of Valley Forge and you have George Washington; raise him in poverty and you have Abraham Lincoln; strike him down with infantile paralysis and he becomes Franklin Delano Roosevelt. Burn him so severely that doctors say he will never walk again and you have Glen Cunningham, who set the world's record in 1934 for the one-minute mile. Deafen him and you'll have Ludwig van Beethoven; call him a slow learner, retarded, and write him off as uneducable and you have Albert Einstein.'

S—STAND FIRM ON YOUR COMMITMENT

The word of God encourages us in 1 Corinthians 15:58; 'Be steadfast, immovable, always abounding in the work of the Lord, knowing that your toil is not in vain in the Lord.' Someone asked James Corbett, the heavyweight boxing champion at the time, what it took to be a heavyweight champion, and he said, 'Fight one more round.' When asked how he had been so successful in his inventions, Thomas Edison said, 'I start where other men leave off.' Napoleon Hill, in his book *Think and Grow Rich*, records that he studied 500 of the wealthiest men in the world and concluded that all wealthy men are persistent. When Winston Churchill went back to his alma mater to speak, the audience anticipated a great speech from the prime minister. He stood before them and said six words: 'Never, never, never, never give up.' That was it; the speech was over. And that is probably the speech for which he is most remembered. Stand firm on your commitment. Don't be a quitter.

S—SURRENDER EVERYTHING TO JESUS CHRIST

Don't ever forget that although you may succeed beyond your fondest hopes and your greatest expectations, you will never succeed beyond the purpose to which you are willing to surrender. Seek first the kingdom of God and His righteousness and all of these other things shall be added to you (Matt. 6:33).

The secret of the surrendered life is giving God the first part of every day, the first day of every week, the first portion of your income, the first consideration in every decision, and the first place in all of your life. When we surrender to Him, then we have a power that really caps off the formula for success. Surrender is what brings power. We fight for power and we lose it; we surrender and we find it.

Jesus Christ has not only shown us the righteous life—many great and good men and women did that before His time—but He has given us the power to live this righteous life. He not only shows us the beauty of God, as others have done, but He gives us the means by which we can become part of that beauty. We can learn the power of hourly surrender to the living Christ. Change in our lives is not brought about by our tense tinkering. It is brought about by the radiant, immeasurable energy of Christ, which has never left the world since He first said yes to God. His yes was complete; He kept nothing back for Himself.

As Flora Slosson Wuellner says, 'There is nothing so tragically ineffectual as trying to live the Christian life without the Christian power. Try turning the other cheek without using the spiritual weapons of Christ's power to love and see what destructive situation develops. Try going the second mile with a neighbor without going all the way to surrender to Christ and see the damage done to the neighbor's personality and your own. Try to love and pray unceasingly without turning daily to the living water of Christ and see how quickly the personal well runs dry.' Surrender to Jesus Christ.

Success is a word that is greatly misunderstood, and we need to grasp what it means biblically to be a success—to love God with all of our heart, our mind, our soul, and our strength; to allow Him to unlock the imprisoned potential in our lives; to set godly goals and not be content to settle for second best when we realize that God gave everything He could give so that we could have the very best of life; and to realize that one of the greatest sins we commit against God is not reaching the potential He has placed in us.

3

STRETCH TO SUCCESS

RUBBER BANDS come in different sizes and different colors and different shapes, but they all work on the same principle: they must be stretched to be effective. Like rubber bands, our personalities, talents, and gifts are different; we're also not effective unless we're stretched. If you're not stretching in your own personal walk with God and in your leadership abilities, then you're not going to be able to be as effective for God as you really need to be.

Leonard Ravenhill relates that a group of tourists were in a village in Europe, and one of them asked an elderly villager, 'Have any great men been born in this village?' The old man replied, 'Nope, only babies.' Every person who has ever achieved anything has stretched for it. There's no such thing as a self-made person; there's no such thing as a person who comes into the world fully equipped for success. Every person who has ever made it to the top, every person who has achieved anything for God, every person who has been effective has learned to stretch. One of the most common mistakes, and one of the costliest, is thinking that success is due to some genius, some magic something or other, which we do not possess. Success is due to our stretching to the challenges of life. Failure comes when we shrink from them. There's no such thing as a man who was born great.

WHY DON'T WE STRETCH?

I would guess that 95 percent of us try to avoid stretching. When we come up against something that is bigger than we are, we tend to back off. What keeps us from expanding? Why do we avoid these stretching experiences?

Fear has to be the number one reason. The unknown out there can really paralyze us. Another reason is that we're *satisfied.* Why stretch? We already like where we are; we have it made. Or perhaps there's a streak of *laziness* in us. There are times when we would just rather take it easy. I have found that *self-esteem* has a lot to do with one's willingness to stretch. A lot of people with low self-esteem have above average ability; they just do not see themselves in the proper light. Some of us just don't want to be *different.* If you stretch, you're no longer ordinary. To stretch is to be out of sync with many of our friends and associates.

I would encourage you to put this book down for a moment and evaluate yourself. Ask yourself why it is that you're not always stretching. Take about five minutes to do some introspection and be honest as you sense God dealing with the reasons for your complacency. If we're trying to avoid stretching, we need to begin to regroup so we can become useful and effective in our ministry and leadership.

MOTIVATED TO STRETCH

Most of us need to be motivated before we will stretch. It's not something that comes naturally. We need to learn how to stretch and motivate ourselves, but we also need to know how to motivate others and help them to reach their potential.

One of my modern-day heroes is Bear Bryant, who was the coach for the Alabama Crimson Tide for many years and who held the record for several years as the college football coach with the most victories. Bear Bryant was an outstanding coach and a tremendous motivator. His players knew they had better play good football. The story is told that during one important game his team was ahead by six points with only a minute left in the game, and they had the ball. It looked as if they had the game sewed up. He sent in a running play to his quarterback, but the quarterback decided to surprise the other team—and Coach Bryant—by calling a pass play. He said, 'They're looking for the run; let's throw a pass.' So he went back and threw a pass, and sure enough, the defensive cornerback, who was the speed champion of the league, intercepted the ball and headed toward the goal line. Alabama was about to lose the game. The Alabama quarterback, who was known for a good arm but not for fast legs, took off after the cornerback and caught him on the five-yard line. He saved the game; Alabama won. The opposing coach went to Bear Bryant after the game and said, 'I thought that quarterback was slow! How'd he catch my world-class sprinter?' Bear Bryant looked at that opposing coach and said, 'You have to understand. Your man was racing for six points. My man was racing for his life.'

Some of us have to be racing for our lives before we're motivated to stretch. What motivates you? What makes you want to be your best for the glory of God? Think about it for a few minutes. For some people, challenge itself is a stimulant. Others are motivated by dissatisfaction with their present situation. Or we can be spurred on by previous successes.

One of the things that helps me stretch is a public commitment, a public goal. I have found that when I tell others what I want to do, it really helps me to keep on track. They can hold me accountable by checking my progress. John F. Kennedy loved to tell stories about his grandfather, Fitzgerald. When his grandfather was a boy in Ireland, he would walk home from school with a whole group of boys. There were a lot of very jagged, high cobblestone fences. They were kind of difficult to climb, and some of them were 10–12 feet high, so they were a little dangerous to climb. But, being adventurous boys, they always wanted to go over the walls, but they were afraid of getting hurt. One day as they were walking home from school, Fitzgerald took his cap off and threw it over the wall. The moment he threw it over the wall, he knew he had to climb over to get it back, because he didn't dare go home without his cap or he would be disciplined. Throwing your cap over the wall commits you to stretch and do something you would not normally do. I encourage you to begin to throw your cap over the wall.

VULNERABLE IN THE STRETCH

Most people are vulnerable when they are stretching. When a rubber band is pulled taut, it's much easier to break. A runner who's stretching for the wire is in a precarious position. If you were to push him a little bit you could knock him clear off his course. Every energy, every muscle, every fiber, is aiming toward a goal, leaving the runner vulnerable.

If you're not stretching, you're in a much better position to defend yourself; your muscles are naturally defensive. Though most people begin their lives by stretching, they soon discover that this position leaves them open to attack, so they begin to withdraw. They start to equate stretching with pain. Before long they're not willing to stretch anymore.

Those who continue to stretch will find themselves vulnerable to criticism. Unfortunately, the road to success is paved with critics. They're ready and waiting to point out how imperfectly other people do what they themselves are unable or unwilling to do.

Jonas Salk, who developed the polio vaccine, was attacked continually for his creative, inventive work in the medical field. He found that criticism came in three stages. The first stage is when people tell you that you're wrong—it won't work. After they've seen you get some success under your belt, they say that what you're doing isn't really that important. Finally, after they see that it's important, they'll say that they knew you would do it all along. If you're stretching, the best defense to these critics is the fruit of your labor. Don't feel that you have to pull out of that stretch position to defend yourself. Just go out and produce the fruit. Those who recognize fruit will appreciate it and those who don't recognize fruit will criticize you whether you produce it or not.

We're also vulnerable to misunderstanding. Often people whose own motives are wrong will feel threatened by us if we are stretching to be our best. They react by questioning the validity of our motives, accusing us of doing our best for some impure purpose.

Not only are we vulnerable to the reactions of others, but we can be vulnerable to ourselves. We are often harder on ourselves than other people are. If we have no goals, we won't recognize failure, but if we're stretching for success, we will fail from time to time. We need to learn how to deal with that. Don't ever let failure become final. Be aware that discouragement is failure's partner. The best way to pull yourself out of discouragement is to surround yourself by people who are encouragers. Get a friend who really understands the value of affirmation, who really believes in you. Do you know the best way to get encouragers around you? Become an encourager yourself.

We've talked about criticism, misunderstanding, failure, and discouragement. Take about five minutes and evaluate yourself: where are you vulnerable?

THE NEED FOR AFFIRMATION

The most important time to affirm people is when they are stretching. If you want to be a cheerleader to a friend, be a cheerleader when he or she is really moving out and stretching. Too many people affirm too late. I think there are times when we're afraid to encourage risk takers, because in doing so we identify with them; we join them out there on the limb. If they fail, we fail too. But remember that even a tombstone will say good things about a fellow after he's dead. Don't be a tombstone encourager. *Affirm early.*

Affirm often. Don't wait for the race to be won, but encourage each step forward. *Affirm immediately.* The effect of an encouraging word loses its strength as time lapses. If you sense that a friend is starting to slip, give immediate affirmation before the slip has a chance to become a fullscale slide. *Affirm personally,* and don't be afraid to affirm in front of others. Nothing is more encouraging than to receive honest praise in front of your peers.

STRETCHING NEVER STOPS

Most people never learn that stretching never stops. We have a pattern of stretching and resting, stretching and resting. I understand the need for recuperation and restoration, but the problem is that most people stretch a little and rest a lot. Pretty soon they have a vacation mentality, a retirement mind-set.

Too many people stop learning because they have come to believe that you go through twelve years of school and then you go to college for four years and then your education is over. But a good education really does nothing more than prepare you to stretch and learn for the rest of your life. Then there are people who stop trying because of bad past experiences. They say, 'I tried that once before,' or, 'I've already done that.' They allow one failure to put a lid on their abilities.

When you stop stretching, you become *boring.* Nothing bores me like people who haven't had a new thought in the last year. They bore the socks off of me. That's why I think it's so important that in every area of our lives we to continue to stretch.

The other day my father, who is retired and living in Florida, called me and said, 'Son, I just want to tell you that life is so exciting. I've got more work than I've ever had in my life. I'm scheduling more meetings; I'm traveling more. My correspondence is getting so heavy that I've got to get a secretary. Life is not boring at all; I've been so busy.' My dad is in his early sixties now, and I have no doubt that in his early eighties he'll still be excited about life. He is determined to live until he dies.

Why do people stop stretching? Let me give you four quick reasons. The first is that they have surrounded themselves with people who are both bored and boring. Stay around people who are vitally alive if you want your own blood to continue to flow. This is the reason so many elderly people die fast when they enter retirement centers where there is nothing for them to do. When all of a sudden they realize all there is to do in life is watch the sun set, they're in trouble. They're going to be setting themselves.

Number two, work ceases to be a challenge. For many people, work is nothing more than an assembly line, and so it becomes automatic. That's why we always need new goals, new visions, or new dreams.

Many people stop stretching because they have learned to get by with shortcuts. Nothing is more damaging to growth than getting by with second best. There is a difference between taking shortcuts and working smart. We all want to work smart. Working smart takes less effort but is more effective. Shortcuts not only require less effort, but they're less effective. So I'm not talking about working smart, knowing priorities and understanding how to arrange your work so you can do it more quickly. I'm talking about settling for less than the best.

I find that many pastors learn early in their careers that they can just open their Bibles, study a text a little bit, and get up and 'wing it.' They stop taking the time to write their messages out and make sure they have developed some depth. I know many pastors who have to move to a new church every three years because they've used up their resources; they've taken shortcuts all their lives and forgotten how to study.

Many times we stop stretching because we see our value based on our relationships, not our resources. Marriage is one example. If we stretched as hard after our marriages to make our mates happy as we did before our marriages, we wouldn't have marriage problems. After the wedding, we figure that our spouses will love us just because we're married. So we stop stretching, and our marriages stop growing.

Let me apply it in another area—work. I've known people to start a new job and work really hard for six months. Then they become friends with the boss and start slacking off. They mistakenly think a relationship means they don't have to pull as hard on their resources. They stop stretching.

STRETCHING—YOUR FINEST HOUR

Most people will look back at their stretching experiences as their finest experiences. Why? *Growth is happiness.* The happiest people in the world are growing people.

We have in our society a lot of false hopes for happiness. We have what I call *destination disease.* People think that when they arrive at a certain point, they'll be happy. When they retire, when they get rid of this job, when they take that trip, when they meet that goal—then they'll be happy. They're goal oriented, and there's nothing wrong with being goal oriented, but they have not learned to enjoy the journey as much as the arrival. Your happiest moments happen along the way, not at the end of the trip.

There's another false hope for happiness that I call *someone sickness*. That's when you say, 'If I could just meet that person; if I could just marry that woman, I'd be happy.' But you are the only one who can make yourself happy. No one can bring happiness to someone who is miserable. When we begin to take responsibility for our own personal happiness and realize that it's through growth and growing experiences, even though they may be painful, that we become happy, then we're really going to achieve.

Another false hope for happiness is what I call *backslider's blues*. That's the affliction of people who are always talking about the good old days. They're always talking about the past, which was always better than the present. They see only the good things, neither remembering, nor wanting to remember, the bad times. As the saying goes, 'If ifs and buts were candies and nuts, we'd all have a Merry Christmas.'

One last false hope for happiness is the *problem-free plague*. There are many people who want to get in a problem-free society, and they're plagued with that hope. They say, 'Boy, if I just wouldn't have problems, I would be happy.' No, no, no! Problems have nothing to do with your happiness. In fact, in your stretching periods you will probably have more problems than at any other time, and those will be the greatest times of your life.

STRETCHING INSPIRES

Few people stretch all their lives, but those few people inspire the rest of us. There is something within us that is thrilled to see a man or a woman attempt the heroic. The pioneer, the successful entrepreneur, and the victorious athlete all speak to us about the ability of the human spirit to achieve monumental accomplishments when properly motivated. Vicariously we share in their achievements and find hope in our own lives through them. What we need to do is to become inspirers of others, and the only way we're ever going to do that is to throw our caps over the wall. When others see us climbing our fences, they too will begin to climb theirs.

In the earlier part of this century, Charles Lindbergh thrilled the world by flying across the Atlantic. In his story, he tells how as he was going across the United States and over Canada and Newfoundland, he would look down, spotting places where he could land in case of problems. But there came a time when all he saw was the Atlantic Ocean when he looked down. 'It was at that moment I realized there was no turning back; there was no place to land.' Charles Lindbergh had thrown his cap over the wall, and he inspires us because of it. He stretched.

PUT IT TO WORK

Let's get to the application of this lesson. How can we stretch to success? *Discover your potential.* Get near somebody who believes in you. Discovery always comes in an encouraging environment. Find someone who will help you discover who you are and what you can do. Do something that you enjoy. I feel so sorry for people who work in jobs they don't enjoy and live in places they don't like. If you don't like where you live and you don't like your work, why don't you quit your work and move somewhere else? Discover your potential by doing something you enjoy. Then remove the 'if onlys' from your life. As long as you have 'if onlys'—if only I could be there and if only I could do this and if only I could be that, you'll never discover your real potential, because you'll always be excusing yourself for what you are.

Dedicate your potential. Give your motives to God. If He has your motives, He has everything. Dedicate your potential by giving your best to others.

Develop your potential. You can develop your potential by beginning to accept personal responsibility. Then, realize that God is interested in your development. God is even more interested in your development than He is in your mistakes. Forget your mistakes; start developing. *Never* limit your potential. Don't you dare sell yourself short. Fifty years ago Johnny Weismuller was the greatest swimmer of all time, with 50 swimming records. Today 13-year-old girls break his records every time there's a swim meet. Don't limit your potential.

4

VICTORIOUS BECAUSE OF A VISION

HELEN KELLER was asked one time what would be worse than being born blind. She quickly replied, 'To have sight and no vision.' I've found that if you ask successful people what has really helped them get where they are in life, invariably they'll talk about a goal, a dream, a mission, a purpose—something that has been motivating them throughout the years to become what they have finally become.

Tragically, our world is full of what I would call mundane men, people who see only what is immediate. They only reach out for things they can tangibly put their hands on. They go for the convenient. They never look beyond themselves, and they never look at what they could be. A mundane man may be a truck driver, a bank president, or a schoolteacher. Mundane men can be found in every profession. A mundane man is really someone who lacks depth because he lacks vision. The poorest person in the world is not the person who doesn't have a nickel. The poorest person in the world is the one who doesn't have a vision. If you don't have a dream—a goal and a purpose in life—you're never going to become what you could become.

There is a distinguishable difference between successful and unsuccessful people: successful people are motivated by a dream beyond them. They have a dream that is bigger than themselves; they have something that constantly keeps them going. It's out of their reach, and yet they believe that if they work hard enough, they will someday hold that dream in their hands. That's a successful person. Unsuccessful people are only motivated by today. They are not tomorrow thinkers. They're not looking beyond themselves. They grab with gusto the present, not even taking into consideration what tomorrow may present them.

DREAM STAGES

When you receive a vision that could change your life or you're grabbed by a dream that could really help you become what you want to be, there's a natural sequence that happens. First there's the *'I thought it'* stage. That's when a dream just flashes by. *Could it be? Maybe this is for me. What would happen if I did that?* That's the 'thought it' stage. Every person goes through this stage. Probably not a week goes by in which we don't dream. *Could this be me? What would happen if I did this?* We go from the 'I thought it' stage to the *'I caught it'* stage. After we think about some of the dreams that we have and the visions that God gives us, we get excited, and we begin to talk about that dream and see ourselves in it.

I think everyone goes through these first two stages. But stage three makes the difference between the person who will be successful and the person who won't be successful. It's what I call the *'I bought it'* stage. After we catch that dream, there's a time when we have to put a deposit down on it. There comes a time when we have to make an investment in it to make it happen. No dream comes true automatically. We have to buy that dream.

The successful person goes into that third stage and buys the dream. They decide to pay the price. But just as the successful person buys it, the unsuccessful person fights it. It's at that stage they begin to rationalize; they begin to think about why it wouldn't work, why it's not possible, and they begin to fight the dream that God may have given them to reach their potential. People who are not going to reach their dreams stop at this third stage. They don't buy into it; they fight it—and they never become what they could become for God.

The fourth stage is the *'I sought it'* stage. This is where desire comes in: we begin to want it so much that it possesses every part of us. Finally comes the *'I got it'* stage: I can touch it with my hands. This is where I say, 'It's mine; I'm glad I paid the price; I'm glad I dreamed the dream.'

I was in college when Robert Kennedy was assassinated, and I remember one of my college friends coming in and sharing with me that morning that Kennedy had been killed. In the days immediately following his death, there was much written about him in the newspapers. I cut out a quotation of his that I've never forgotten. I'm not sure it was original with Kennedy, but it was said about him, and I hope it can be said about all of us. 'Some people look at things as they are and say, why? Some people look at things as they could be and say, why not?' There are people who see only what is and constantly butt their heads up against the wall and back away with Excedrin headaches. They haven't figured out that if they stand on their tiptoes and peek over that wall, they will see that there is life beyond. They're always asking, Why did this happen to me? Why am I a victim of my circumstances? But there are other people who have learned to look beyond limitations and barriers. They can see beyond and say, Why not? Why can't this happen to me?

When Hubert Humphrey died, I began reading a lot about his life. He wrote a letter to his wife in 1935, during his first visit to Washington, D.C. Here's what he said. 'I can see how someday if you and I just apply ourselves and make up our minds to work for bigger things, we can someday live in Washington and probably be in government, politics or service. Oh, gosh, I hope my dream comes true. I'm gonna try anyhow.'

STOPPED BY A VISION

Let's look at the Apostle Paul. I think one of the key ingredients in his life was his vision. Not only did he see what he was, but he also saw what the grace of God could enable him to become. It was that vision that kept him steady throughout his ministry. In Acts 26:19, when he stood before King Agrippa, he said, 'Consequently, King Agrippa, I did not prove disobedient to the heavenly vision.' In spite of all the problems he had run into in his ministry, in spite of what was about to happen to him, he had been obedient to the dream God had given him. The vision Paul was given by God did several things for him. First, it stopped him. If we have a great dream, if we have a challenging vision, it will stop us right in our tracks.

> *While thus engaged as I was journeying to Damascus with the authority and commission of the chief priests, at midday, O King, I saw on the way a light from heaven, brighter than the sun, shining all around me and those who were journeying with me. And when we had all fallen to the ground, I heard a voice saying to me in the Hebrew dialect, 'Saul, Saul, why are you persecuting Me? It is hard for you to kick against the goads.' And I said, 'Who art Thou, Lord?' And the Lord said, 'I am Jesus whom you are persecuting.' (Acts 26: 12–15)*

Our visions may not be quite that profound. Few of us have a Damascus road experience. But like Paul, if we have a great vision, it will stop us in our tracks and let us glimpse what we have the potential to become.

What happened in Paul's life can happen in our lives. When we see ourselves properly, there are a couple of things that will happen. One, we'll see our *position.* We'll see who we are. We'll see what we are doing. We'll see where we are going. This can be discouraging because we may think, *I'm not accomplishing what I want to accomplish; I'm not being what I want to become.* But all people who have the potential for greatness first of all have to see themselves as they are, and usually that's discouraging. When Paul saw that he had been persecuting Christians, when he saw that he had been thwarting the plan of God, when he saw that he had been buying into a wrong religion, no doubt he was discouraged. Remember when Isaiah had a vision of God? It stopped him. He began to see himself, and his first comment was, 'Woe is me.' In effect he was saying, 'Wow! I'm in trouble. I'm not what I should be; I'm not what God wants me to become' (Isa. 6:5).

When we have a vision from God and it stops us, we not only see our position, but thankfully, we also see our *potential.* We see our possibilities. The good news is that God believes in you, and He will not allow you to see yourself and your problems without allowing you to see your potential. He's not going to frustrate us; He's going to encourage us and help us see what we can become. Isaiah went from 'Woe is me' to 'Here I am, Lord. Send me' (Isa. 6:8).

Five things happened to Isaiah. He saw God, and when he saw God, he saw a holy God. That took him aback. When we see the holiness of God, we see our own uncleanness. Second, he saw himself, and he saw that just as God was holy and perfect, he was needy and imperfect. Then he saw others; he looked at the multitudes around him. He saw God, he saw himself, he saw others, and then he allowed God to change him. At that point one of the seraphim picked up the coal from the altar and placed it on Isaiah's tongue. God took him through a purification process. Fifth, Isaiah began to stretch. He began to say, 'OK, God, allow me to be part of this dream. Allow me to reach out and be what You want me to become.'

The value of a vision is that it encourages you to give up at any moment all that you are in order to receive all that you can become. In other words, once you've had a glimpse of what God can make of you, you'll never be satisfied with what you now are. You will be willing to let go of whatever might keep you from actually realizing that vision. You can probably think of times in your life when this happened to you. Do you remember when you first fell in love with the person you married? All of a sudden other members of the opposite sex were not that interesting to you anymore. You were willing to trade in the pool for the one.

I have found that you do one of two things in life. You either pay the price now and enjoy later, or you enjoy now and pay the price later. But you will always pay the price. I'm constantly amazed at the short-sightedness of people who are not willing to pay the price now. Some people are short-sighted about their bodies. They're not willing to give up those pleasurable things that are destroying their bodies now in order to gain a few good years later. Some people are short-sighted about their finances. They can't give up any of today's luxuries in exchange for tomorrow's financial security. And some people are short-sighted spiritually. They are so caught up in the pleasures of today that they can't see the pain of tomorrow: they're not willing to totally sell out for God. They're trying to avoid the price, but the price will always be there. You can either pay it today and enjoy life tomorrow, or you can enjoy life today and pay the price, plus interest, tomorrow. You cannot avoid the price.

I have always been very goal conscious. For that reason, even though Margaret and I had been dating since high school, I decided we would not get married until I graduated from college. While I waited through four years of college, I watched a number of my friends marry during their sophomore and junior years. You can guess what happened to many of them: grades fell, financial hard times hit, and discouragement set in. Even so, they were encouraging me to go ahead and get married. But I remember thinking, *You guys weren't willing to pay the price. I'll set my goals and pay my dues. The time will come when I'll be enjoying a fantastic marriage, plus the fruit of my ministry, and you guys will still be struggling.* I can point to five or six of my closest friends from college who are still struggling. They sold their birthright for a mess of pottage. We either enjoy life now and pay for it later or we pay for life now and enjoy the fruits of it later.

SENT BY A VISION

When Paul had a vision, it stopped him, but it also sent him. Any God-given dream will never *just* stop you; it will always send you. The vision or the dream God has for you will always allow you to touch other lives. So, Paul was stopped, he saw himself, he saw his potential, and then he was sent. After the vision had stopped Paul, the Lord said to him, in effect, 'OK, Paul, you've looked at yourself long enough; stand on your feet.'

> *For this purpose I have appeared to you, to appoint you a minister and a witness not only to the things which you have seen, but also to the things in which I will appear to you; delivering you from the Jewish people and from the Gentiles, to whom I am sending you, to open their eyes so that they may turn from darkness to light and from the dominion of Satan to God, in order that*

they may receive forgiveness of sins and an inheritance among those who have been sanctified by faith in Me. (Acts 26:16–18)

Like Isaiah's vision, Paul's vision would help him touch others. A vision first requires that we see ourselves and then that we see others. No person is successful in fulfilling God's dream for his life until he has begun to positively affect the lives of those around him. This is the 'I bought it' stage. You may have thought it and caught it, but have you bought it? Have you made the decision? That decision requires that you involve yourself in people's lives.

I remember reading an article in 1972 in *Life* magazine. It was entitled, 'One Man's Life of No Regrets.' It was about a 47-year-old man who had set out at the age of 15 with 127 specific goals in his life. By the time he was 47, he had reached 105 of his goals. He talked about how he had the rest of his life to reach out and grab the other 22. His goals stopped him, and then they sent him. They changed not only his life but the lives of others around him.

STRENGTHENED BY A VISION

If the vision is God-given it will stop us, it will send us, and it will strengthen us. As Paul stood before King Agrippa, he talked about some of the setbacks that he had had (Acts 26:19–23). The key is where he says that he has obtained help from God. The goal strengthened him. We receive a visitation from God, and then we pursue our visions for God. He visits us, and as He comes upon us and empowers us and strengthens us, then we begin to fulfill His vision. In 2 Corinthians 11:23–28, Paul writes about some of the problems he came through. He writes of many labors and many imprisonments, of being 'beaten times without number, often in danger of death.'

Five times I received from the Jews thirty-nine lashes. Three times I was beaten with rods, once I was stoned, three times I was shipwrecked, a night and a day I have spent in the deep. I have been on frequent journeys, in dangers from rivers, dangers from robbers, dangers from my countrymen, dangers from Gentiles, dangers in the city, dangers in the wilderness, dangers on the sea, dangers among false brethren; I have been in labor and hardship, through many sleepless nights, in hunger and thirst, often without food, in cold and exposure. Apart from such external things, there is the daily pressure upon me of concern for all the churches.

Now, what helped Paul to come through all those difficulties? It's very simple. He had a vision. The vision makes the difference. Any problem is a problem when there is no purpose. But no problem is a problem when there is a purpose. How true that is! When you really have a dream, you aren't a problem-conscious person. When you see a problem, you also see a dream, and the dream takes you through the problem.

STRETCHED BY A VISION

Paul's vision stretched him; it helped him become what he would never have become without it. The same holds true for us. We will never reach our potential unless we follow our dreams, unless we fulfill our visions.

When I was in fourth grade, I went to my first high school basketball game. I stood in the balcony, looking down on the basketball court and the guys getting ready to play. They were in their warmups, and I'll never forget the moment all the lights went out and the spotlight came on, aimed at the middle of the floor. A drum roll preceded the booming announcement of each player's name. The player would then run out under the spotlight to the sound of thunderous applause. Totally entranced, I turned to brother, Larry, and said, 'There's gonna be a day when they'll do that for me!' After the game I went home and formally announced my intention to become a basketball player.

I became consumed with being a basketball player. My dad made a cement drive, put up a backboard and rim, got me a Spaulding basketball, and I began to play basketball in fourth grade. When I got to fifth grade, I played in the little basketball league.

Sometimes we went to that same high school gym to play intramurals. The first time I walked down on the main floor of that gymnasium, looking all around as only a fifth-grader can, I began to replay my vision. I saw myself in the starting line-up. I sat down where I'd seen those big high school basketball players sit, and I closed my eyes so I could turn the lights off in the gym and hear the drum roll in my mind; then I ran out in the middle of the floor and just stood there like the other guys had. All the other kids watched me, wondering what in the world was wrong with me. I was simply replaying my dream.

I will never forget the night in my sophomore year when the coach said, 'You're going to start this evening,' and the lights went off. That dream stretched me. During good weather and bad, I was always playing basketball; I was always seeing myself as I could become. That's what a vision will do for you.

There's a difference between a dreamer and a person who has a dream. There are thousands and thousands of dreamers, but there are very few people who have dreams—and there's a world of difference between them. Dreamers talk much but do little. They may hatch up wild plans and ideas, but you never see them happening. Dreamers lack discipline. On the other hand, a person who has a dream talks little but does much. You may not hear all about the dream, but if you watch, you'll see it happen. This kind of person is driven by the dream.

SATISFACTION GUARANTEED

Let's look at the fifth thing that happened to Paul. His vision, or his dream, satisfied him. When he stood before King Agrippa, it was with a sense of satisfaction that he said, 'I did not prove disobedient to the heavenly vision' (Acts 26:19). He sensed great satisfaction in having been obedient, in having followed through on his dream.

One of the mountains of the Alps that is popular with climbers has a rest house about halfway up. Now, for amateurs, it's a good day's climb from the base to the top. If they start out early in the morning, they get to the rest house about lunchtime. The owner of the house has noticed over the years that an interesting phenomenon happens on a regular basis. When the climbers get into the house, where they feel the warmth of the fire and smell the good food cooking, several will always give in to temptation. They'll say to their companions, 'You know, I think I'll just wait here while you go on to the top. When you come back down, I'll join you and we'll go to the base together.'

A glaze of satisfaction comes over them as they sit by the fire or play the piano and sing mountain-climbing songs. Meanwhile, the rest of the group get on their gear and trek on to the top. For the next couple of hours, there's a spirit of happiness around the fireside; they're having a good time in the cozy little lodge. But by about 3:30, it starts to get quiet. They begin taking turns at the window, looking at the top of the mountain. They're silent as they watch their friends reach the goal. The atmosphere in the house has changed from fun to funereal as they realize they settled for second best. Those who paid the price reached the goal.

What happened? The temporary comfort of the shelter caused them to lose sight of their purpose. It can happen to any of us. Don't we all have little sheltered places in our lives where we can retreat from the climb—and lose sight of our goals?

Who are the happiest people in the world? Are they young people? Are they healthy people? Are they wealthy people? No, not necessarily. The happiest people in the world are those who are living out their dreams. In giving themselves to something bigger than they are, they're giving themselves the impetus to rise above their problems. If you want to know real happiness, dream a dream that is bigger than you are; find something you can lose your life in. Jesus said if you keep your life you will lose it, and if you lose your life you will keep it (Luke 9:24). Isn't there something better than watching 'As the World Turns' every afternoon? Isn't there something better than waiting for a vacation every year? Isn't there something better than waiting for retirement by just killing time? Isn't there something better than just settling for average? Average doesn't look so good when you realize it's the worst of the best and the best of the worst.

When I counsel people, I find that their number-one problem is that they've lost their dreams. They've lost their goals; they've lost their purpose. When you lose a dream or your purpose in your marriage, you lose your marriage. When you lose your purpose in your job, you lose your job. When you lose your purpose for your health, you die.

Think of the great men and women who continued to pursue their dreams into old age. Think of people like Moses, who at 80 years of age led three and a half million people out of captivity. Or Caleb, who at 85 years of age said, 'Give me that mountain.' Or Colonel Sanders, who at 70 years of age discovered 'finger lickin' good' chicken. Or Ray Kroc, who after 70 introduced a Big Mac to the world. Then there's Casey Stengel, who at 75 became the manager of the Yankees baseball team. And there's Picasso, still painting at 88, and George Washington

Carver, who at 81 became head of the Agriculture Department. There's Thomas Edison, who at 85 invented the mimeograph machine, and John Wesley, who was still traveling on horseback and preaching at age 88.

Don't ever be content with having reached a goal; don't rest on your laurels. History is filled with examples of people who, though they had accomplished great things, lost sight of their vision. When Alexander the Great had a vision, he conquered countries; when he lost it, he couldn't conquer a liquor bottle. When David had a vision, he conquered Goliath; and when he lost his vision, he couldn't conquer his own lust. When Samson had a vision, he won many battles; when he lost his vision, he couldn't win his battle with Delilah. When Solomon had a vision, he was the wisest man in the world; when he lost the dream God had given him, he couldn't control his own evil passion for foreign women. When Saul had a vision, he could conquer kings; when he lost his vision, he couldn't conquer his own jealousy. When Noah had a vision, he could build an ark and help keep the human race on track; when he lost his vision, he got drunk. When Elijah had a vision, he could pray down fire from heaven and chop off the heads of false prophets; when he lost the dream, he ran from Jezebel. It's the dream that keeps us young; it's the vision that keeps us going.

When I went to Arizona for a convention a couple of years ago, the fellow who was in charge of the convention picked me up at the airport. The conference was going to be at the church where he was the pastor. We got in the car, and we hadn't left the airport parking lot before he started saying things like, 'I'm really not sure why you're here. I don't know if you've spoken to older people before, but I have heard you before, and you're enthusiastic. The people that are going to be here are going to be mostly retired, and they've worked hard all of their lives in churches back East. They've come here to settle down and just enjoy the sunset years.' As he talked, I was getting the message that he wanted me to go easy on them, maybe just give the old folks a devotional. His attitude was going against my grain. *This guy doesn't understand people,* I thought to myself. People want a cause—they need a goal. If you're not yet dead, you must be still alive; you want something to live for, whether you're 18 or 81.

So, on our way to the conference that night, I got my pen out and began reworking my whole sermon. The more I listened to this pastor, the more convinced I became that I had to preach what he didn't want his people to hear. By the time the service had begun, I had developed what I would consider a real motivational message for these old-timers. I got up and shot both barrels of enthusiasm out into that congregation. I preached on the subject, 'Why Retire When You Can Reenlist?' I talked about their potential, the experience they had, their wisdom, and the trials they had come through. At the end, I said, 'If you'd like to reenlist in your local church and help fulfill a dream and a cause, come forward.' The place was packed that night, and about three quarters of those retirees came up to say, 'Yes, sir, we want to have a cause.' The pastor was wondering what had happened to his saints. It was not his saints that were the problem. They wanted a dream; they wanted a cause. The pastor was the problem. He had lost that dream; he had lost that vision and settled down for second best.

Do you remember the sequence of a successful dream? Let's go through it one more time, because in this sequence there's one more point that I want to give you. The first stage is 'I thought it,' followed by 'I caught it,' 'I bought it,' 'I sought it,' and 'I got it.' But there is still one more step if you're going to be a great leader. You should move on to step number six, which is, 'I taught it.' You should never live out a dream without sharing it with someone else. That's discipleship. In the Winter 1983 issue of *Leadership* magazine, Terry Muck writes,

> *According to a survey of* Leadership *readers, communicating vision is one of the most frustrating parts of leading a local church. 'It is also a task young pastors feel poorly equipped to handle. In a comprehensive 1982 study, one major seminary found that its alumni felt least prepared in their ability to get people working together toward a common goal. Apparently, putting a vision in a form that inspires and energizes is a major hurdle.' One fact is true. Leaders who effectively communicate goals to their followers are paid far beyond those who do not.*

The key is not only getting to the 'got it' stage, where you have the dream personally, but it's passing that dream on to others.

THE DAILY DOZEN

Here are a dozen exercises to help make your dream come true.

- ✦ *Examine* your life at the moment. The first step toward making your dream come true is to find out where you are right now. That takes close scrutiny.
- ✦ *Exchange* all of your little options for one big dream. Every dream has its price.
- ✦ *Expose* yourself to successful people. It is true that birds of a feather flock together.
- ✦ *Express* your belief in your dream. Write it down or talk about it frequently.
- ✦ *Expect* opposition to your dream. Every nitpicker who doesn't have a dream will oppose yours. Regretfully, there are ten nitpickers for every person with a dream. You will never rid yourself of them. As long as you understand that, you won't

let them hinder you. Remember that those who have no dream cannot see yours, so to them it is impossible. You can't have what you can't see.

- *Exercise* all of your effort, all of your energy, toward the dream. It's worth it. Pay that price!
- *Extract* every positive principle that you can from life. Constantly be on the lookout for anything that will enhance that dream.
- *Exclude* negative thinkers as close friends. You're going to have some friends who are negative thinkers, and no doubt some are members of your family. But if their negative thinking drags you down, which it will, you don't need to spend much time with them. There are people in my own family and in my wife's family who are spirit-dampeners. We have chosen, for the sake of our kids as well as ourselves, not to spend a lot of time with them. You may need to put some distance between yourself and your negative-thinking friends.
- *Exceed* normal expectations to make your dream come true. If you're to reach your dream, you'll have to do that which is beyond the normal. Dreams are not achieved by average energy.
- *Exhibit* an attitude that is confident. I believe that if you are outwardly confident, you will become more confident inwardly. The way we act outwardly affects what we are inwardly.
- *Explore* every possible avenue to reach your dream. Don't let any detour or dead-end street stop you on your way to a dream God has given you. There are more routes up a mountain than just the east side. Go around to the south side. See what else you can do.
- *Extend* a helping hand to someone who has a similar dream,

and both of you will climb together. Mountain climbing is not an individual sport. It's a team sport. One holds the line for the other. As we hold the lines for others, we can all make it to the top, and our dreams can come true.

5

THE BIGGER THEY ARE, THE HARDER THEY FALL

I WANT TO bring some principles out of the story of David and Goliath that will help us to charge the giants in our lives in a more effective way. Before you read any farther, stop and think for a minute: What is your biggest problem? What giant is standing in your path?

This chapter is dedicated to enabling you to be victorious over some seemingly insurmountable barrier or difficulty in your life. Victory requires more than positive thinking; positive thinking is nothing more than a thought pattern. It requires more than enthusiasm; enthusiasm is only a feeling. It even requires more than action. Victory becomes ours when we think right about our problems, feel right about our problems, and then act right about our problems. We need more than just a positive mental attitude.

THINKING RIGHT

I read an interesting article recently about Karl Wallenda, the great tightrope artist. He died a few years ago in Puerto Rico, after a 75-foot fall from a tightrope. On one occasion he said, 'Being on a tightrope is living. Everything else is waiting.' He lived for the thrill of the moment. Wallenda's wife, who was also an aerialist, had some interesting observations concerning what happened before that fateful fall. She said, 'All Karl thought about for three straight months prior to walking across the tightrope was falling. It was the first time he'd ever thought about that. And it seemed to me that he put all of his energies into not falling, rather than walking the tightrope.' Mrs. Wallenda added that her husband went so far as to personally supervise the installation of the tightrope, making absolutely certain that the guy wires were secure. He had always trusted his crew to do this in the past.

He walked the tightrope with the fear of falling in his mind, and his thinking created his feeling of insecurity; we know what happened. He poured all his energy into not falling, and that's exactly what happened to him. I think that's what so often happens to us when we face giants. We look at the Goliaths of our lives in the same way the army of Israel looked at them, and our thoughts focus on not being defeated. That was all they could think about—not being killed, not being destroyed. When we focus on the pitfalls rather than the prize, we often fall right in. We should never allow ourselves to lose sight of our goal, for we may never see it again.

STONE NUMBER ONE—CHECK YOUR CAUSE

How did David kill Goliath? With a slingshot and a stone. We need some stones to knock off the giants in our lives too. Stone number one—check your cause. That is the first thing I would encourage you to do. Identify your purpose. What is the cause that makes you need to tackle your problem? Is it worthy enough to consume your energy, effort, time, commitment? Is it worth the risk you'll be taking? You can be sure that David had a cause. When he arrived on the scene, the first thing he found was a very frightened Israelite army. The second thing he saw was Goliath—and he realized why they were scared to death. David had a giant of a problem to deal with.

I've found that little minds have wishes, and great minds have causes. Many of us are like Woody Allen, who said, 'No matter what I'm working on, I'd like to be doing something else.' I know a lot of people like that! They have never developed a purpose great enough to hold them steady or a commitment strong enough to make a real difference. Behind every great accomplishment is a purpose, not a wish. Our purpose is what keeps us from giving up. Behind every enjoyable experience is a purpose, because purpose puts the seasoning in life, and makes it tasty and exciting.

Here's an acrostic that may help you understand and remember what a sense of purpose will do for you, how it will lift you out of the realm of the ordinary. A purpose will cause you to

Pray more than the ordinary person
Unite more than the ordinary person
Risk more than the ordinary person
Plan more than the ordinary person
Observe more than the ordinary person
Sacrifice more than the ordinary person
Expect more than the ordinary person

A purpose will cause you to spend more time in *prayer.* If your purpose is bigger than you are, you'll need to continually ask God for His wisdom and strength. Prayer is how the power of God is unleashed. We need to look at prayer as taking hold of God's eagerness, not overcoming God's reluctance. Throughout the Scriptures we are challenged to boldly claim victory through prayer: 'Call to Me, and I will answer you, and I will tell you great and mighty things, which you do not know' (Jer. 33:3). 'And whatever you ask in My name, that will I do, that the Father may be glorified in the Son. If you ask Me anything in My name, I will do it' (John 14: 13–14). 'Therefore I say to you, all things for which you pray and ask, believe that you have received them, and they shall be granted you' (Mark 11:24). Through prayer we have the power and privilege to be used of God for a great purpose. The disciples of the first century knew how to pray and claim in faith the power of our omnipotent God to help change the course of history. We serve the same God today.

A purpose will cause you to *unite*—to look for others with similar goals. A good example of this is found in Genesis at the time of the building of the Tower of Babel. Because the people were united in a purpose, they were able to do things that had never been done before—extraordinary things.

A purpose challenges us to *risk* more. We're willing to put ourselves out a little bit farther on the limb; we're willing to get closer to our Goliaths.

If we have a purpose, we will do extraordinary *planning* to see it accomplished. If a cause is bigger than we are, it will require our best organizational skills. Goals aren't met by accident.

A purpose also makes us extraordinarily *observant.* It makes us more sensitive to people and needs around us. We will look for opportunities to move forward.

Having a purpose enables us to *sacrifice* beyond the call of duty. We're willing to lay more on the line. And last, having a purpose allows us to *expect* more than we ordinarily would.

What I'm really saying is this: purpose makes the difference between the ordinary and the extraordinary. A person with a purpose does things out of the ordinary, above average. Personality doesn't make a person extraordinary. Neither does intelligence nor education. What makes a person extraordinary is purpose—the consuming desire to accomplish something in life.

There was only one reason for David to charge Goliath: he had a purpose. The God of Israel was being ridiculed by the Philistines because the Israelites were afraid to tackle their problem. Was their God not able to help them? When we're confronted by the Goliaths in our lives, what is it that makes us want to attack? Our first step should be to identify and examine our causes.

Not long ago I picked up an article about a doctor who had studied the care of the elderly. He found that people who lived to be over 100 years of age all had one thing in common. Now, I expected to read about healthful diets and disciplined exercise programs—subjects that make me uncomfortable. But that wasn't it; the one thing these centenarians had in common was purpose. They each had a positive outlook on life. The future looked bright; they had a reason to live.

THE SECOND STONE—COUNT THE COST

After we check our cause, we need to pick up the second stone with which to fight a Goliath: count the cost. What's it going to cost me to tackle this problem? When God measures a man He puts the measuring tape around his heart, not his head. David not only knew what he wanted, which was Goliath, but he knew what he had to do to achieve his goals; he knew what it was going to cost him.

To defeat Goliath, David had to pay a twofold price. Number one, he had to pay the price of criticism. When he charged his giant, he was going to be criticized.

> *Now Eliab his oldest brother heard when [David] spoke to the men; and Eliab's anger burned against David and he said, 'Why*

have you come down? And with whom have you left those few sheep in the wilderness? I know your insolence and the wickedness of your heart, for you have come down in order to see the battle.' (1 Sam. 17:28)

Notice that the criticism leveled at David came from his brother. While his enemies laughed at him, his friends and relatives criticized him. They said things like, 'You don't belong here. You're too young. You're too inexperienced. You're proud.'

I've found that before any great accomplishment is achieved in reality, it's believed in the heart. If we need to hear the applause of the crowd before our Goliath is down, we will never slay him. We have to begin our attack in the face of criticism, believing that the applause will come later.

In addition to criticism, you should count on some loneliness too. I want you to notice that when David charged up the hill, he didn't charge up there with the army. They were all in their tents with their knees knocking. I can picture them, hundreds of heads peeking out their tent flaps, probably ready to run in the opposite direction when David was destroyed. And I can see David, steadfast in purpose, moving on up the hill alone. When you face your Goliaths, you won't be backed up by an army either. You will have to face them by yourself.

When I think of loneliness, I think of an Olympic competitor. He displays his personal skill, while the world just watches. No one jumps out of the stands to run with him. I think of Christopher Columbus when he wanted to sail due west to Asia, believing that the world was round. 'Oh, no,' everyone else said, 'the world is flat.' I think of Henry Ford and the car. One of my great-great-uncles was a good friend of Henry Ford's. He once told Mr. Ford, 'I have no doubt that you can invent an automobile, but once you've invented it, where will you drive it?

There are no roads! There will be no place for you to go.' My uncle didn't realize that if you have a great enough idea, people will literally move mountains to make that idea become reality. But you have to have the strength of your convictions to launch your dream alone.

Every person who has never killed a giant will tell you that it's impossible. They will tell you it can't happen. So if you set out to confront a Goliath, expect to meet criticism and feel loneliness; it's all part of the process. David understood that. Another David, David Livingstone, charted great paths for missions in Africa. One time a missionary society wrote him a letter saying, 'We have some people who would like to join you. Do you have some easy access roads to get where you are?' Dr. Livingstone wrote back and said, 'If you have men who will come only if there are good roads, I don't want them. I want men who will come even if there is no road at all.' Count your cost. It will cost you something to be victorious in battle. You cannot knock giants off easily.

STONE NUMBER THREE—CHART YOUR COURSE

The third stone that you need in order to knock off your giants is this one: chart your course. Let's look at how David charted his course in 1 Samuel 17:31–40. 'When the words which David spoke were heard, they told them to Saul and he sent for him' (v. 31). I think this verse holds a great lesson for us. The moment that you commit yourself to any great project, you will be tested. As soon as David said he was going to charge Goliath, someone was willing to take him up on it.

I think every person who sets a great goal knows the trauma of first publicly declaring that goal. Many times when I knew that God was calling me to do something that was different or difficult, I had to go through an inward emotional struggle to get myself to say it publicly, because I knew that once I said it publicly, somebody would hold me accountable for what I had said. When I was called to preach, I struggled until I was 17 years old to publicly say it, because I knew that once I announced it, my friends and my family would take it seriously. In 1973, as a young preacher, I felt that I should lead to the Lord 200 people who were outside of my church. I remember driving from Chattanooga, Tennessee to Lancaster, Ohio, wrestling with God for the entire eight-hour trip over whether I should declare this goal publicly. I knew that as soon as I told people, they would really jump on it. I declared it publicly, and for a week I knocked on doors and did everything you're supposed to do to win somebody to the Lord Jesus Christ, but nobody was getting saved. On Saturday night when I came in to do some last-minute study in the church office, a friend was out in the lobby, and he said, 'Pastor, I've been praying for you all week since you declared you want to win 200 people to the Lord. I just wondered, how many have you won this week?' And I remember telling him, 'None—but I'm going to win somebody before tomorrow night.' I turned around and walked out of the church. I went clear across town to do some serious soul-winning—and led a couple to the Lord. They were in church the next morning. What happened? The moment you publicly announce that you're going to charge a Goliath, somebody in the crowd will hold you to it.

As soon as David said, 'I'm going to charge Goliath,' what did the people do? They took him to King Saul. David said to Saul, 'Let no man's heart fail on account of him; your servant will go and fight with this Philistine' (v. 32). In verse 33, Saul says to David, 'You are not able to go against this Philistine to fight with him; for you are but a youth while he has been a warrior from his youth.' The moment you commit yourself to a great project, not only will your statements be tested, but others will express their doubts. As soon as you say what you're going to do, there will be the King Sauls of life who will tell you that it has never been done before and you can't do it either.

> *But David said to Saul, 'Your servant was tending his father's sheep. When a lion or a bear came and took a lamb from the flock, I went out after him and attacked him and rescued it from his mouth; and when he rose up against me, I seized him by his beard and struck him and killed him. Your servant has killed both the lion and the bear, and this uncircumcised Philistine will be like one of them, since he has taunted the armies of the living God.' And David said, 'The Lord who delivered me from the paw of the lion and from the paw of the bear, He will deliver me from the hand of this Philistine.' And Saul said to David, 'Go, and may the Lord be with you.' Then Saul clothed David with his garments and put a bronze helmet on his head, and he clothed him with armor. And David girded his sword over his armor and tried to walk, for he had not tested them. So David said to Saul, 'I cannot go with these, for I have not tested them.' And David took them off. (1 Sam. 17:34–39)*

When you make a commitment to charge a Goliath, the third thing that will happen is this: people will want to tell you how to do it. Can you relate to that? You see, they'll express their doubts, but when they find they can't talk you out of the project, then they'll want to give you instructions on how to handle it. They'll try to put their armor on you. Saul, who himself was unwilling to face Goliath, was more than willing to tell David how to do it. Do you know people like that? The very guy who could not handle the problem himself was willing to tell someone else how to handle it.

As a leader, I will listen to anybody. There's no one who can't teach me something. But the only ones I'm really going to take seriously are those who have an investment in my cause and are willing to charge the hill with me. When they give me their advice, they're putting their lives on the line with me. There are all kinds of people who are willing to stay in the background and tell you how to do it—but they're not willing to be part of it themselves.

Notice that David, when he charted his course, was confident in mapping out his strategy because of his past successes. David knew that the God who helped him with the bear and the God who helped him with the lion is the same God who would help him with the giant. God had delivered him before; God would deliver him again. I can't emphasize enough the importance of getting success under our belts. We've got to have some victories. It is winning that gives us confidence. I find that people who won't handle problems are people who have histories of failure; they're afraid of problems.

When I was a kid, I was very frail and anemic. I ate liver all the time—in fact, I ate it so much that I learned to like it—and I had to take medicine to spinach myself up a little bit. Even so I always had a competitor's heart, and I loved to wrestle my older brother, who was much bigger than I. We'd shove all the living room furniture up against the wall, much to Mother's disapproval, and go at it! Dad not only allowed this regular evening activity, he was our referee. Have you ever watched fake wrestling on TV? That's what we did every night—only it was real—and guess who got killed every night? So one time Dad said to my brother, 'Larry, this week you can't wrestle Johnny. You referee; I'm going to wrestle him.' Every night my dad and I would wrestle for 15 or 20 minutes, and I would finally whip him. I would finally get him down and make him say uncle. I felt so good! After I had defeated my dad every night for a whole week,

Dad said, 'OK, Larry, you and John wrestle again.' And my brother never pinned me again. Did I get strong in a week? No, physically I was about the same, but mentally I had grown a lot. All of a sudden I had deduced that if I could beat my father, I could beat my brother. Dad said it took almost an hour the first night. Larry would almost pin me, but I'd think 'Hey, wait a minute! I whipped Dad; I can whip him.'

That's what had happened to David. David was mentally tough. So he charted his course based on his past successes. That doesn't mean we handle our problems the same way every time, but it does mean that our attitude is the same.

Let me give you another acrostic, this one a formula for planning ahead when you get ready to tackle the Goliaths in your life.

Predetermine your course of action
Lay out your goals
Adjust your priorities
Notify key personnel
Allow time for acceptance
Head into action
Expect problems
Always point to success
Daily review your plan

The letter *P* stands for *predetermining your course of action*: decide what you want to accomplish. David knew what he wanted to have happen. He wanted to kill Goliath; he wanted to take Goliath for the glory of God.

After you determine a course of action, *lay out your goals*. Ask yourself, How do I want to achieve that? Think of the course of action as your umbrella; that's your main purpose. Then set goals that will enable you to accomplish your purpose. David decided to take off the armor of Saul, pick up a slingshot he had used before—a proven, trusted victory tool—and take up the stones. Each of these goals had to be reached before his mission was accomplished.

Third, *adjust your priorities.* That's so important! Once you have determined your course of action and laid out your goals, you'll discover priorities you have to discard, because they won't be effective. You'll have to discard Saul's armor, whatever it is, and pick up what you need.

The *N* stands for *notifying key personnel.* David even did that, didn't he? He went to King Saul and said, 'Here's what is going to happen; here's what I'm going to do.'

The letter *A* stands for *allowing time for acceptance.* After you've predetermined your course of action, laid out your goals, adjusted your personal priorities, and notified the key personnel, you need to allow time for acceptance. Why? Because the world is not used to defeating giants. The more difficult the project, the longer it takes people to accept it. If in your leadership you are finding that people don't need time to accept some of your goals, it's probably because your goals are way too small. You've got to take bigger steps, make bigger plans, meet bigger giants.

Head into action. That comes right after the time for acceptance. Some never defeat their Goliaths because they think that allowing time for acceptance means they have to have a consensus. They think they have to have everybody approve of their plans. You will never kill giants in your life if you need everyone's support. Give them time to understand and accept what you're going to do, but don't expect them to agree with it. They may not vote for it, but allow them time to swallow it, and then head into action.

The letter *E* stands for *expecting problems.* The bigger the project, the bigger the problems. It's always that way. If you're having too easy a time achieving your goal, maybe your goal is not big enough. Don't let problems surprise you; expect them.

I once had breakfast with a fellow in the construction business. He made a statement I'll never forget. He said, 'I have made my money off everybody else's problems.' And he's made a lot of money! He was willing to tackle what no one else would tackle. What others drew back from and were intimidated by he was willing to take on.

Always point to success. There will always be people pointing in the other direction, aiming you toward failure. But keep your eyes focused on success.

Daily review your plan. Check your position every day. The giants move around on the hillside, and what you did yesterday to kill the giant may not work today.

STONE NUMBER FOUR—CONSIDER YOUR CHRIST

Let's go on to the fourth stone we have to pick up if we're going to kill the giants in our lives: consider your Christ. David didn't charge that hill all by himself. He considered his Christ.

> *Then the Philistine came on and approached David, with the shield-bearer in front of him. When the Philistine looked and saw David, he disdained him; for he was but a youth, and ruddy, with a handsome appearance. And the Philistine said to David, 'Am I a dog, that you should come to me with sticks?' And the Philistine cursed David by his gods. The Philistine also said to David, 'Come to me, and I will give your flesh to the birds of the sky and the beasts of the field.'* (1 Sam. 17:41–44)

That is an example of positive thinking. Goliath said, 'Come here, I want to make mincemeat out of you.' But there's a difference between positive thinking and positive faith, and in verse 45 we see positive faith.

> *Then David said to the Philistine, 'You come to me with a sword, a spear, and a javelin, but I come to you in the name of the Lord of Hosts, the God of the armies of Israel, whom you have taunted. This day the Lord will deliver you up into my hands, and I will strike you down and remove your head from you. And I will give the dead bodies of the army of the Philistines this day to the birds of the sky and the wild beasts of the earth, that all the earth may know that there is a God in Israel, and that all this assembly may know that the Lord does not deliver by sword or by spear; for the battle is the Lord's and He will give you into our hands.' (vv. 45–47)*

That's the difference between positive thinking and positive faith. Paul made that great statement, 'I can do all things through Him who strengthens me' (Phil. 4:13). This verse includes four positive things. The 'I can' is the positive *thinking.* When Paul goes on to say, 'I can do,' that's positive *action.* If your positive thinking is right, it will result in positive action. When he says, 'I can do all things,' that's positive *faith.* A less confident person would have said, 'I can do *some* things,' but Paul believes he can do *all* things. He also had positive *power.* 'I can do all things through Him,' meaning Christ. When we measure our possibilities, we should do so not by what we see in ourselves, but by what we see of God in us. Our God 'is able to do exceeding abundantly beyond all that we ask or think, according to the power that works within us' (Eph. 3:20). We cannot even imagine what God wants to do in our lives.

STONE NUMBER FIVE—CHARGE YOUR CHALLENGE

If you want to be effective, charge your challenge. Go get it! David seized his chance to get into action.

> *Then it happened when the Philistine rose and came and drew near to meet David, that David ran quickly toward the battle line to meet the Philistine. And David put his hand into his bag and took from it a stone and flung it, and struck the Philistine on his forehead. And the stone sank into his forehead, so that he fell on his face to the ground. Thus David prevailed over the Philistine with a sling and a stone, and he struck the Philistine and killed him; but there was no sword in David's hand. Then David ran and stood over the Philistine and took his sword and drew it out of its sheath and killed him, and cut off his head with it. When the Philistines saw that their champion was dead, they fled. And the men of Israel and Judah arose and shouted and pursued the Philistines. (1 Sam. 17:48–52)*

I consider that last verse to be the key to the whole story. The reason we need to kill the giants in our lives is this: those whom we lead will never kill the giants in their lives until we first kill the giants in our lives. When did the people shout? When did they charge? They did it after David had killed the giant. When leaders fail to conquer their own problems, their followers never become victorious. This is the number-one problem in leadership in the country. There are too many people in leadership positions who are not successful because they're not facing problems head-on. If they are unwilling to confront their giants, if they are not overcomers, neither will their followers be. When the leader fails, the people fail. When the leader fears, the people fear.

All over the country I see congregations trying to survive in the midst of major problems because they don't know how to deal with them. They don't know how to knock off a giant because they've never seen their pastors do it. Think of how we would release our people if we became giant killers. Imagine what that would do to their faith! The number-one problem in the church is that we're not seeing miracles; we're not seeing God do His work. We think of miracles as history, and we think of victory as history. We ought to pray that God will give us a seemingly insurmountable barrier so that our people can see the power of God at work in us to defeat giants.

My first church was in a rural area of Indiana. We decided we wanted to have 300 people in our Sunday School. One sincere member of that congregation, Mike, was convinced it couldn't be done. One Sunday he stood up right in the morning service and said, 'Pastor, we can't *do* that.' Mike had a sincere heart, a loving, wonderful, pure gold heart, but he didn't have an expanded mind. I remember looking at him and smiling, and saying, 'Mike, if we do it, will you stand up and apologize and tell this congregation you'll never think small again?' It was kind of a brash thing for a twenty-four-year-old kid to say, but it didn't offend Mike; he said he would. The day we had 301 in Sunday School, Mike stood up, tears streaming down his face, and he told the whole congregation, 'I'll never think small again.'

I did something for Mike that day. It was great to have 301 in Sunday School; but for Mike it was greater to have the lid taken off his thinking. One of his giants had been slain.

In 1954 there were medical articles that said that the human body can't run a four-minute mile. They said that physically the body was not able to withstand that much pressure. And then what happened? In 1954 Roger Bannister, a young medical student, went out and ran a mile in under four minutes. Today, any miler that's going to have any kind of national recognition runs a mile in less than four minutes. Between 1954 and 1956, 213 men ran under four minutes, all because one guy broke the barrier.

In the 1900 Olympics Irving Baxter high jumped 6'2". People said the impossible barrier was 7 feet—no one would ever jump over 7 feet. Then a guy by the name of Fosbury figured out that high jumpers were jumping the wrong way over the bar: they shouldn't go over feet first; they should go over head first backward. Everyone else laughed and ridiculed while he worked on an unorthodox way to jump over the high bar. Critics dubbed his method, 'the Fosbury flop'—but he 'flopped' over 7 feet. Recently an East German jumped 7'8¾".

Back in 1956, 15 feet was thought to be the limit for a good pole vault. Then someone discovered that a fiberglass pole gave a little higher lift than the conventional pole. Now a Polish athlete has pole vaulted 18' 11¾". Nineteen feet will be the next record, and perhaps sometime down the road, 20 feet. Why? Because somebody broke the record. A giant was killed, so everybody else decided to charge. That's what can happen every day in your life. No matter what your ministry is, the moment you begin to knock those giants down, people will say, 'We can do that too!' And off they'll go. It gives them permission; it gives them confidence.

What are some lessons we've learned from David's encounter with Goliath?

We fail, not because of big problems, but because of small purposes. Our failures are not caused by giants. Goliaths don't defeat us; small purposes defeat us.

We usually have to charge Goliaths by ourselves. Don't expect a whole crowd of people to gather around you, waving banners and patting you on the back. Whoever steps out first will step out alone.

Small successes lead to greater successes. Begin to have some victories over small things in your life. Make every day a victory day over something, and build a track record of success.

Success for most people comes after someone else has done the impossible. Success for the army of Israel came after David defeated the giant. Help someone else be a success—knock off a giant. Remember, the bigger they are, the harder they fall.

What would you say *you* have learned from David and Goliath? What have you picked up that may help make a difference as you face giants in your life? Take a few minutes to consider what you've learned—then go meet your giants!

6

SEE IT—SAY IT—SEIZE IT!

THERE ARE three levels of living. First is the see-it level, which is the bottom level. Anybody can live on this level. Everybody has the opportunity to see. Now when I say 'see-it,' I'm not talking about visual acuity; I'm talking about faith's opportunity. Some of us are visually acute; but blind to opportunity.

In my church in Ohio there was a fellow who was a great hunter. We sometimes drove together to Columbus, a 25-mile freeway ride. As we drove, he would say things like, 'Did you see that groundhog?' No, I didn't see that groundhog. 'Did you see that rabbit?' I didn't see the rabbit. 'Did you see that duck?' I didn't see the duck either. We'd drive all the way to Columbus, and he'd see about 10 animals and all I would see was the freeway. All those animals were in my range of vision, but I didn't see them because I had not been trained to look for them. The see-it level of living is faith's opportunity. We can all be looking from the same spot and not see the same thing.

The second level is the say-it level, and that's what I call faith's word. To see it is the opportunity for faith; to say it is the word of faith. That is where we begin to verbally commit ourselves to what has gripped our vision. The Bible is full of say-it faith. The

Word of God teaches us, 'If you confess with your mouth Jesus as Lord . . . you shall be saved' (Rom. 10:9).

Then comes the seize-it level of living. This is the level at which faith becomes action. It's more than verbiage, and it's more than vision—it's a vital action within our hearts and lives.

Since everyone starts on level one, the see-it level, we all have the opportunity to grab hold of faith's opportunity. As you climb the steps, however, fewer and fewer people climb with you. When you get to the seize-it stage, the action stage, you will find yourself in an elite group; most people never climb this high. They have missed faith's opportunity and life's action.

THE EXAMPLE OF CALEB

There is an example in the Bible of a person who reached the seize-it level, and his name is Caleb. When we pick up Caleb's story, it is 45 years after he spied out the land of Canaan, bringing back a good report. Now the Israelites are in the process of taking the land for their own. In Joshua 14 Caleb is talking to the elders, those in leadership. 'I was forty years old when Moses the servant of the Lord sent me from Kadesh-barnea to spy out the land' (v. 7). That's the see-it stage; he has seen the land. Caleb goes on, 'I brought word back to him as it was in my heart' (v. 7). That's the say-it stage.

The vision began to seize him. It not only got into his head through his eyes, but it got into his heart. He began to *feel* what he had seen. 'Give me this hill country about which the Lord spoke on that day, for you heard on that day that Anakim were there, with great fortified cities; perhaps the Lord will be with me, and I shall drive them out' (v. 12). Joshua, having seen Caleb's commitment to the vision 45 years earlier, gave Caleb the land: Caleb *seized* what he *said* he *saw.* Caleb is not alone in the pages of Scripture. I have found that most great men of God, went through these three stages before their visions became realities.

SEE IT—FAITH'S OPPORTUNITY

Moses. Let's look first at the see-it stage in some of the Bible's great leaders. Moses is a prime example of a leader who saw faith's opportunity. When I look at the life of Moses as the author of Hebrews sums it up, I am impressed by the fact that Moses was motivated by his vision.

> *By faith Moses, when he had grown up, refused to be called the son of Pharaoh's daughter; choosing rather to endure ill-treatment with the people of God, than to enjoy the passing pleasures of sin; considering the reproach of Christ greater riches than the treasures of Egypt; for he was looking to the reward. By faith he left Egypt, not fearing the wrath of the king; for he endured, as seeing Him who is unseen. (Heb. 11:24–27)*

Moses was a great see-it leader, a great visionary. I want you to see four things that Moses' vision helped him to accomplish. Number one, it helped him to make difficult decisions. He refused to be called the son of Pharaoh's daughter. That was a difficult decision; he was giving up his royal position; he was giving up all the pleasures of Egypt. He was able to make that decision because he saw a greater calling, a greater vision.

The second thing that Moses' vision helped him to do was to be willing to pay the price. The price was enduring ill-treatment with the people of God rather than enjoying the passing pleasures of sin. He was going to endure instead of enjoy—because he had a vision.

Third, Moses' vision helped him to live for the eternal and not for the temporal. Because he had a vision, he did not have to live for today; he could live for tomorrow. He considered the reproach of Christ more valuable than the treasures of Egypt. Why? The treasures of Egypt were present, but he was looking to a future reward. He didn't have that reward in his hands as he could have had the pleasures and the treasures of Egypt. Because he was a visionary, he lived for tomorrow instead of for today.

Fourth, Moses' vision helped him overcome fear in his life. By faith he left Egypt, not fearing the wrath of the king.

I have discovered that having a vision will do the same things for us that it did for Moses. It will help us make difficult decisions. People who cannot make difficult decisions may feel torn between good things. What keeps them from being able to choose the best is that they have no purpose because they have no vision.

A vision will help us pay the price. It provides the motivation for us to give up good things now for better things later. A vision will also help us rise above fear. It keeps us from becoming immobilized by monsters so that we will be able to move mountains.

Caleb. We've already looked briefly at Caleb, but let's see what Caleb's vision helped him accomplish. First, it helped him develop conviction. He says in Joshua 14:7 that when he saw the land, he told Moses that his heart had seized it. His vision gave him conviction. He was able to stand up against the other spies, to follow through on his vision.

His vision helped him obey God. Others' hearts began to melt with fear, but Caleb said, 'I followed the Lord my God fully' (Josh. 14:8). Why? Because he had a vision.

It helped him stay young. We all hear about vitamin B and vitamin C, but the best vitamin you can have is vitamin V, the vision vitamin. When people take vitamin V, they are revitalized daily. Age never becomes an issue because they still have a goal, they still have a dream, and they still have a vision. At 85 years of age Caleb was ready to go to war for the land. His strength had not abated. Why? Vitamin V. He had a vision.

His vision helped him secure the land. He eventually possessed it—because he first of all saw it.

I often meet people who are drowning in life's problems. Yet it really isn't their problems that are weighing them down; it's their lack of vision. A big vision will help you overcome any problem, but a small vision or no vision at all will cause the smallest of problems to trip you up and keep you from becoming what you should be.

Abram. The prerequisite for possessing new territory is sight. The story of Abram and Lot provides a great example. When Abram and Lot separated, Abram gave Lot the first choice of land; Lot took the well-watered plains of Jordan. Abram had what was left, which was the supposedly second-rate land. 'And the Lord said to Abram, after Lot had separated from him, "Now lift up your eyes and look from the place where you are, northward and southward and eastward and westward; for all the land which you see, I will give it to you and to your descendants forever"' (Gen. 13:14–15). Abram was encouraged to do three things. First God said, 'Look.' Then He added, 'from the place where you stand.' Now, this is more complex than it sounds. He was telling Abram that all the opportunities for being a success could be seen from where he was right then. The roving commentator for the local TV station would have been following Lot down to the well-watered plains of Jordan, because it looked like Lot took the best, but God told Abram to look beyond what looked plush and lush and green and fruitful and to look from where he was standing. He told Abram to see what opportunities lay before him.

Too often we want to go stand on someone else's spot; we want to get on their mountain and look around at their green grass. But God was telling Abram, 'Abram, there's no need to run over there where Lot is; you stand right here and look. Where *you* are standing are opportunities.' The good news is that where you are, whatever your lot in life is, under your feet is gold. All you have to do is see it and believe it.

The third thing He told Abram is, 'Look in every direction.' I don't think it's an accident in the Scriptures that He spelled it out: northward, southward, eastward, and westward. To miss seeing a section was to miss possessing it. He had to spell it out because some of the areas that Abram could see didn't look too promising. Maybe if God had said, 'Abram, I want to give you the best land,' Abram wouldn't even have looked at some of those areas because he knew the land well.

Vision always comes before victory. James said, 'You do not have because you do not ask' (James 4:2). Could it be that we don't ask because we don't see? My wife and I know better than to take our son Joel into any store. He's a little Abram. That little guy can walk into any store and see opportunity. There are very few things for sale for which he couldn't find a use. Be it a toy store or a drapery store, he never fails to find something he desperately needs and thinks he should have. He's always ready to go out and possess the land. We would prefer to possess him and stick him back in the car, because what he doesn't see, he doesn't desire to have. The point is this: to have something you have to first see it.

FOCUS YOUR VISION

There are four areas in which we need to fine-tune our vision. First, do I see *myself* correctly? How can we see ourselves accurately? Spend time in prayer and meditation. Notice problems that continually arise in your life. What kind of problems are they and when do they occur? If your problems are similar in nature and they occur in the same types of situations, you've never really dealt with the cause. Ask yourself some questions: What kinds of circumstances cause me to show strong emotion, either positive or negative? What kind of people do I spend my time with? What spiritual gifts do I possess, and am I using them? How am I living in the light of my knowledge of God? If there are areas in which you're falling short, try to identify the reasons why.

The second thing we need to see is our *inner desires.* If you could be anything you wanted to be and do anything you wanted to do, what would you be or do? What would really bring joy to your life? If you can answer this question, you have identified your inner desires. Knowing this will help you reach your potential.

We need to see our *resources,* both internal and external. What are your personal strengths? What can you draw on to help you possess the land? Do you surround yourself with supportive people? Do you use past experiences to your benefit? Do you take advantage of opportunities as they arise?

Fourth, we need to get a clear sight of our *God.* We need to see Him as the God 'who is able to do exceeding abundantly beyond all that we can ask or think, according to the power that works within us' (Eph. 3:20).

SAY IT—FAITH'S WORD

In Hebrews 11 there is a list of examples of active faith. The possessors of this faith are described in summary in verse 13:

> *All these died in faith, without receiving the promises, but having seen them and having welcomed them from a distance, and having confessed that they were strangers and exiles on the earth.*

First they *saw* the promises—that's see-it faith. Then they confessed, or *said*, that they were strangers and exiles—that's say-it faith.

STEPS TO SAYING IT

There are four steps toward possessing a say-it faith. How do you make your inward belief an outward confession? First you need the *confidence* to say what you believe. Many great dreams die because the dreamers lack the confidence to declare them. Whenever we are unsure of ourselves or our projects, we usually remain silent. We don't say it because we want to save face.

Saying it takes *commitment*. Many great dreams die because dreamers lack the commitment to declare them. Other people cannot follow our inward hopes; they follow our visible commitments. It's seeing the dream consume us and seeing the commitment that makes us act on that dream that causes others to follow it. Commitment is contagious. People will only catch what has caught you.

The third step to say-it faith is good *communication*. Many great dreams die because dreamers lack the communication skills to get it across. This is very important. There are four ways that people learn: listening, discussing, watching, and discovering, or participating. Discovering, or participating, is the most effective way to learn. You need to help your people discover that dream for themselves by allowing them to participate. They need to hear about it, discuss it, and see it happening. You will not have effectively communicated your dream, however, until they participate in it.

If we're going to say it, there's a fourth thing we need, and that's *conviction*. Many great dreams die because the dreamers lack conviction to act on them. There's a difference between commitment and conviction. Commitment keeps me going when things get tough. Conviction keeps others going when things get tough. People around us are motivated by emotion, our conviction, that tangible sense of morale. People do not follow a leader because of character; they follow a leader because of conviction. People do not do things because it is right; they do things because they feel that it's right. When we act on our conviction, others are drawn to us. Without conviction we may communicate truths, but we'll develop no disciples. We will have people who have the right answers, but we won't have people who live the right lives.

Saying it, then, requires confidence, or knowing it; commitment, doing it; communication, showing it; and finally, conviction, feeling it. To have say-it faith you have to know it, do it, show it, and feel it, and then you'll be able to say it.

SEIZE IT—FAITH'S ACTION

Few will cross the Jordan to seize the prize. I think there are four reasons why some of us get right to the edge of the river and then don't go on across and possess the land. First, we're too close to success to risk failure. Fear of failure probably keeps more people from positive action than anything else.

The second reason that we do not seize it is that this level requires *discipline.* If you're going to act on your dream, it takes more than just sitting around on the sofa. You have to roll up your sleeves and go to work. It does not take any discipline to dream, but it does take discipline to make those dreams real.

The third reason that many people do not seize it is that this level *divides the concerned from the committed.* I have found that you can get almost anybody to agree to almost anything. You can get almost anybody to show some kind of concern for something. But there are few people willing to leave the ranks of the concerned to join the committed.

This level takes *time.* If you're going to seize your dream, you'll have to make a time commitment. You can say your dream in a moment, but you can seldom seize a worthwhile dream in less than a lifetime.

SECURE THAT DREAM!

How are we going to secure that dream of a life? I would suggest six things:

State dreams
Examine motives
Consider options
Utilize resources
Remove nonessentials
Embrace essentials

The first thing to do is state your dreams. Write them out on a piece of paper. Look at them. Then examine all your motives. You have to ask yourself, *Why am I doing this? Do I have pure, right motives?* If the motive isn't right, the dream will die. Make sure in the beginning that your motive is right.

Consider all your options. Now that you have stated your dreams and examined your motives, sit down and consider all of your options. How many ways can you reach this goal? There is more than one option. Everybody needs a backup plan; everybody needs a plan B and a plan C and a plan D. Next, utilize your resources. Find people around you who have a similar dream and work with them.

The letter *R* stands for removing your nonessentials. Get the excess baggage off your back, anything that keeps you from achieving your dream. The letter *E* stands for embracing your challenges. Picture difficulties in front of you and practice reacting positively instead of negatively. Learn to wring out of those challenges the best that God has for you.

In February 1973 when bus ministries were really big, I went to a conference in Lynchburg, Virginia. Jerry Falwell was talking about buses, and he challenged the 5,000 of us there to get a dream for a bus ministry. God began to speak to my heart, saying, 'John, you could have in one year as many people on buses as what your church was averaging when you came.' Our average attendance had been 418. I didn't even have a bus. I remember going back to the Holiday Inn and lying on the floor saying, 'God, do You *really* want me to do this?' Falwell had said, 'Tomorrow, we're going to give you a card and you're going to write down your name and the number you're going to have on buses within one year. And you're going to bring them forward and we're going to read them.' I thought, *Oh, no, they're going to read this in front of 5,000 people from all over the world!* I wrestled with it all night. The next day I took that card and put 418 on that card—and I didn't have a bus! With fear and trembling I handed in my card, and it was read in front of 5,000 people. I thought, *This is the worst thing I've ever done in my life.* But I became motivated because I had said it. Falwell wrote a letter to my church board telling them my goal, and I had to go out and raise money for buses before we ever brought it to the board. The great thing is that in one year's time, literally one year from that day, we had 438 people on buses. Why? Because we went out and seized it.

A FIRST STEP TOWARD SEEING YOUR DREAM

What do you see God challenging you to do or be in the next year? Whom will you share this dream with in the next two weeks? How will you seize this goal and make it become a reality? Take fifteen minutes right now and write down the answers to these questions on a 3" x 5" card. Then write down some steps of action you're going to take to seize that dream. Place your card in a visible location. Read it in the morning, act on it during the day, evaluate it in the evening, and pray about it at night. Don't let this opportunity pass you by. There are many people in this world who *see* it. There are some people in this world who *say* it. But there are only a few people in this world who *seize* it. Filling out this card is the first step toward seizing your dream.

7

THE 101 PERCENT PRINCIPLE

THE EFFECTIVENESS of our leadership is determined by our ability to relate to others. Leadership is *influence.* Whether it's effective, positive leadership or ineffective, negative leadership, when people are leading others, they have influence—what they say, what they think, and what they do influence those who follow them.

Your relationship with others determines how you will influence them. Are they under your care? Are they accountable to you? Are you consistent and approachable? Do you project a positive attitude? Your relationships with the people around you will do more to determine your effectiveness as a leader than anything else. Too often we try to separate leadership from relationships. We look at leadership as position, title, or a name.

JESUS' RELATIONAL LEADERSHIP

John 10 gives us a biblical understanding of relational leadership. Jesus, describing the Good Shepherd, says,

> *The sheep hear his voice, and he calls his own sheep by name, and leads them out . . . He goes before them, and the sheep follow*

him because they know his voice. And a stranger they simply will not follow, but will flee from him, because they do not know the voice of strangers. (John 10:3–5)

There are three components of relational leadership in this Scripture passage. The first is that the shepherd knows his sheep intimately. His relationship with them is such that he recognizes them instantly. The sheep know his voice, and he knows their names. He is personally acquainted with each one.

The second component of relational leadership is that the relationship is built on trust. The shepherd not only knows the name of his sheep, but his sheep trust him. They hear his voice and come to him, but they will run from a stranger. From this we can learn that leaders must be worthy of their followers' trust.

The third component is that relationships are modeled. The shepherd walks ahead of his sheep, and they follow him.

Someone asked chief executives of major companies in the United States to name the characteristic they wanted most in potential employees. By far the great majority of these executives said that what they wanted to see more than anything else in people who came into their companies was the ability to work with other people. Of course they want them to have certain abilities and skills, but more than that, they want people who can work well with others. If you can relate well with others, you can survive almost any situation in life. John Rockefeller, the builder of giant corporations, said, 'I will pay more for the ability to deal with people than any other ability under the sun.'

A survey was sent out to 2,000 employers, asking respondents to check the files of the last three persons they dismissed from their jobs and tell why they were fired. In two out of three cases, the answer was the same: the employees could not get along with other people. People did not lose their jobs because they lacked skills; they lost their jobs because they lacked ability to relate effectively with others.

We're going to deal with two things in this chapter: handling conflicts in relationships, which I find to be the number-one problem of people in leadership positions, and creating effective relationships.

HANDLING CONFLICTS

The secret to handling conflicts successfully is to live according to the 101 percent principle. If there is someone under your umbrella of leadership who tends to be obstinate, find the 1 percent on which the two of you agree, and give it all you've got—100 percent of your effort and ability. Let that 1 percent shred of agreement be the tie that binds you together.

There's a tendency for us to generalize and idealize relationships. Remember the Parable of the Lost Sheep? One sheep disobeyed and disappeared; it left the security of the flock to go out and do its own thing. The shepherd could have said, 'We're better off without you—be some lion's dinner!' But no, the shepherd left the 99 that were secure and went in search of the one that was lost (Luke 15:4–6). That's a perfect example of the 101 percent principle. The shepherd looked until he found it; he expended a great deal of energy to develop that relationship with the very one who had not been in kilter with the rest of the gang. That's the 101 percent principle.

And I want to give you ten commandments for handling conflicts. I think they'll be helpful to you because all of us have times when we have to take a relationship that's not healthy and try to bring healing to it.

TEN CONFLICT COMMANDMENTS

Follow the 101 percent principle. I had a friend in my last church who had caused me all kinds of difficulties. He had done the same with the two previous pastors. In fact, I'm pretty sure he was the reason both of them left the church. For months I thought and prayed about ways to develop a relationship with him. I was looking for that 1 percent. He and his wife had adopted two children into their family, and we had adopted two in ours. One Halloween night I took my daughter, Elizabeth, who was then about two years of age, to his house and knocked on the door. I'd already programmed her to go over and give him a big hug and tell him she loved him. She did and he melted. As he stood there crying, I knew I had found the crack in his tough exterior and the 1 percent that we had in common—adopted children. That began to build a relationship that became very successful. That's the 101 percent principle.

Love people more than opinions. Anyone who loves his opinions more than he does his friends will defend his opinions and destroy his friends. People who are not effective in relationships usually have a higher regard for their opinions than they do for people. We need to step back and look at what is really important to us. Is it helping or hindering our relationships with people?

Give others the benefit of the doubt. We usually rule ourselves with our hearts, but we rule others with our heads. We have mercy on ourselves but not on the other person. If you want to build relationships, follow this rule: when working with yourself use your head; when working with others, use your heart. Give other people the benefit of the doubt.

Learn to be flexible. Thomas Jefferson once said, 'In matters of principle, stand like a rock. In matters of taste, swim with the current.' In my last church when they were decorating the sanctuary, I really didn't like what they were doing, but I also realized that it wasn't that important. If the issue is evangelism, I'm not going to waver for anybody—that's a matter of principle. But if we're talking about the color of the carpeting or the stain on the pews, I'll swim with the current. Learn to be flexible in your life. The greater the man, the more flexible he is. Good leaders learn how to say 'I'm sorry' more quickly than followers. Effective leaders know how to back down; they don't constantly feel the need to defend their rights; they've learned to differentiate between principles and taste; they've learned to be flexible.

Provide an escape hatch for the person in conflict. I have watched people defend their actions, not because they knew they were right, but because their pride kept them from backing down. It takes a strong leader to allow someone who has been defeated to ease out of a situation and save face. Once the point has been made, back off.

Check your own attitude. Many times wrong relationships develop because of wrong attitudes. You need to ask yourself questions to help you know whether your attitude is right or wrong. For instance, if you're having conflicts with several people, there's a good chance the problem is you, not them. Ask yourself, Am I constantly in conflict, or is this an exception? If it's an exception, your attitude is probably fine. The attitude with which we view people determines to a large extent our perception of how they feel about us. Check your attitude.

Don't overreact to conflicts. You're going to have conflicts; don't make them worse by overreacting to them. Don't drop a bomb when a slingshot will work. If you expect conflicts, you will be better prepared to handle them sensibly.

Don't become defensive. You never win in relationships when you're defensive. A secure leader knows how to say, 'I'm sorry. I was wrong. I misunderstood. Please forgive me.' The moment that you defend yourself, the moment that you stand up for your rights, you're going to start a battle. We never resolve differences by being defensive.

Welcome the conflict. Make it a learning experience. Most of us will never enjoy conflicts, but we can be thankful for them if we learn from them. Conflicts will either give you ulcers or understanding: you choose which it will be.

Take a risk. Many people do not handle conflict in relationships because they are afraid to put their hands out first. If my relationship with you is shaky and you extend your hand toward me in a gesture of friendship, how do you feel if I don't clasp it? First, you feel ridiculous standing there with your hand in the air. Then you feel rejected. Many people don't handle their conflicts because they don't want to be rejected. They're unwilling to take that risk.

When I realized that I was going to be a leader, I sat down one day and wrote down all the ways a leader can be hurt. After I wrote them down, dozens of them, I categorized them. I decided that leaders will always be hurt. Don't let anybody sell you on the idea that everybody's going to love you all the time. If you are out front leading people, you will be hurt. The issue is not will you or won't you but in what way will you be hurt? I decided that I would be hurt because I trust people and make myself vulnerable to them. I know people who say, 'I won't get close to people, so they won't hurt me.' I've watched people build themselves into glass cases; they make good mannequins but poor leaders. Because I am willing to be hurt in that area, I find that there are people I have trusted, people I have believed in, who have grown because I risked getting close to them; I risked being rejected by them. Many times more often than not, it's worth the risk. Allow yourself to be vulnerable.

CULTIVATING GOOD RELATIONSHIPS

Fortunately, we don't always have to handle conflicts. We do have some good relationships. How can we make them better? In John 10 we can find three things to do to cultivate relationships: know them, grow them, and show them. Relationships start with knowing, continue with growing, and climax with showing. Know them: Jesus called His sheep by name. Grow them: they heard His voice and came to Him. Show them: Jesus walked ahead of His sheep, and they followed Him.

Know them. Let me give you the ABCs of beginning effective relationships. *Acknowledge* your need for others. For your relationships to be cultivated effectively, you have to admit that you need other people in your life. Paul teaches that 'there are many members, but one body. And the eye cannot say to the hand, "I have no need of you"; or again the head to the feet, "I have no need of you"' (1 Cor. 12:20–21). A complete Christian is filled with God's Spirit but is also complemented by different gifted friends. Friends are essential. Acknowledge your need of them. Until you do that, you'll never cultivate effective relationships.

Believe in the value of others. Carlisle said, 'A great man shows his greatness by the way he treats the little man.' The value you place on people determines whether you are a motivator or a manipulator of men. Motivation is moving together for mutual advantage. It's all of us moving together because it benefits all of us; manipulation is moving together for my advantage. There's a difference. With the motivator, everybody wins. With the manipulator, only the 'leader' wins.

Concentrate on people, not programs. The only things that God will ever rescue from this planet are His people. Therefore, if you want a ministry of permanence, you must build into the lives of others. Changing programs won't establish permanence; changing people will. Some of the most miserable people I know are program changers and builders. On the other hand, the happiest people I know are people builders and changers. Where are you going to put your life? Concentrate on people.

Grow them. If you want to help people grow, you need to be available to them when they need you. People going through hard times have deeply felt needs that you can reach out to meet. As you do, you will find your relationships with them deepening. Timing is more important than time in a relationship. Walking into the lives of people when they really need you is more important than being with them all the times when they don't really need you. Timing is essential.

Be a reliable leader. Relationships grow on consistency; they shrink on moodiness. Be approachable: have you ever wanted to see somebody who had tremendous mood swings but hesitated because you didn't know whether that person would love you or bite your head off? As a leader, be reliable so your people can always feel comfortable coming to you.

Be a reassuring leader. Relationships grow in an atmosphere of affirmation. Most people are insecure; because they need encouragement, you need to be an encourager. Margaret and I recently had a talk with our daughter's gymnastics instructor. He has had trouble grasping the importance of affirming people: he's quick to tell the kids in the class when they do something wrong, but he doesn't know how to say, 'That was good. You're doing well there.' We encouraged him to use some positive reinforcement with Elizabeth. Affirm your people. That's how they grow.

Be a resourceful leader. Relationships grow when someone has answers to questions. Become a problem solver. Have something to contribute. We all like to be around people who can stretch us, teach us, and help us grow.

Show them. People do what they see. In cultivating relationships we have to model for others good people skills. People do not care how much you know, but they know how much you care, and they know how much you care by the way you act, not by what you say.

In studies of the leadership of American businesses, it has been shown that executives spend three-fourths of their working days with *people.* The largest single cost in most businesses is *people.* The most valuable asset of any company is its *people.* All executive plans are carried out, or fail to be carried out, by *people.* Our relationships with people will determine the success of our leadership. We can either work with people or war against them. We can be plows or bulldozers: the plow turns over the earth, stirring it up, cultivating it, making it a good place for seed to grow; the bulldozer scrapes the earth, pushing obstacles aside. Both plows and bulldozers are useful instruments, but one wrecks while the other cultivates. The plow type of leader sees in people riches waiting to be uncovered and cultivated; the bulldozer type of leader sees in people obstacles to be destroyed. Be a cultivator!

8

SOLVE OUR PROBLEMS, BUT SAVE OUR PIGS!

WHEN I conduct church leaders' clinics, I ask the pastors to tell me all the ways they can think of to grow a church. We take about 15 or 20 minutes, and I fill up a blackboard with ways to get a church growing. We have on that board every essential ingredient for building a church. After reviewing the list, I point out to them that we all *know* how to build a church. We already have 50 church growth books on our shelves. We already have all those answers. The issue is not whether we *know* how to build a church; it's whether we're willing to *pay the price* to make it happen.

One time when Jesus went over to the Gadarene country, a couple of demon-possessed men met Him. He cast the demons out of them and sent the demons into a herd of pigs. The pigs rushed into the sea and drowned (Matt. 8:28–34). Until Jesus came, there had been a real problem in that community. Every time people went near the graveyard, the demon-possessed men came out, wild and naked, and attacked them. But the people weren't happy when their pigs drowned, even though the demons were disposed of too. They wanted to get rid of the demon-possessed men, but they didn't want to lose their pigs.

They remind me of people who want God to solve their problems without its costing them anything. They want all the solutions, but they want them for nothing.

There are some observations about this incident that begin to float to the surface. The people themselves were unwilling to pay the price to see the problem solved. I think that's the most obvious lesson. They wanted to get rid of the demon-possessed men, but they also wanted to save their pigs. It is also interesting to me that the demons didn't want to leave the Gadarene country. They wanted to stay right there. They obviously knew a good thing when they saw it; they found the people in that area easy prey.

We don't want to be confronted with changes or problems. Even when God Himself brings them into our lives, we want to escape them. We want deliverance without disturbance. We want the benefits without the bills. We want success without sacrifice. But it just doesn't happen that way. We cannot afford to drift into a lifestyle that places repose above results. We must welcome the changes that God's Spirit brings and accept them on His conditions and not ours. And it's up to us to set the pace for those who are following us, whatever the cost.

Let's talk about the costs of leadership. What do we really have to pay in order to have credibility, power, and authority in our leadership?

LEADERSHIP MEANS DISCOMFORT

If you are going to be a successful leader, you are going to experience a great amount of discomfort.

In *Success* magazine in October 1985 there was an excerpt from *Doing It Now* by Edwin C. Bliss (Scribners) that really grabbed me.

> *We live in a culture that worships comfort. During this century we have seen the greatest assault on discomfort in the history of the human race. We have learned to control our environment with central heating and air conditioning. We have reduced drudgery with machines and computers. And we have learned to control pain, depression, and stress. We even provide electronic antidotes to boredom with television sets and video games. Most of this is to the good, but unfortunately it has created an impression that the purpose of life is to attain a blissful state of nirvana, a total absence of struggle or strain. The emphasis is on consuming not producing; on short-term hedonism rather than long-term satisfaction. We seek immediate gratification of our desires, with no penalties.*

Life just doesn't work that way, at least not for many and not for long. One of Benjamin Franklin's favorite sayings was 'There is no gain without pain.' The great goal of becoming what one is capable of becoming can be achieved only by those who are willing to pay the price, and the price always involves sacrifice, discomfort, unpleasantness, and even pain.

OUR GRATIFICATION CULTURE

What are some of the signs in today's society of the pursuit of immediate gratification? How about fast-food restaurants? Credit cards? Abortion clinics? An abundance of divorce lawyers? The list could go on and on. We want to play; we don't want to have responsibility. We want the position and the paycheck, but we don't want to do the work.

Consider the life of the Apostle Paul, one of the greatest leaders in the first century. He understood perhaps better than any of his peers that we have to pay the price to solve our problems. In 2 Corinthians 11:23–29 Paul describes the price he paid for his apostleship, the cost of his success in leadership. There are three things I want to draw out of this chapter as we look at the relationship between leadership and discomfort.

Paul would tell us to *never get comfortable.* When you look at all the affliction he went through, you can see that Paul never thought that he had a claim on comfort. When he wrote about being beaten, shipwrecked, and abandoned, he wasn't asking for pity. He was simply describing his very real experiences. He understood that if comfort is our highest aim, we will miss out on the riches of the kingdom of God.

An American professor was talking to a Christian from the Soviet Union about Christianity in both lands. The Russian woman commented on the difference between receiving Christ in the United States and receiving Christ in the Soviet Union. In American the new Christian is led to a comfortable church and a padded pew, while in the Soviet Union the new believer is prepared for death. Paul tells us not to get comfortable. A person cannot be committed to comfort and at the same time be committed to Christ.

Never allow for plan B. When I say that, I'm not talking about administration. Wise leaders understand that something may go wrong, and they have to cover their bases with subsidiary plans, but this is not a lesson on administration. This is a lesson in paying the price; there is no plan B in the area of commitment; either you are committed or you're not. Get rid of the exit signs in your life. As long as there is a way out, a fire escape, you'll be tempted to take it rather than pay the price. You don't have to survive. The Apostle Paul didn't have to survive; he was committed beyond the point of survival. He had no plan B to fall back on.

Never fall into a maintenance mind-set. Nowhere do you find that the Apostle Paul was satisfied to just maintain the work. He never settled for the good when the best was a possibility. He pressed on, not leaving it up to his co-workers to carry on the work. What I'm saying here is that Paul did not have a maintenance mindset; his goal was not just to maintain the status quo. He was willing to make waves and be unpopular at the cost of his comfort. Don't be content to *carry* on when you need to *press* on.

LEADERSHIP MEANS DISSATISFACTION

Dissatisfaction is a tool God can use to motivate us to greater things. I'm not saying we will be great leaders if we are unhappy. Miserable leaders have a great capacity to make miserable followers. When we lose our drive and motivation, we're in danger of losing our vision.

The average church in America, regardless of denomination, has about seventy regular attenders, because that's about how many people it takes to survive. Generally speaking, a congregation of seventy can afford to buy that acre plot of ground, turn the lights on, and partially pay a pastor. That is the survival level, and once churches get there, many of them stop growing because they can meet their own basic needs. Dissatisfaction doesn't set in unless they look beyond their basic needs and examine their overall purpose.

John Wesley was one who understood that leadership means dissatisfaction. He averaged three sermons a day for 54 years, preaching more than 44,000 times altogether. To do this he traveled by horseback and carriage more than 200,000 miles, or about 5,000 miles a year. He was greatly devoted to pastoral work. During a later period in his life, he was responsible for all the churches in England. To get his work done, he rose at 4 every morning and worked solidly until 10 at night, allowing brief periods for meals. At age 83 he was upset to discover that he could not write more than 15 hours a day without hurting his eyes. At age 86 he was ashamed to admit that he could not preach more than twice a day and he was angry that he would sleep until 5 A.M.

Charles Spurgeon was known as the prince of preachers. Like Wesley, he was not satisfied with just being a great orator; he had a passion for the work of God, and he was never satisfied with the number of souls that he had won. At the age of 30 he preached to 5,000 people at Metropolitan Tabernacle, and he still wasn't satisfied. He was once invited to lecture at a university where all of his expenses, his wife's expenses, and his personal secretary's expenses would be covered, and in addition he would receive $1,000 per lecture over a 50-day period. Spurgeon, however, turned down this offer, suggesting that instead of taking their $50,000, he would stay in London and attempt to win 50 souls for Jesus Christ.

I was privileged to meet E. Stanley Jones when I was in high school. My dad set up an appointment with him, and we had 15 minutes together. He signed a couple of books for me and talked about how great it was to be in the ministry. He was woven from the same fabric as these great men were. In the twilight of his life he wrote these words from his beloved India, where he was a missionary: 'I have often said, half jokingly, that when I get to heaven I will ask for 24 hours to see my friends and then I shall go up to my Master and say, ''Haven't You a world somewhere which has fallen people who need an evangelist like me? Please send me there, for I know of no heaven beyond preaching the Gospel to people. That is heaven to me. It has been and it ever shall be.'' '

We have been talking a lot about the Apostle Paul, a man who was not satisfied and was not about to quit as he pressed toward that high mark. But there are other men and women in the Bible who were driven to greatness by dissatisfaction with their present conditions. Nehemiah was fairly well off as the cupbearer for the king in the royal court. He was surrounded by luxury, but he was willing to leave all of that to go back and help rebuild the wall of Jerusalem. Or consider Esther, the queen who chose to risk death in order to rescue her people from suffering. Joshua and Caleb could have settled for the wilderness with all of the other people, but they were unwilling to settle for second best. Why live in the wilderness when you can live in the land that flows with milk and honey? Moses could have stayed in Pharaoh's court and enjoyed all the pleasures and the riches of Egypt, but he chose to lead his people out.

LEADERSHIP MEANS DISRUPTION

You show me a person that is in a strategic leadership position and I'll show you a person who will be disrupted. We must get used to disruptions because working with people means there are no guarantees of smooth sailing. Just about the moment we think we're going to accomplish a lot on our agenda, another hurting, needy person comes along.

We have to be like an airline pilot. We know our destination, but we have no control over the weather. Unexpected squalls may make it necessary for us to vary from the flight plan. I was flying from Phoenix to San Diego recently and the weather was pretty bad, rainy and foggy. We started our descent, and I thought we were going to make it until all of a sudden we were in a big cloud. Up we went, circling again. That pilot understood something about flying. He had a time schedule; he wanted to get there at 9:10 in the morning, but he also understood that bad weather patterns may necessitate changes. Instead of 9:10, it may be 10:10 or 10:20 or it may mean going to an alternate airport and reaching the original destination some other way.

Like the airline pilot, we leaders will often have to deal with disruptions—sometimes very unpleasant disruptions. The issue is whether we *respond* or *react* to those disruptions. To react means to act negatively. To respond means to act positively. If you go to your doctor's office, and he prescribes some medicine for you, your body will either react or respond to that medicine. When you come back three days later, the doctor may tell you that your body is reacting to the medicine—he means that your body isn't allowing the medicine to accomplish its purpose. Or he may say that you're responding to that medicine—he means that the medicine is healing your body; you're getting well.

When we have disruptions, do we react or respond? I need to continually remind myself of the importance of responding. People who are schedule oriented, who have their to-do lists, and who have strong goals will always have some tension over disruptions. We have to remember that leadership is more than taking a pen to our to-do lists and marking off numbers. Leadership is meeting needs. I'm afraid sometimes we're marking off numbers instead of meeting needs, and that keeps us from being as effective as we could be.

One key to being an excellent leader is not to let disruption throw you: handle your disruptions but don't be consumed by them; keep your eyes on the goal. Too many people detour around the need in order to hit the goal, or they meet the need but forget the goal. We have to do both. We must minister to the need as we press on to the goal.

A good example of somebody who knew how to deal with his disruptions positively was the great boxer Gene Tunney, who took the heavyweight title from Jack Dempsey. When Gene Tunney was in World War I, he broke both his hands. His doctor, who was also his manager, told Tunney that he had brittle hands; he would no longer be a boxer. But Tunney decided to try a strategy change. Instead of relying on the hard punch, as he had before, he became a strategic boxer; he learned to move well, to score points, and to be an artful dodger. He changed his strategy but not his goal. That is exactly what we have to do with our disruptions. We have to change our tactics, manipulate our circumstances, but continue to aim for the goal. I have found these three guidelines to be helpful in dealing with disruptions.

Number one: Find out the specific will of God for your life. Nothing will keep us on track better than knowing what God's purpose is for us individually.

Number two: Don't give in to the desires of the flesh. If you give in to the flesh you will always take the easiest way out. Make yourself do what has to be done, and you will develop character. As you exercise your character-building muscles, you'll find they become stronger each time they're used.

Whenever you are going to do something great for God, there are 27,000 people around you that will try to tell you why you can't, shouldn't, and won't. All they are doing is testifying to their own experiences. They haven't paid the price for greatness, so they don't understand how you can do it. Effective leaders, however, leaders who have paid the price, know the value of character-building exercises. They know that they can not give in to fleshly desires, whether their own desires or the desires of other people.

Number three: Don't try to survive. Look at Galatians 1:15–17. You will see these three principles in action. Once Paul saw his goal, he looked neither to the left nor to the right for the easiest path; he simply headed in the direction in which God's finger was pointing. His goal wasn't to survive—and yours shouldn't be either. It is amazing what will happen in your leadership when you do not gauge the happiness of your life or the greatness of your day by how easy it was.

'HAVE A GOOD DAY!'

Do the circumstances of your day have to be smooth and easy for you to have a good day? Some people's only happiness comes on vacation—so they can only be happy two weeks out of the year. It's a sad thing when people can't enjoy the problems of life. It's a sad thing when you rise up in the morning and realize that it's going to be a bad day because you're going to work, where there are problems that you don't want to deal with. It's a sad thing when you start looking for an escape instead of a challenge.

We have developed a society in which people would rather take the easy way out; we have become a relief syndrome culture. This type of society does not make good leadership training ground. But those who are willing to pay the price will make it, and the world will sit back and wonder how these successful men and women ever got so lucky. Luck has nothing to do with it; they were simply willing to do what all the rest of the people were unwilling to do.

What conditions do you set on your service to God before you'll be happy in ministry? I would encourage you to put down the book as you finish this chapter and spend some time answering that question. Write down what you need to have before you'll be happy. Is it a place where you must live? Is it a salary you must receive? What conditions must be met?

Are we really attacking the problems in our personal lives? We're not in a Boy Scout camp; we're in the army of God. We need to trust God for the courage to go forth and pay the price to help build the kingdom.

9

YOUR PROBLEM IS NOT YOUR PROBLEM

YOU CAN tell it's going to be a rotten day when you call Suicide Prevention, and they put you on hold. You can tell it's going to be a bad day when you turn on the news and they're showing emergency routes out of the state. You can tell it's going to be a rotten day when your car horn goes off accidentally and remains stuck as you follow a group of Hell's Angels on the freeway. Have you ever had a day like that? I think we all have. Yet as I work with and study people, I find that they do not all attack their problems in the same way. In fact, I meet people who have huge problems and yet seem to be just whistling along, making out fine; then I meet others who have relatively small problems and they're devastated by them. I have concluded that your problem really is not your problem. Surface problems do not make or break us.

Let me give you some examples. I've done a lot of marriage counseling, and I've seen couples with incredibly large problems decide that they really want to live together and make their marriages work and they go out and do it. I've had other couples whose problems appear very small. They're a little bored, but they just need to make a few changes and their marriages could be revitalized. I've watched their marriages fall apart and end in divorce.

I've watched people who had incredible financial problems work their way out of trouble. I've watched other people with small financial problems sink, unable to handle the stress.

It is popular in our society to believe that we are victims of our situations. Society looks at a person and says, 'That poor person was born on the wrong side of the tracks and doesn't have a chance.' Society emphasizes the problem rather than the person. That's a major mistake. Your problem is not your problem. If you can get the person right, the problem will be fine.

HOW WE RESPOND TO PROBLEMS

In one of our Sunday night baptism services, a fellow walked into the baptistry and shared a testimony the like of which I had never heard. When this guy was fourteen, his sister died. Two years later his father was killed. His first two marriages ended in divorce. His oldest daughter died of cancer at the time of his second divorce. Last year his brother was killed during a robbery at his place of business. Grief piled on top of grief caused this man to renew a bad relationship with drugs and alcohol, which caused his third marriage to fall apart. For a guy in his early thirties, he had known a lot of tragedy. And yet at the end he talked about how God had changed his life and given him a bright outlook. There was a smile on his face, he was confident about his future, and he was confident in God. His focus had shifted from his problems to God's promises. Your problem is not your problem.

We respond to problems based on two things. We respond to problems based on *what we see* and *what we seek.* What we see is determined by our perspective in life and our level of discernment. What we seek is our desires, our values, and our purpose.

Before we can understand and tackle problems effectively, we must identify what we see and what we seek. If I can see the problem but lack the desire to solve it, I'll begin to observe problems as they are, but I'll never solve them. To flip that coin, if I desire very much to take care of my problems but don't see them in the right light, I will never be as effective as I could be.

WHAT WE SEE

The Apostle Paul viewed problems accurately. In 2 Corinthians Paul writes about how we are handicapped on all sides.

> *We are afflicted in every way, but not crushed; perplexed, but not despairing; persecuted, but not forsaken; struck down, but not destroyed. (2 Cor. 4:8–9)*

Paul had been through shipwrecks, beatings, humiliation, and imprisonment, but he saw that the difficulties he was experiencing were very small in comparison with the glory of God (Rom. 8:18). Paul overcame his problems because he saw them in the right light.

So often we take a little speck of a problem and make it a huge barrier in our lives. That's usually because we see the problem in the wrong light. We don't see it in the light of God's glory.

One day little Bobby's father came into the front room and saw the boy looking out on the street through the big end of a telescope. He said, 'Son, that's not the way you look through a telescope. If you look through it that way, you make the objects look much smaller. A telescope is to make things look bigger.' But Bobby smiled and said, 'Daddy, the bully who's always beating me up is out on the street. I turned the telescope around because he's my main problem, and I want to see him smaller than he really is.' Most of us, instead of taking the big end of the telescope and reducing our problems, take the small end of the telescope and magnify our problems so that they look much bigger than they really are.

PAST EXPERIENCES

We see our problems based on three things, past experiences, present environment, and personal evaluation. Let's start with past experiences. How we have handled problems in the past will greatly influence how we view them today. A sculptor begins his work with a chunk of granite, a mallet, and a chisel. The novice expects a chip of the rock to fall every time he hits the chisel with his mallet, but often nothing happens. After a while he lays down his mallet and chisel, too discouraged to go on. Why? Because every time he strikes the chisel he expects to see a tangible result. The professional working by his side has been doing it for years. He patiently takes that mallet and taps that chisel, and to the inexperienced eye, nothing's happening at all. The veteran knows that a chip doesn't have to fall every time the chisel is struck, because he understands that every time he strikes the chisel, he weakens the stone. If he's patient long enough, the piece he wants to chip off will depart from the main rock.

Seeing your problems based on your experience can be good or bad. If we've had good experiences in handling problems, we will be able to handle them in the future; if we've had bad experiences, then we will probably continue to do so until we get a better understanding of how to deal with difficulties.

A couple went camping in the mountains, and their guide said, 'Now, you'll see snakes, but don't worry about it; they're not poisonous.' Even though the man had a tremendous phobia for snakes, he went hiking alone the next day. When he got back to the cottage where they were staying, his clothes were torn, and he was battered and bleeding. His wife said, 'My goodness, what happened?'

He said, 'Oh, I was hiking on one of the high trails and I saw a snake. I jumped off a 50-foot cliff.'

She said, 'But honey, don't you remember, the guide said those snakes weren't poisonous.' He said, 'They don't have to be poisonous if you jump off a 50-foot cliff.' The damage was already done. What was his problem? His problem wasn't snakes; it was fear of snakes. His bad experiences in the past caused him to see the problem wrongly.

PRESENT ENVIRONMENT

We also see our problems in the light of our present environment. Here is a key idea you need to remember: the problems surrounding us are not as crucial as the people surrounding us. We are not overcome by our problems, but if the people around us don't know how to handle problems, then we may be overcome.

There are two ways to respond to an environment filled with problems. We can be like the gardener who took great pride in his lawn. He kept it beautiful. One year his lawn was besieged with dandelions. He tried everything and still couldn't get rid of them. Finally, in his frustration, he wrote the Department of Agriculture explaining all the different dandelion deterrents he had tried and asking what he should do next. The answer came back from the Department of Agriculture, 'Try getting used to them.' That's not what he wanted to hear. That's not what we want to hear either, but sometimes it's the best advice we'll get. The person who expects to live in a problem-free society is going to be as frustrated as the fellow who thought that he was going to rid his lawn of all the dandelions.

I saw a cartoon the other day which showed a little boy in a car watching his dad outside in the pouring rain fixing a flat tire. The boy has the window down, and he's asking his father why this is happening to them. The father looks at the boy and says, 'Son, don't you understand? This is life. This is what is happening. We can't switch to another channel.'

There's something else that we need to realize. We may always have dandelions in our yards, but we don't have to let those dandelions mess up our lives. During World War II a young soldier married a woman and brought her to his post in the California desert. She didn't like the desert; she didn't like the barrenness; her husband was away on active duty most of the time and she was very lonely and bored. Finally she wrote her mother and said, 'Mom, I'm coming home. I just don't like the desert, and I don't like the dryness, and I don't like the fact that my husband's gone. It's an ugly place to live.' Her mother wrote back to her these two lines: 'Two men looked out through prison bars; one saw mud and the other saw stars.' That young wife got the message; she decided to look for stars. She began to learn as much as she could about desert flowers and cacti. She studied the language, folklore, and traditions of the Indians who were her neighbors. By the time her husband's tour of duty was over, she had become so engrossed with the desert that she wrote a book on it. Her problem was not her problem. It was how she saw it.

In the fifteenth century in Europe, the whole continent was filled with despair. It was probably the most discouraging time in European history. In 1492, in the *Nuremburg Chronicle,* a German wrote that the end had come; there was nothing left worth living for. At the close of his book he left several blank pages on which he proposed that the reader fill in any discouraging events or situations that he had left out. The next year, 1493, a young buck sailor returned to his Portuguese port with the most exciting story. In the midst of this negative environment, Christopher Columbus came home saying, 'Guys, there's a whole new world out there. Get your eyes off your problems. Rip those pages out of your book!' Christopher Columbus was not willing to let the environment of his day determine his dream; he refused to let present problems order his future.

PERSONAL EVALUATION

We tackle problems our own size. Big people tackle big problems, and small people tackle small problems. The better a person's self-image, the more willing he or she is to take a risk and handle a big problem. The more fragile a person's self-image, the less willing she or he is to tackle a big problem.

Problems can stop you temporarily, but only *you* can stop yourself permanently. We cannot continually handle problems in a way that is inconsistent with the way we see ourselves. If you evaluate yourself as a person of worth, then you will begin to tackle big problems. One of the ways you can tell whether you're growing emotionally and spiritually is by the size of the problems that you're willing to tackle.

WHAT WE SEEK

The size of your problem is determined not only by how you see it but by what you seek in life. Again, your problem is not your problem. Problems defeat us when we lack purpose in life. Goal-oriented people don't let problems deter them from their goals. If they want to reach them badly enough, they're going to reach them.

The night before my son's first soccer game, his coach sat the kids down, and she said, 'I'm really not interested in winning this year; I'm interested in having you kids learn how to play soccer—learn the rules, the fundamentals.' I understood what she was saying, but I was so proud of my boy, Joel, when he blurted out, 'But Mrs. Jones! I want to *win!*' My last advice to him was to get the ball and go for the goal.

People who regularly allow themselves to get sidetracked by problems are people who have no clear purpose in life. When we have a purpose, when we really seek and desire the best of life, our problems begin to shrink. Here's the way it works. As our purpose increases, our problems decrease. As our goal decreases, our problems increase.

LEARNING INSTEAD OF LEISURE

Our problems are no longer problems when we seek learning instead of leisure. You show me a person who loves to learn about life, and I'll show you a person who handles problems well. On the other hand, people who want to live lives of leisure, to whom life is nothing but a big vacation, become frustrated with their problems. M. Scott Peck, a psychiatrist, has written several best-selling books in the last few years, including *The Road Less Traveled.* Peck had decided to do some case studies on the subject of evil. As he did the case studies, he became convinced that evil was a reality, and he became a Christian. In *The Road Less Traveled* (Simon and Schuster) he writes, 'It is in this whole process of meeting and solving problems that life has its meaning' (p. 16). Peck says that life doesn't have meaning unless we learn how to handle our problems. He said, 'Problems are the cutting edge that distinguishes between success and failure. Problems call forth our courage and our wisdom; indeed, they create our courage and our wisdom. It is only because of problems that we grow mentally and spiritually. . . . It is through the pain of confronting and resolving problems that we learn. As Benjamin Franklin said, 'Those things that hurt, instruct' (p. 16). Notice what he says about people who want to avoid the pain of problems: 'Fearing the pain involved, almost all of us . . . attempt to avoid problems. We procrastinate . . . forget them, pretend they do not exist. We even take drugs to assist us in ignoring them, so that by deadening ourselves to the pain we can forget the problems that cause the pain' (p. 16). Then he gives the clincher. He says, 'This tendency to avoid problems and the emotional suffering inherent in them is the primary basis of all human mental illness' (p. 17).

The writer of Hebrews said of Jesus, 'He learned obedience from the things which He suffered' (Heb. 5:8). Problems create situations in which we can grow. The very things we want to avoid in life are the things that nurture us and shape us into the persons we should be. The author of the Book of Hebrews doesn't say that Jesus learned obedience *in spite of* the things He suffered; He said that He learned obedience *from* the things He suffered. Effective leaders have learned this principle, and they almost *welcome* problems into their lives, knowing that it will drive them closer to God and closer to the people with whom they must relate. They have discovered that dealing with problems successfully develops a sense of security, not only in themselves but in Christ Jesus.

HOLINESS INSTEAD OF HAPPINESS

If you study the lives of those who have suffered greatly, such as Helen Keller and Joni Eareckson Tada, you seldom find skeptics among them. The skeptics are the people who have not suffered a great deal themselves, but who have been in the observation towers watching others suffer. They're the ones who ask why. They're the ones who become calloused.

Seeking holiness rather than happiness is a hard thing to do in the culture in which we live, because so much is geared to happiness—whatever makes you feel good. In a secular society, happiness is the aim of life. In a spiritual society, holiness is the thing that we strive for. Jesus said, 'Blessed are the pure in heart' (Matt. 5:8). That word *blessed* means 'happy.' Happiness is really found in holiness. But if we try to bypass holiness in our search for happiness, we'll miss it altogether. Happiness is a by-product of holiness; it's a benefit of living a pure life, rightly related to God, self, and others. So if you want to live a happy life, seek to live a holy life.

SOLUTIONS INSTEAD OF SYMPATHY

When we seek solutions instead of sympathy, we begin to see our problems in a different light. A woman had been confined to a wheelchair all her life, and a friend who was trying to encourage her said, 'You know, afflictions really color life, don't they?' The woman in the wheelchair replied, 'Yeah, but I choose the color.' A lot of people would have their problems solved if they would just go for the solution instead of the sympathy. We need to realize that our problems are going to be there until we tackle them. Some people choose to hang on to their problems because they enjoy having other people feel sorry for them. I would challenge those people to dare to attack their problems. It's far more gratifying to receive admiration than to receive pity.

I want to close by giving you some problem-solving principles. We handle our problems based on what we see and what we seek. If we see our problems correctly and if we have a goal that is bigger than our problems, there's no problem that we can't solve. The happiest people on earth are not people without problems. The happiest people on earth are people who have learned to appreciate the possibilities for growth that problems bring.

PROBLEM-SOLVING PRINCIPLES

Never believe any problem is unsolvable. These six words will give you the right attitude toward problem solving. Whenever I deal with somebody who has a problem, that's the first thing I tell them. Now you may be thinking that there *are* some unsolvable problems. But I would reply that they're only unsolvable to you. Don't bring everybody else into your arena: speak for yourself. I don't know how to solve every problem, but that doesn't mean every problem is unsolvable. It just means that I haven't found the right person to help me; I haven't worked hard enough on it; I haven't worked long enough; I haven't thought it through. I need to bring in some other resources. Every problem is solvable.

One day in an upper-level doctoral seminar in mathematics a professor wrote an unsolved problem on the blackboard. Mathematicians had been trying for years to solve this problem. The professor was trying to emphasize to the students that there are no easy answers. He told them, 'This problem is unsolvable, but I want you to spend the whole hour trying to solve it.' One student came in about five minutes after the professor had given the assignment. He sat down, saw the problem on the board, and began working on it—and he solved it—all because he had never heard anybody say it was unsolvable. I wonder how many problems you and I have not solved only because we've heard there's no solution. The first key to handling problems is to get the right mind-set: every problem is solvable.

Define your problem clearly on paper. You need to see it before you. Don't think your problem; write your problem. Until you can see it, there's a danger of confusing the symptoms with the problem. By writing it down clearly you can separate the symptoms from the real problems. Once you begin to visualize the whole issue, your mind can begin to see solutions.

Organize to divide and conquer your problems. Generals who understand effective military strategy do not attack all fronts simultaneously; they look for a weak area up at the front and they attack that spot until they break through. This particular tactic works in any kind of warfare. If you have a problem that needs attacking, divide it into parts. Suppose you look at it and see five areas of difficulty; ask yourself which area you could handle most quickly. Then take care of that need. Now the problem has been reduced a little. There are not five parts, just four. So take the next part—and keep going until the problem is gone.

List people and other idea sources that might help you solve your problem. Begin to collect resources that can help you solve the problem—books, tapes, people. No man is an island, and no man solves problems by himself. This is an area that is too often overlooked in problem solving. People too often try to solve their problems by using their own limited resources instead of using the expertise of outside help.

List all the possible courses of action that you can think of. Write down five or six possible solutions. Many people are not problem solvers because they only try one solution. If that doesn't work, they decide the problem has no solution. I have found that if I take the time to write down all my options and then begin to attack the problem from different perspectives and from different viewpoints, at least one option will be a workable solution.

Visualize these different courses of action. Think through the process before you try to actually attack the problem. You may be able to eliminate some of your options, because it will be obvious that they won't work.

Choose the best course of action and get going. Don't stop at choosing—get going. Don't play the philosopher, who sees the problem but doesn't seek the remedy. Look at the problem, choose the best course of action, and go after it.

Never let problems stop you from making the right decision. So many times we are tempted to live with problems because if we solve them, someone may get hurt. Don't forfeit the right solution for an easy way out. This is especially crucial in spiritual leadership, because we tend to do that which is most palatable to those we are leading. We don't want to hurt anybody; we don't want to rock the boat. I learned a long time ago that true leaders will make the right decision regardless of its palatability to others.

I've also learned that a lot of people never solve their problems because they wait. Even after they know which option to take, they wait, hoping that the problem will eventually work itself out. Thomas J. Peters and Robert H. Waterman, in their book *In Search of Excellence* (Harper and Row), make the point that a laboratory may produce solutions, but it doesn't make those solutions work. You can stay in the lab with the mice all day, but your problems won't dissolve. You have to take your solution out and introduce it to the problem.

What you see and what you seek determine your success or failure. Success in problem solving is more related to the person than the problem. You may not choose your problem, but you do choose your response. It's not what happens *to* you; it's what happens *in* you. Your problem is not your problem—once you see it correctly and once you seek high goals in your life.

10

FAILURE IS NOT FINAL

THIS MAY be hard for you to believe, but successful people experience failure almost as often as unsuccessful people. In fact, on the average, successful people fail two out of every five times they attempt something and unsuccessful people fail three out of five times. That's not a lot of difference, is it? Actually, there are several similarities between the person who fails three out of five times and the person who fails two out of five times, even though one would be classified as successful and the other one would be classified as unsuccessful.

The first similarity is that all fail. There's not one person who does not experience failure. The second similarity is that we all fail often. We don't just fail once and walk gingerly through life so that we'll never fail again. Failure is something that we experience every day. And third, we will continue to fail until we die. Death itself is the only thing that's going to keep us from failing. Sometimes I have a feeling that people are trying to tiptoe safely to the grave without goofing up somewhere along the way.

Why is it that failure destroys some and builds up others? How can I allow failure to make me a better person?

CONCENTRATE ON SUCCESS

Too many people concentrate on failure instead of on success. Too few concentrate on success instead of on failure. Herein lies the key.

Have you ever heard a person say, 'I'm not going to make a mistake here; I'm going to avoid that pitfall'? Then they do exactly what they were trying so hard to avoid. What happened is that they concentrated on the fall, the failure, the fault, the problem that was looming out in front of them. As the proverb goes, as a man 'thinks within himself, so he is' (Prov. 23:7).

Ray Meyer, basketball coach for DePaul for 42 years, had 42 consecutive winning seasons before he retired a few years ago. One season his team had a 29-game winning streak at the home court; then they lost a game. Reporters were anxious to get in the locker room to interview Meyer to ask him about that loss and to see how it affected him. He was all smiles; he said, 'This is great. For the last ten, twelve days we've been thinking about the winning streak. We've been trying not to lose, every game. Now that we've lost a game, we can go back to concentrating on winning.' Those who concentrate on failure program themselves to fail.

One day when the Raiders were in Oakland, a reporter visited their locker room to talk to Ken Stabler. Stabler really wasn't known as an intellectual, but he was a good quarterback. This newspaperman read him some English prose: 'I would rather be ashes than dust. I would rather that my spark should burn out in a brilliant blaze than that it should be stifled by dry rot. I would rather be a superb meteor, every atom of me in magnificent glow, than a sleepy, impermanent planet. The proper function of man is to live, not to exist. I shall not waste my days in trying to prolong them. I shall use my time.' After reading this to the quarterback, the reporter asked, 'What does this mean to you?' Stabler immediately replied, 'Throw deep.' Go after it. Go out to win in life.

TREAT FAILURE AS A FRIEND

The second observation I want you to see is that too many people treat their failures as enemies. They look at a flop and see a foe. This kind of thinking, in itself, is a mistake; failure should be treated as a friend. Your reaction to failure determines what you do with it. If you treat your failure as a foe, for example, you'll hide it. Whenever you fail in a certain area, you'll want to get out of that area, whatever it is—a job, a marriage, a relationship, even a hobby. If you treat your failure as a foe, you will take your mistakes too seriously. You'll be ridden with anxiety. Every mistake will be a life-or-death situation. On the other hand, if you can see failure as a friend, a helper, then you'll react positively to it. Only when you're honest and open about a mistake can you learn from it. When you stop and think how many times you've really blown it, it seems a shame to let those failed attempts go to waste. So learn from your mistakes—and then learn to laugh at your mistakes. No failure is significant enough to sink a person.

When I was pastoring my first church, a college friend was also serving his first pastorate about 20 miles down the road from me. We got together once or twice a month for meals with our wives. Being brand new at the job, I was making lots of mistakes—blowing it in a big way every day! So when we came together I would share my flops and failures. After two or three dinners, I realized that Mike wasn't communicating; he and his wife were on the defensive. His wife was saying things like, 'Oh, Mike wouldn't do that,' or 'Mike has never let that happen.' My wife, on the other hand was saying, 'You should have seen John handle that!' and, 'John blew it royally yesterday.' Mike never seemed to make a mistake. If there was ever a problem at his church, it was the people's fault.

I did a series of meetings for him after his first year, and over dinner one night he was talking about the 'ding-a-lings' in his church. 'That ding-a-ling won't do this, and this ding-a-ling won't do that.' After about 30 minutes Mike's conversation was making me nauseated. I thought, *I can't let this go on forever*, and I put down my fork and said, 'Mike, I want to tell you. Do you know why you have so many ding-a-lings in your church?' He put down his fork and said, 'No, but I'd like to know.' So I told him, 'It's because you're the biggest ding-a-ling of all.' Suddenly, my digestion improved tremendously, but now Mike couldn't eat!

Two years afterward he called me on the phone to say he was going to leave these ding-a-lings and go to another state, to a really *good* church. He hadn't learned a thing from his failures because he saw them as foes. I remember hanging the phone up and telling Margaret, 'Mike's going to another church in another state. I give him six months and he'll find ding-a-lings there. If he doesn't start admitting that he's the problem, that he needs to make some changes, he's going to have more problems.' Sure enough, he lasted about six months. This time, it was not only the ding-a-lings in his congregation, but it was the ding-a-ling district board, the ding-a-ling district superintendent, and all the other ding-a-lings around him. So he decided to build an independent church. The last time I heard, he was out of the ministry. What happened? He had always looked at his failures as enemies, and he had always blamed them on someone else.

There is truth in the statement that a person is not a failure until he or she places the blame on someone else. Remember Jimmy Durante, the comedian with the big nose? Many people would have taken that nose and hidden in the corner of life—but not Jimmy. Someone asked him one time how he managed to accept his larger-than-life nose, and here's what he said, 'All of us have schnozzles.' He meant that we all have peculiarities. If our 'schnozzle' is not on our face, it's somewhere else—maybe in our mind or in our habits. When we admit those schnozzles instead of defending them, regardless of where they are, we can begin to laugh at ourselves, and when we laugh at ourselves, the world will laugh with us.

Take a moment and write down the last big mistake you made. It should take about three seconds to remember it. How did you react to it? Is it your friend? Or is it your foe?

VIEW FAILURE AS A MOMENT

Too many people, when they fail, erect a *monument* to their failure and spend the rest of their lives paying homage. Not enough of us view failure as a *moment*—a fleeting experience. Do you make a monument when you fail, or do you look at it as just something that happened in a moment and is over and done with? Charles Kettering said, 'Virtually nothing comes out right the first time. Repeated failures are fingerposts on the road to achievement. The only time that you don't fail is the last time you try something and it works. One fails forward.' I like the expression, 'fails forward.' Fail forward toward success.

People make monuments out of their mistakes by saying things like, 'I tried it, and it didn't work. They said it couldn't be done, and they were right.' Mark Twain said that if a cat sits on a hot stove, the cat will never sit on a hot stove again. The problem is, the cat will never sit on a cold stove either. The cat just won't sit on stoves, because every time he sees a stove he sees a burning failure. Abraham Lincoln wisely stated, 'My great concern is not whether you have failed, but whether you are content with your failure.'

What else do people put on their monuments to failure

besides 'I tried it and it didn't work' and 'They said it couldn't be done'? How about 'I wish I had done that'? There are people who spend their whole lives wishing instead of getting out and doing. They never venture into the arena of action; they sit sadly on the sidelines and wish.

Others say, 'I'll never get hurt again.' They stay so far away from anything that is risky that life will pass them by. They'll see the joy of the risk takers, but they won't share in it.

Another common inscription on monuments to failure is 'I can't change. It's just the way I am.' This goes on monuments of people who say, 'Leaders are born, not made, and I'm not a leader. I grew up on the wrong side of the tracks. I can't help myself.'

There's a curious thing about people who build great monuments to failure: they don't want to accept responsibility for the construction. They're not willing to take blame. They find it much easier to attribute their failures to other people. Their philosophy of life is 'My circumstances make me who I am.'

VIEW FAILURE INWARDLY

My fourth observation is this: too many people have too broad a view of failure. They're too quick to judge an attempt as a failure. If they don't see immediate outward positive results, they see a major mistake. Failure is not the external result; it's the internal activity.

Thomas Edison was once experimenting in search of a natural rubber. In his search he had 50,000 failures. His assistant said, 'Mr. Edison, we have made 50,000 experiments, and we have no results.' He was ready to quit. He viewed failure outwardly. Edison replied, 'Results! We have had wonderful results. We now know 50,000 things which won't work.' Thomas Edison knew that there was only one thing that was failure, and that was quitting.

So often people who fail frequently follow this philosophy: if at first you don't succeed, destroy all the evidence that you ever tried. They view failure outwardly. What the world judges as obvious failure is many times not failure at all. If you study history, you'll find that the world has put labels of failure on some events that have been some of the greatest successes of mankind. Some examples: the Iowa banker who told Alexander Graham Bell to remove that toy (a Bell telephone) from his office; the Hollywood producer who scrawled *Reject* on the movie screenplay for *Gone With the Wind*; the fellow who was Henry Ford's greatest investor, who in 1906 asked that his stock be sold; Mr. Roebuck, who sold his part of the Sears, Roebuck firm for $25,000 because he thought it would never fly. (The last I read on Sears was that they sell $25,000 worth of goods every 16 seconds.) Do you view failure from the outside or from the inside?

SUCCESSFULLY FAIL

Too many people fail, and then they never use that failure to their benefit. There is such a thing as a successful failure. Any time you have learned from a mistake, you have made a major step towards success.

I read a great article on leadership not long ago in which the author discussed the fact that one characteristic that distinguishes successful leaders and followers is that successful leaders learn from their failures. Let me just quote a couple of statements. 'Leaders use their energy well because they learn from failure, and they can therefore reach higher goals. Almost every false step is regarded by them as an opportunity, not as the end of the world. They are convinced that they can learn and, more important, that their organizations can learn from failure.'

Tom Watson, Sr., who founded IBM, had a top junior executive who spent $12 million of the company's money on an experiment that failed. The executive put his resignation on Watson's desk, saying, 'I'm sure that you want my resignation.' Watson said, 'No, I don't want your resignation. I've just spent $12 million educating you; it's about time you get to work.' Watson knew that there is such a thing as successful failure.

We successfully fail when *it stirs us to keep trying.* The setbacks that look as though they will finish us off can spur us on to come out on top. A Louisiana farmer's favorite mule fell into a well. After studying the situation, the farmer came to the conclusion that he couldn't pull the mule out, so he might as well bury him. He got a truckload of dirt, backed up to the well, and dumped it on top of the mule at the bottom of the well. When the dirt hit the mule, it started snorting and tramping. As it tramped, it began to work itself up on top of the dirt. So the farmer continued to pour dirt in the well until the mule snorted and tramped its way to the top. It then walked away, a dirtier but wiser mule. What was intended to bury it turned out to be its salvation. That's a successful failure.

We successfully fail when *we see our mistakes and are willing to change.* The greatest mistake we make is not correcting the first mistake. When we see where we went wrong, we should make every effort to make sure that it doesn't happen again.

We fail successfully when *we discover our true selves.* In reading the biographies of great men, I've been impressed with two things. One, some of the most successful people in the world started out as failures; two, because they failed, they found themselves and their purpose in life. I'll give you a few examples. Nathaniel Hawthorne was fired from his position in a custom house in Salem, Massachusetts. He came home after losing his job feeling utterly defeated, and his wife said to him, 'Now you can write the book that you've wanted to write all your life.' Out of that came *The Scarlet Letter.* James Whistler failed at West Point. He became an engineer, and he failed in business. Then he decided to try painting. We all know his success. Phillips Brooks started out as a teacher, but he couldn't make it in the classroom, so he went to seminary and eventually became an outstanding preacher. These men were successful failures.

NEVER QUIT BECAUSE OF FAILURE

Too many people never start because of failure; too few never quit because of failure. Samuel Johnson said, 'Nothing will be attempted if all possible obstacles must first be removed.' Have you ever not started something because you wanted all the conditions to be perfect before you began? If this is your criterion for taking a risk, you'll never accomplish anything. Perfection does not guarantee success; if anything, it's a hindrance.

Starting is the first step to succeeding. Too many of us don't make it to the top of the ladder because we don't try often enough. We're afraid of failure. In 1915 Ty Cobb set the record for stolen bases, 96. Seven years later, Max Carey of the Pittsburgh Pirates became second best with 51 stolen bases. Does this mean that Cobb was twice as good as Carey, his closest rival? Look at the facts: Cobb made 134 attempts, Carey, 53. Cobb failed 38 times; Carey only failed twice. Cobb succeeded 96 times, Carey only 51 times. Cobb's average was only 71 percent. Carey's average was 96 percent. Carey's average was much better than Cobb's. Cobb tried 81 more times than Carey. But here's the key: his 81 additional tries produced 44 more stolen bases. Cobb risked failure 81 more times in one season than his closest rival and Cobb goes down in history as the greatest base runner of all time. Why? Because Ty Cobb refused failure.

Babe Ruth hit 714 home runs. He struck out 1,330 times. If

Ruth was in a batting slump, it never bothered him. He kept smiling, and he kept swinging the bat. During a low period an interviewer asked him, 'How do you keep from being discouraged?' Ruth said, 'I realize the law of averages will catch up if I just keep swinging. In fact, when I'm in a slump, I feel sorry for the pitcher because I know that sooner or later he's going to pay for it.'

KEEP SWINGING THE BAT

My nephew Eric was in his first Little League baseball game three years ago. He was the youngest member of his team, so I went along to encourage him. It was Eric's first time at bat, and he was scared to death. Out on the mound was the biggest kid on the opposing team. The biggest kid is always the pitcher, and his name is always Butch. Sure enough, Butch threw that ball hard—strike one, strike two, strike three. Eric never got the bat off his shoulder. I could see how relieved Eric was when he struck out and got to go back to the dugout. But the coach was mad; he was hollering at Eric for not swinging the bat—forget not hitting the ball—and the fans were just going wild. I decided not to let this happen to one of my relatives, so I went over to him and said, 'Eric, I don't know what this coach has told you, but let me tell you something. The object of this game is *not* to hit the ball. The object of the game is to *swing the bat.* Don't even try to hit the ball. Just go up there next time and swing the bat. Every time Butch pitches the ball, you take the bat and swing all three times, and I'll cheer for you.'

Eric's turn came up again. This time the ball was already in the catcher's mitt before Eric realized it had gone by, but he swung the bat. I stood on my feet and yelled, 'Great swing, great swing!' The rest of the fans kind of looked around at me as though I was a little odd. On the next pitch, Eric swung and missed. It didn't matter. 'Great swing, great swing!' He struck out; I was on my feet cheering for him. He was so proud, because he did what he was supposed to do—swing the bat. So Eric was happy; I was happy. Margaret was at the game with me, and she was not happy. She thought that I was making a fool of myself, so she said, 'I think I'll go to the car and read a book for a while.'

I went over to Eric, tousled his hair, and said, 'That was great. Next time Butch pitches, three swings again.' He got up with a little more confidence now, because all he had to do was swing the bat. Butch struck him out, and I gave him a standing ovation.

I knew that sometime during the Little League season, if Eric kept swinging the bat, the ball would eventually make contact with it. Sure enough, when Eric was up the fourth time, the ball accidentally hit the bat. I ran right alongside him to first base, cheering him on all the way. 'Don't stop, Eric! Keep on going!' As Eric rounded third I was running alongside him again and we slid safely into home together.

Too many people stay in the dugout of life. They never swing a bat; they never face the challenge of a fastball or a curve. They may play manager, or be a batboy, but they never get into the game. Someday they're going to wonder why they never saw any action.

Now it could be depressing to think that life is passing you by—but here's the good news: *failure is not final.* So you never got into the game, or you tried and struck out? I strike out every day of my life—but that's OK. Get that bat off your shoulder and swing—give it the very best you've got, and then watch God make up the difference in your life.

11

YOUR DECISION DETERMINES YOUR DESTINY

TODAY IS a day of decisions—as is every other day of my life. In fact, I began the morning with the decision to get out of bed. My next decision, which apparently wasn't well thought out, was what I should wear. As I confidently stepped out of the bedroom to face the world, my 10-year-old Elizabeth took one look and said in her most gentle and loving way, 'Dad, the tie is OK, but I think maybe you could have done better with the jacket.' Ten minutes into the day and I had already made a wrong decision!

In this chapter I want to help you understand that decision-making is a process which, if practiced, will enable you to make better decisions for the glory of God. Joshua, in the well-known 'choose you this day' passage, provides an excellent example of what goes into making right choices. As he is about to die, Joshua gives his farewell address to the people. First, he reviews the history of God's blessing the Children of Israel; then he says:

Now, therefore, fear the Lord and serve Him in sincerity and truth; and put away the gods which your fathers served beyond

> *the River and in Egypt, and serve the Lord. And if it is disagreeable in your sight to serve the Lord, choose for yourselves today whom you will serve: whether the gods which your fathers served which were beyond the River, or the gods of the Amorites in whose land you are living; but as for me and my house, we will serve the Lord. And the people answered and said . . . 'We also will serve the Lord.' (Josh. 24: 14–18)*

We can draw several conclusions regarding decision-making from these few verses. First, *leaders bring people to a point of decision.* Joshua *led* his people in the decision-making process. As leaders, you and I are responsible for bringing our people to some needed decisions in their lives. Our journey through life is nothing but a process of decision-making. As leaders, the better we are in bringing our people to right decisions, the more effective our leadership will be.

The second conclusion that we can draw from this portion of Scripture is this: *many things in life are decided for us and are therefore beyond our control.* Joshua realized this when he assumed that people, by nature, are subservient to someone. We have no choice. There are many other circumstances of life over which we have no control. We had no part in deciding whether or not the sun would rise this morning. We didn't decide to have a thunderstorm today. We didn't choose when, where, or to whom we would be born.

As we grow up and become independent, though, conclusion number three comes more and more into play: *there are many choices in life which we* can *make.* Joshua realized that his people could not choose *whether* they would serve, but they could choose *whom* they would serve. We can't always choose what our circumstances are, but we can choose what we'll do with them.

The fourth conclusion has to do with responsibility: *not only* can *we make right decisions, we* are responsible *to make right decisions.* I find it interesting that as Joshua laid out the possible options for the Children of Israel, he made this statement: 'Choose for yourselves.' In other words, Joshua looked them right in the eye and told them they were responsible for their own decisions. He was saying, 'I may be your leader; I may do my best to bring you to a point of decision; but the choice is still yours. You have to choose for yourselves.'

The most important point I can make in this chapter and the most important one you can take away is that where you are today, in all probability, is a result of decisions you made yesterday. Until you take responsibility for your decisions and resulting actions, you will always be looking for a scapegoat to blame for your problems. You and I are responsible for our choices. This is one of the most important lessons we can teach our children. When we have taught our children to accept responsibility for their decisions, to be able to say 'I was right' or 'I made a mistake,' we have moved them to the head of the class in maturity.

Conclusion number five follows: *the sooner we make the right choices, the better.* Notice that Joshua said, 'Choose for yourself *today.*' He didn't add, 'if you feel up to it' or 'if it's convenient.' Joshua knew that delaying a decision could lead to destruction.

Sixth, *leaders must decide first.* Often, as I observe a leader who is not moving his people forward, it becomes obvious that the leader is waiting for the followers to decide where they want to go next. This tactic never works. There is a reason 'it's lonely at the top.' Someone has to stand in front of the crowd and make choices. A good leader has to be willing to stick his neck out and give direction.

Joshua did exactly that. He stood out from the crowd and declared unashamedly, 'But as for me and my house, we will serve the Lord.' He didn't know where his people were going to go, what direction they were going to take. But he boldly declared where he was going. He knew that leaders make choices first; they don't wait for the people to decide what to do and then hop on the bandwagon with them.

Conclusion number seven is a corollary of number six: *the leader's choice influences other people.* If you are a successful leader, the moment you make your choice, people will follow, as in Joshua's case. Actually, this is the acid test of leadership. When you make a decision, do people follow?

Read verse 18 again: 'We also will serve the Lord, for He is our God.' Did you notice that word *also*? In effect, the people were saying, 'We'll serve the Lord, because you're serving Him, Joshua.' And verse 31 says, 'And Israel served the Lord all the days of Joshua and all the days of the elders who survived Joshua, and had known all the deeds of the Lord which He had done for Israel.' A tremendous amount of influence lies with the leader who recognizes the power of decision-making.

There is, of course, more to making a decision than saying, 'Let's do it.' In fact, the decision-making process is a complex one. But if you are to be a leader that people follow, it will be worth your while to understand this process. It involves five progressive phases. By way of illustration, I'm going to walk you through a major decision-making process in my own life—the call to come as senior pastor of Skyline Wesleyan Church.

STAGE ONE: THE FOUNDATION STAGE

Before you can make a wise decision, you need to understand the background of your situation. Why are your people where they are right now? Who made the decisions that led them here? It is impossible to jump into a situation and take control without ascertaining some historical information.

When Skyline's pastoral search committee called and asked if

I would consider being a candidate, I answered yes. I was familiar with the church; my impressions were favorable. But there was a great deal I needed to know before committing myself. Returning home to Ohio from my first trip to meet with the search committee, I spent the entire time on the plane examining a large box of background information. I read year-end reports, financial statements, anything and everything that would help me better understand the church's history.

There are seven questions that I needed to answer and that you will need to answer before you have thoroughly worked through the foundation stage:

- *What is the track record?* Does the organization have a history of success or failure? Before I came to Skyline, I knew that it had a history of continued growth, godly leadership, and a good reputation in the community.
- *Who are (or were) the key players?* What kinds of people have been in leadership positions? At Skyline, Pastor Orval Butcher held the key leadership position, but other people and organizations were very influential. I came to find out that two groups in the church commanded the most respect: musicians and missionaries. Knowing this bit of information enabled me to know what was important to the people.
- *What has been their philosophy?* Has it been positive, progressive, visionary? Is it compatible with mine?
- *What is the organizational pattern?* How is the structure run? Does the staff have control of the total operation, or do the lay people? One of the appealing things about Skyline was that it was (and continues to be) a staff-run church. I would never accept the senior pastorale of a church in which the lay people choose the staff.
- *What were the major problems?* As you examine the background of the situation in question, clearly identify what the main

problems have been. I identified what I felt were two problem areas in Skyline's past. One involved a plateau period, a certain length of time during which the church did not grow. Another was that the staff was not strong in leadership. I've often joked with Pastor Butcher that if he were working with my staff, he would have church attendance running 5,000 now.

- *What were the major accomplishments?* What qualities stand out? I recognized that Skyline's major asset was the tremendous spirit of unity in the church body. The people had learned how to pull together. I knew that because of the love and warmth in the church, it would be easy to walk in and lead them.
- *What are the present goals and expectations?* It is often the case that your own goals and expectations are much different than those which other people have for you. And many times those under your leadership won't agree what their goals for you are.

After the pastoral search committee had grilled me for several hours, they began to draw the meeting to a close, satisfied that they had all the pertinent information. But I said, 'Wait a minute! It's my turn to ask you guys some questions.' They had found out what my goals were. Now I needed to know what their expectations of me were. 'What do I have to do if I come to this church?' We all agreed that I would be expected to show up on Sundays and have a sermon ready. Besides that, the search committee expected me to build a great church. But then I discovered that there were a number of people who were counting on me to make home visits on a regular basis. Others expected me to perform all weddings and funerals. Not everybody's expectations of me were compatible. I had to evaluate their goals and my goals and then decide what was important.

If you are able to answer these seven questions about any

leadership situation which calls for decisive action, you are on your way to making a wise choice. You have laid a solid foundation and are ready to move on.

STAGE TWO: THE FACT STAGE

At this point of the decision-making process you go on a fact-finding mission to help you better assess the situation as it really is. There are three key questions to ask at this stage:

- ✦ *What do I need to know?* Before I came to Skyline, I needed to know what my job description would be. I needed to know exactly what I was responsible for and to whom I was accountable. I needed to know what my salary and benefits would be. These are the hard, cold facts of the job.
- ✦ *What do I know?* After you have decided what facts you need to know, mentally check off the questions that you already have answered.
- ✦ *What do I not know?* In my own situation, I knew what the search committee would be expecting of me. I knew what they were going to pay me. I knew that they were behind me. I did not know, however, whether or not I would be so readily accepted by the congregation. I did not know where I would live or where my children would go to school. It can be difficult to make a decision when all the facts are not in.

Once you have answered these three questions to your satisfaction, you are in the position to make a decision, *so make it.* At this point, many people fall into the 'what if . . .' syndrome. These people rarely do anything decisive. What they need more than answers is a swift kick.

STAGE THREE: THE FEEDBACK STAGE

At this phase of the process, you may get strong reactions. People will either confirm your decision or question your wisdom. This is a crucial time because emotions come into play. You will hear such comments as, 'This is the way we've always done it!' or 'But my grandpa helped build this church.' Expect to take some heat after you have lit a fire. The secret here is to develop an 'inner circle.' In my case, my inner circle is my staff. Your inner circle should be made up of people who are closely involved in your project, people who are knowledgeable, positive, and unintimidated.

How do you determine whose feedback is going to count? Let me give you six factors that should be taken into account:

Knowledge of the subject. Obviously, this is critical. If, for instance, I have to make a decision involving the music department, I am much more likely to listen to members of our music staff than to our comptroller.

Skill. Not only should the person know the subject in question, he or she should be good at it. Our comptroller may have some knowledge in the field of music, but he can't carry a tune in a bucket.

Experience. This means *successful* experience, of course. There is no substitute for experience in giving a person expertise in any area. I am ready to listen to the person who has already lived through what I may be going through.

Responsibility. Someone who has successfully shouldered the responsibility of seeing a plan carried out will certainly have more credibility than a novice.

Strength of feeling. This is an intuitive thing, but when someone has strong feelings about an idea, it comes through. I love people of conviction. If a person is willing to lay his life on the line, he has my attention.

Principle. Am I well enough acquainted with the person to know that he runs his life on the same general principles that I do mine? If his principles are in violation of mine, he's not apt to be in my inner circle.

If a person qualifies in all six of these areas, he or she has my ear. If a staff member comes to my office to sell me a program and he passes all six tests, I'm in a position to buy.

The feedback stage is crucial in the decision-making process. If we don't spend enough time here, we're in danger of making the wrong decision. If we spend too much time here, we may never get the decision made. Actually, the greatest difficulty is not in *knowing* the right decision but in *making* it. After you know the facts, the history, and have feedback, you need to make your decision without delay.

STAGE FOUR: THE FOCUS STAGE

At this point my attention turns from 'What decision should I make?' to 'How shall I make my decision work?' Here I move from the inner circle to the 'outer circle.' In this stage I need to focus on two concerns:

PROBLEMS—What might torpedo the decision?
PROCEDURES—How can the decision be effectively communicated?

I discussed handling difficulties in chapter 9, 'Your Problem Is Not Your Problem,' but here I want to give you a concise four-point outline for responding to problems:

1. *Anticipate them.* Don't let problems take you by surprise.
2. *List them.* Write down all the problems you're aware of.
3. *Address them.* Examine each problem thoroughly and think of a solution.
4. *Outsmart them.* If plan A doesn't work, be ready with plan B.

When we first began dealings to purchase land on which to relocate our sanctuary, the chairman of the relocation committee wrote to the congregation *answering* the potential questions and problems before they had a chance to ask. It kind of lets the wind out of a possible opponent's sail when he discovers you're one step ahead of him. Address the possible problem before it becomes a reality.

Once you have faced the issue and decided what to do about it, how do you proceed? There are five steps to take in order to make a decision effective:

Communication. Make others aware that you're aware.

Consideration. Enable your outer circle to visualize the positive results of your decision.

Comparison. Evaluate your decision honestly. Compare the pros and cons.

Conviction. This is the climax of the decision-making process. This is the step at which you reach a consensus.

Commitment. Once you and your circle have agreed on the decision, they should stand with you in seeing that decision through to fruition.

STAGE FIVE: THE FORWARD STAGE

This is the part of decision-making that I like; it's the time to move ahead. The critical element at this stage is timing; if your timing is off, all of your preparatory work may not save your decision. A good formula to remember regarding timing is this one:

The wrong decision at the wrong time = disaster

The wrong decision at the right time = a mistake

The right decision at the wrong time = unacceptance

The right decision at the right time = success

Now you have the five stages of decision-making. Don't underestimate the value of understanding and practicing this process. A leader's ability to make decisions and see them work means the difference between success and failure. Remember, success is not for the chosen few, but for the few who choose.

12

I DON'T HAVE TO SURVIVE

SURVIVE—IT'S the most natural thing we do. We were born with an instinct to try to survive. We are born fighters.

But that natural desire to survive creates a conflict. In Galatians 2:20, Paul said, 'I am crucified with Christ'—that's not survival. We're caught between resurrection and death. We all want the resurrection, but most of us don't want the crucifixion. This is a major problem in the church, both among church leaders and laymen.

WHAT'S THE PROBLEM?

The desire to survive keeps us at a mediocre level of living. It eats away at our conviction until we find it too easy to compromise and next to impossible to confront. The result of this survival mentality in the church is spiritual stagnation—maybe not death, but not exactly life either.

If our number one goal is to survive, we're no longer free to make the best decisions. I find this all the time in leadership. We make decisions that are acceptable instead of making decisions that are right and godly. We take a poll and do what satisfies the people rather than what we know in our hearts is really right.

Also, if we desire to survive, we are encouraged to excuse our lack of effectiveness. We talk a lot about being faithful in the church; we talk very little about being fruitful. A fruitful person has to die first, so since most of us haven't died, we would rather talk about faithfulness. We may not really accomplish much, but at least we're consistent.

Another thing our desire to survive does is to sap our freedom and joy in the Lord. That's why there's a lot of talk in the Christian community today about burnout instead of move-out. We are trying so desperately to survive that we're operating in the flesh, and that is just wearing down our emotional and physical faculties.

Our desire to survive hinders us from completely obeying God. The Bible's heroes were characterized by wholehearted obedience. But if we are survivors, when it comes to the point in our walk with God where we may lose our skin, we cease walking in the light in order to preserve our flesh.

Our desire to survive robs us of the power and the blessings of God. When we strive for man's approval, that's about all we'll get. What we'll miss out on are the riches of God.

THE BIBLE'S EXAMPLES

There are a number of survival seekers in the Bible who, because of their desire to save themselves, lost the best that God had for them.

Lot is a good example. He chose the well-watered plains of Jordan. He took what was best for himself, and he lost his family in the deal. Ananias and Sapphira withheld from God what was rightly His and lost their lives because of it. King Saul wanted to keep his throne and his kingdom. He also wanted to keep all the glory to himself.

There's something common to all these people who tried to

survive: they lost what they tried to keep. Whatever the survivor holds tightest he loses. It's a paradox evident in the teachings of Jesus. 'Whoever wishes to save his life shall lose it, but whoever loses his life for My sake, he is the one who will save it' (Luke 9:24).

Sometimes we think that the people who have the most are the ones who hold on to it the tightest. The rich young ruler is a good example. But this is not necessarily the case. If you're a survival seeker, it's because of your mind-set, not your position or your possessions. Survivors have an 'I want to stay alive at any cost' attitude. Anybody can adopt this philosophy of life.

How about Peter and his denial? There was a survival tactic if I've ever seen one. He tried to save his own skin. We could go on and on giving examples of those in God's Word who tried to survive. They paid a terrible price for their survivor mind-set. Solomon had an empty life; the rich ruler went away sadly after Jesus tried to minister to him; Peter will never forget the look on Jesus' face when He saw that His disciple had been unfaithful to Him.

The Bible also provides us with numerous examples of men and women who did not have to survive; they achieved great things for God because they were willing to put their lives on the line. Let's look at some examples here.

Shadrach, Meshach, and Abed-nego believed God would deliver them, but if He didn't, that was all right too. Caleb and Joshua came back with a different report from that of the other 10 spies, which again shows you that we aren't compelled to strive for survival even in a survivor climate. They saw the same place, and they came back with an attitude that said, 'Let's go possess that land!' David is another who didn't have to survive. The survivor would have said of the giant, Goliath, 'He's so big he will hurt me.' David said, 'He's so big I can't miss.'

How about Abraham sacrificing Isaac? Gideon didn't have to survive; he took just a few hundred men against thousands of Midianites. The widow with two mites was willing to give up all she had. She didn't have to survive. Again, it does not matter how much or how little you have; it's what percentage are you willing to give up? It is not a position in life. The widow gave everything that she had. The Apostle Paul is a classic example of one who didn't have to survive. We'll spend more time with him later.

'I DON'T HAVE TO SURVIVE' CHARACTERISTICS

Let me give you four characteristics of 'I don't have to survive' people.

They have faith in God, not in themselves. They understand the value of placing their trust in God, because they recognize their own limitations.

They change people, nations, and generations. A leader who is willing to step out in faith may step out alone, but he will soon have followers. Together they will change lives. Many have changed the course of history.

They are willing to stand alone. A person who doesn't have to survive chooses to make the right decision even if it's not a popular one.

They possess unusual powers. God gives selfless people spiritual power. That's what makes the difference.

Some risk takers are getting a lot of attention in the world today—terrorists. This is certainly a negative example, but the terrorists provide a very fitting example of what happens when somebody doesn't have to survive. The world doesn't know what to do with terrorists, because they do not care about surviving. We have no leverage on them. Even great powers like the United States are powerless against terrorists, because their lives are less important to them than their cause. They're willing to lay it all on the line.

Look at Israel's ability to keep their land even though surrounded by enemy nations. They know what it is to almost be extinct; they know what it is to face death, and they're willing to pay any price they have to pay to keep their freedom. They're a nation of people who don't have to survive.

We in the United States have enjoyed so many blessings for so long that we can't imagine being without them. We're not willing to risk loss because we have too much at stake. So we have become guardians of the goods, survivors to the end. We desperately need to shake off this mind-set.

PAUL'S SECRET

I was reading Acts 20 one day, and I really think I found the secret to the Apostle Paul's life. Why was this guy so effective for the glory of God? On his way to Jerusalem, Paul met with the Ephesian elders and reviewed with them some of his ministry. 'I did not shrink from declaring to you anything that was profitable, and teaching you publicly and from house to house . . . And now, behold, bound in spirit, I am on my way to Jerusalem, not knowing what will happen to me there, except that the Holy Spirit solemnly testifies to me in every city, saying that bonds and afflictions await me' (Acts 20:20, 22). Paul doesn't shrink from the message. He doesn't know what's going to happen except he knows it's going to be bad. He went on to say, 'I do not consider my life of any account as dear to myself' (v. 24). This is a classic 'I don't have to survive' statement. What mattered to the Apostle Paul was finishing the work God had for him. And he adds in verse 25, 'I know that you all . . . will see my face no more.'

No wonder Paul was such a change agent in the early church.

No wonder he was willing to stand at the Jerusalem council and say that the Gospel was for the Gentiles as well as the Jews. No wonder he was willing to be the first missionary. The Apostle Paul didn't have to survive. No one could stop him. Those who didn't like some of the statements he was making on the council floor couldn't take away his position. Paul didn't have a position to lose. Those who wanted him to quit preaching could throw rocks at him, but that had happened before, and it didn't stop Paul. He would have counted it a privilege to suffer for Christ. They could threaten him with prison, but Paul could laugh and say, 'Which one? Can I go back to Rome? I was witnessing there the last time I was in prison. Maybe I could help lead that guy to the Lord this time.' Or they could threaten to kill him. 'Would you? I have had such turmoil inwardly. I don't know whether I should stay with the saints or be present with the Lord; if you would just knock me off, that would take care of my dilemma.' What could be done with the Apostle Paul? Absolutely nothing. Why did Paul choose to live this kind of life? So he could be independent? So he could call his own shots? No. He wanted to be crucified with Christ, knowing that in his own flesh he was powerless to preach the Gospel. And that should be our highest aim too. Only when we die to self can we live for Christ.

THE SECURITY PROBLEM

One of areas we are going to have to face is our insecurity. Insecure people are survivors; they're not willing to take risks, especially life-threatening risks. They have to have a second option; they have to have a plan B in their lives. They have a difficult time with failure. They tend to rely on things other than God. The person who doesn't have to survive says, 'Here I stand; I can do nothing else. It's God and nothing else.' The survivor says, 'Well, it's God, but in case God doesn't come through, I have four other options to fall back on so I won't lose my hide.' Paul writes in 1 Corinthians 4,

> *Let a man regard us in the manner as servants of Christ . . . To me it is a very small thing that I should be examined by you, or by any human court; in fact, I do not even examine myself. I am conscious of nothing against myself, yet I am not by this acquitted; but the one who examines me is the Lord. (1 Cor. 4:1, 3–4)*

Paul isn't saying he isn't going to submit to authority, but he is saying his security is not dependent on human decisions. He is saying, 'I'm accountable to God.'

What would happen if church leaders would be prophets instead of puppets? What would happen if we all became secure people who wait on the voice of God instead of insecure people who panic waiting on the voice of other people? This is not to say that the people don't matter. But if you can become secure in God, you will gain a freedom that people can never give you.

I grew up in a denomination where the greatest thing that could happen to a pastor was a unanimous vote from the congregation. When the pastors came together at district conference, all they talked about was their votes. I will never forget my first pastoral vote; the result was 31 yes, 1 no, and 1 blank. I remember getting on the phone in a panic, as a 22-year-old, calling my dad and saying, 'Dad, should I stay at the church or not?' He said, 'Well, what was your vote?' And I said, 'Thirty-one said yes, one said no, and one didn't say anything at all. Is God telling me it's time for me to move on?' Dad just laughed and said, 'John, that's a great vote. Quit worrying about it! Get on with it.' That was probably the best vote that I ever had in my career. If my goal were to keep all the members of the congregation happy all the time, I would many times have to compromise my convictions, but I would more than likely get a 100 percent vote. There are times when, as a pastor, you need to listen to the voice of the people; it may be God's voice. But you should not be led by popular opinion; your sense of security should be anchored in the approval of God, not man.

THE SUCCESS PROBLEM

Another problem we have to face if we want to develop an 'I don't have to survive' attitude is in the area of success. If we've had any success, we'll be tempted to guard it, to want people to continue thinking how wonderful we are. So we take fewer risks. We become a fortress instead of a moving army. We build fences and walls around ourselves so that nobody can walk into our lives and destroy that which is so very precious to us.

Paul talks about the success problem in 1 Corinthians. He says some very humbling things. 'God has chosen the foolish things . . . the weak things . . . the base things . . . and the despised . . . the things that are not, that . . . no man should boast before God' (1 Cor. 1:27–29). In chapter 2 he writes that when he came to Corinth he chose to come to them in weakness and in fear and in trembling, not in persuasive words, but in demonstration of the spirit and of power (1 Cor. 2:1–4). One thing that the Apostle Paul says in this passage of Scripture is that we have a choice. Paul, though he was wise and brilliant, chose to come in weakness and fear. He could have come in and snowed them with all his languages. He could have come in and impressed them with the wealth of his knowledge and the breadth of his experiences. But he decided to put all that on the shelf and come talking about the cross of Jesus Christ. He decided to come in simplicity, not in profundity; in humility, not in arrogance.

One of the most important experiences of my life happened

a few years ago when I was to speak at a large youth conference. For six months I told the church board to pray for me. I was sure this was going to affect many people. The organizers wanted a thousand young people to come forward and answer the call to full-time ministry, so I felt a tremendous responsibility. I prepared and prayed like I'd never prepared and prayed before in my life. Then in the Ramada Inn the afternoon of the evening I was going to speak, I sensed God saying, 'Hey, John, by the way, I'm not going to use your message tonight.' I don't get upset very often, but all of a sudden I realized that there were going to be 7,000 people there, and God was saying He wasn't going to use my message. I had worked a long time on that message. It was soul stirring, and those young people needed to hear it! But God said, 'No, John. Listen to Me.' I might as well have gotten on a plane and gone home.

But I stayed, trusting God had a better plan. He was impressing upon me that the success of the evening would depend on Him, not me. He directed me to read the passage in 1 Corinthians 1 and share with the kids that God was going to move mightily in the service because people had been praying. All He meant for me to do was to read the Scripture, pray, and give the invitation.

But I didn't do that. I read the passage, then I thought, *Well, I think it would help the Scripture a little bit to just use three or four great illustrations,* since I thought God needed me to bail Him out of this terrible problem. I told the first illustration and it bombed. I forgot the second one, so I finally just said, 'Let's bow our heads.' A wonderful peace came over me when I started to do what God had told me to do from the very beginning. Fifteen hundred kids came forward to say, 'God has called me to preach in this service.'

I'll be honest: when they came down that evening, I was both glad and sad. I was glad at what God was doing, but I was sad He didn't use me to do it. God was teaching me to stop worrying about my reputation, my success. He was telling me that if I'm to be successful for Him, He needs my listening ability, not my preaching ability.

If you're running in the reputation race, you need to decelerate and get off the track. I'd like to suggest five courses of action that will help you do this.

Don't take yourself too seriously. We're constantly concerned about what other people are thinking of us, especially others who are running the race. When we begin taking God more seriously, we become less important; we can laugh at ourselves.

Create a climate of unqualified acceptance. We need to create a climate where we accept each other just because we're brothers and sisters in the Lord Jesus Christ.

Fear God more than man. We'll get out of this success syndrome and reputation race when we begin to recognize the frailty, the humanness, of man and the awesomeness of God. We will want to please God above all else.

Turn accomplishments into challenges. Too often we rest on our accomplishments and don't take on any more challenges; we have too much to lose. What we ought to be doing is using those accomplishments as building blocks in the construction of God's Kingdom, not pedestals to rest on.

Make room for innovators, entrepreneurs, to work. We need to make room for people who don't fit the average mold, people who are daring enough to risk failure. We need to be their cheering section.

THE SATISFACTION PROBLEM

In Revelation 3 we see that the church at Laodicea had the satisfaction problem. God said, 'I know your deeds, that you are neither cold nor hot; I would that you were cold or hot. So because you are lukewarm, and neither hot nor cold, I will spit you out of My mouth . . . You say, "I am rich, and have become wealthy, and have need of nothing," and you do not know that you are wretched and miserable and poor and blind and naked' (Rev. 3:15–17).

When we feel satisfied with ourselves, we lack the compassion needed to reach out to others. It's hard to care for others when you don't understand need. When we are satisfied and full, it's hard to help the people who are hungry and hurting. That's why Christians who have been in the church for a long time sometimes lack the compassion and desire to reach out to other people; they've forgotten what it was like to be out there. They have isolated themselves from the people who need to hear the message of the Gospel, the people who are still hurting and needy; they are no longer rubbing elbows with the crowd. Unfortunately, this is a real problem in the Christian community. Satisfaction has gripped the church. We have what we want and are happy with ourselves.

What are some characteristics of people who are in a state of satisfaction? First, they are unwilling to pay the price. They're unable to make *right* decisions. You show me a satisfied person or a satisfied church, and I will show you one that is not able to make the right decisions, because the right decisions are the hard decisions, and the hard decisions are going to cost them something.

People in a satisfaction climate are more concerned about maintaining what they have than they are about meeting the needs of others around them. They have a maintenance mindset. They want only to keep themselves happy. Their commitment in the church is not to the great commission at all but to clean rest rooms, neat bulletins, and potluck suppers. I see this in the denominations who have programs that are palatable to everyone, decisions that are accepted by everyone, plans approved by everyone, and progress witnessed by no one.

THE SELFISHNESS PROBLEM

Another problem we have to deal with if we want to develop an 'I don't have to survive' attitude is selfishness. One of the reasons people want to survive is that they want to be able to protect their rights. But if we want to be like Jesus, we have to give up our rights. Paul wrote,

> *Have this attitude in yourselves which was also in Christ Jesus, who, although He existed in the form of God, did not regard equality with God a thing to be grasped, but emptied Himself, taking the form of a bond-servant, and being made in the likeness of men. And being found in appearance as a man, He humbled Himself by becoming obedient to the point of death, even death on a cross. Therefore also God highly exalted Him. (Phil. 2:5–9)*

I'm continually impressed when I think of the life of Jesus. He is the ultimate example for people who don't have to survive. He was in the robe of flesh, as we are; He had the same basic needs that we have; and no doubt He had moments in His life when He thought of surviving. The issue of survival confronted Him at the very beginning of His ministry, when He went to the wilderness and fasted for forty days. Satan came to tempt Him, to entice Him to survive. He offered bread for His body, a throne for an earthly kingdom, and the world bowing down before Him. Satan was setting Jesus up for survival.

It was before He began His great ministry that He was confronted with the issue of survival. Satan will use the same tactic on you. Before you accomplish anything great for God, I promise you, the issue of survival will arise in your life. Jesus said some remarkable things about Himself.

- ‘The Son can do nothing of Himself, unless it is something He sees the Father doing.’ (John 5:19)
- ‘My judgment is just, because I seek not My own will, but the will of Him who sent Me.’ (John 5:30)
- ‘I do not receive glory from men.’ (John 5:41)
- ‘I have come down from heaven, not to do My own will, but the will of Him who sent Me.’ (John 6:38)
- ‘My teaching is not Mine, but His who sent Me.’ (John 7:16)
- ‘I have not come of Myself, but He who sent Me is true.’ (John 7:28)
- ‘When you lift up the Son of Man, then you will know that I am He, and I do nothing on My own initiative, but I speak these things as the Father hath taught Me.’ (John 8:28)
- ‘I did not speak on My own initiative, but the Father Himself who sent Me has given Me commandment, what to say, and what to speak.’ (John 12:49)
- ‘The words that I say to you I do not speak on My own initiative, but the Father abiding in Me does His works.’ (John 14:10)

Did you see all the *nots?* Not My words, not My teaching, not My judgment, not My deeds, but the Father’s; not I, but the Father; not My own glory, but the Father’s.

How was Jesus able to cope with the pressures of His ministry? How was He able to minister to such a diverse group as the disciples? How was He able to have patience with them; how was he able to face the pressures of a crowd who wanted to put an earthly crown on His head? How was He able to withdraw from all those pressures and pray? Here’s the reason: Jesus didn’t have to survive. If I’m to be like Jesus, I too have to give up all my rights. You do too. The first step in ‘becoming of no reputation’ and relinquishing our rights is in coming to the clear understanding that everything we are and everything we can ever hope to be can only be due to the power and grace of the Lord Jesus Christ. Could it be that we need a mission bigger than ourselves, a purpose beyond our limited vision?

DYING FOR A GREATER CAUSE

In the first part of the fifteenth century a French peasant by the name of Joan of Arc was called to save her country from its enemies. Her sacred sword, her consecrated banner, and her belief in her mission helped her to sweep away the armies that were before her. She sent a thrill of enthusiasm through the French army such as neither a king, a statesman, nor a president could produce. On one occasion she said to one of her generals, 'I will lead the men over the wall.' The general said, 'Not a man will follow you.' Joan of Arc replied, 'I won't be looking back to see if they're following me.' It was that kind of commitment that made Joan of Arc a national hero for the French. She was successful in delivering them from their English enemies, but she herself fell into English hands. As she was being burned at the stake, this 19-year-old was given a chance to recant; she was given a chance to betray her country; she was given a chance for liberty and freedom. But she chose the fire, and going to her death, she made this statement: 'Every man gives his life for what he believes, and every woman gives her life for what she believes. Sometimes people believe in little or nothing, and yet they give their lives to that little or nothing. One life is all we have; we live it and it's gone. But . . . to live without belief is more terrible than dying, even more terrible than dying young.' Joan of Arc had a purpose beyond herself; she didn't have to survive.

Let me give you the three characteristics of people who have been willing to die for a greater cause than themselves.

A purpose worth the price. People who don't have to survive have a purpose that is worth the cost of their very lives.

A vision that is bigger than life. They have the ability to see beyond their horizons. They are willing to make a sacrifice that they know will affect future generations.

A power that is greater than theirs. People who don't have to survive aren't limited by their own weakness; they have a God-given power. Their purpose is God's purpose; their vision is God's vision; their power is God's power. His Spirit living in them makes the difference.

13

COMMITMENT IS THE KEY

BACK IN the middle '70s, I reached a major decision-making period in my life. I was facing choices that would determine the course of my life and the effectiveness of my ministry. For over a year during that period I carried in my pocket a card, which I pulled out and read time and time again. After making my decision, I would waiver—and then reach for my card. I've read it hundreds of times. Because commitment is the key to success, I want to begin this chapter with the words that helped me in this area:

> *Until I am committed, there is a hesitancy, a chance to draw back. But the moment I definitely commit myself, then God moves also, and a whole stream of events erupt. All manner of unforeseen incidents, meetings, persons, and material assistance which I could never have dreamed would come my way begin to flow toward me—the moment I make a commitment.*

The greatest days of your life are the days when you sense your commitment to its highest degree. Your greatest days are not your days of leisure. Your greatest days are not even times when you have your closest friends around you. When something has seized you and caused you to have a high level of commitment to it, those are your greatest days. They may be your days of struggle, they may be your days of suffering, and they may be the days of your greatest battles in life, but they will be your greatest days.

If I could choose only one word to describe what it's like to be committed, I think I would choose the word *alone.* If you become a person who is deeply committed to a cause, the world won't understand you; you will be alone. It's human to stand with the crowd; it's divine to stand alone. It's manlike to follow the people, to drift with the tide; it's godlike to follow principles, to stem the tide. It's natural to compromise conscience and follow social and religious fashions for the sake of gain and pleasure; it's divine to sacrifice fashions on the altar of truth and beauty. 'No one supported me, but all deserted me' (2 Tim. 4:16). Those were the words of the battle-scarred Apostle Paul in describing his first appearance before Nero to answer for his life. Truth has been out of fashion since man changed his robe of fadeless light for a garment of faded leaves. Think about it for a moment.

Noah built the ark and voyaged alone except for his family. Abraham wandered and worshiped alone. Daniel dined and prayed alone. Elijah sacrificed and witnessed alone. Jeremiah prophesied and wept alone. Jesus loved and died alone. On His lonely way Jesus said to His disciples, 'For the gate is small, and the way is narrow that leads to life, and few are those who find it' (Matt. 7:14).

Margaret and the kids and I went to the East Coast for a vacation last year. It was kind of a founding-and-forming-of-our-country vacation. It struck me that every historical site we visited was a monument to somebody's commitment in life. We went to New York City and saw the Statue of Liberty. There on Ellis

Island stands the lady with her torch, the first thing so many immigrants saw in our country. I listened to the guide talk about some of the things that happened to the immigrants when they landed at Ellis Island. They had such great hopes for life in America, yet they couldn't speak the language and didn't have a friend in the country. Sometimes they were detained on the small island for weeks or months; some died there. But many got to New York City and worked hard to carve out a place for themselves in this free society. That's commitment.

Then we got on a train for Philadelphia, a city rich in American history. As we sat in Constitution Hall, where the Declaration of Independence was signed, I realized the commitment level of our nation's founders. By signing their names to this document, these wealthy men were risking their lives and all they possessed. We also visited the graves of many of the signers, many of whom died penniless.

We went to Williamsburg, Virginia, where Patrick Henry began his leadership. He was the first American governor there, the man who said, 'Give me liberty or give me death.'

Two of the most impressive monuments we saw in Washington, D.C., the Washington Monument and the Lincoln Memorial, were built to honor the presidents who had the greatest struggles. One had the struggle of forming the nation, and the other had the struggle of keeping the nation. These are all monuments to commitment.

THE WORLD'S REACTIONS TO COMMITMENT

In Scripture God gives us many great examples of committed men and women, with Shadrach, Meshach, and Abed-nego among them. King Nebuchadnezzar, the ruler of Babylon, has taken Israel captive and selected some of the promising young Hebrew men to be trained to serve in his court. Of course, the one known best is Daniel, but we're going to look especially at his three friends.

Nebuchadnezzar built a golden idol and instructed his people that at the sound of the music they were to bow down and worship this idol. It seemed that everybody was cooperating, but then some Chaldeans came to the king with an upsetting report: 'There are certain Jews whom you have appointed over the administration of the province of Babylon, namely Shadrach, Meshach, and Abed-nego. These men, O king, have disregarded you; they do not serve your gods or worship the golden image which you have set up' (Dan. 3:12). The world reacts in several ways to people who are committed. The first response is brought out in this verse: the world takes notice of our commitment. These three guys really stood out.

'Then Nebuchadnezzar in rage and anger gave orders to bring Shadrach, Meshach, and Abed-nego; then these men were brought before the king' (Dan. 3:13). The second thing that happens is this: the world will be annoyed by our commitment. Nebuchadnezzar was downright mad; he flew into a rage. He couldn't handle somebody who didn't think the way he thought, believe the way he believed, or walk the way he walked.

'Nebuchadnezzar responded and said to them, "Is it true, Shadrach, Meshach and Abed-nego, that you do not serve my gods or worship the golden image that I have set up?" (Dan. 3:14) This verse brings out the next reaction: the world will question our commitment. Nebuchadnezzar had to double-check; he couldn't believe these guys had such strong backbones.

Nebuchadnezzar then said he would give them another chance to bow down to the image. 'But if you will not worship, you will immediately be cast into the midst of a furnace of blazing fire; and what god is there who can deliver you out of my hands?' (Dan. 3:15) The fourth reaction is this: the world will test your commitment.

As those three Jews stood there that day, I imagine several thoughts went through their heads. They probably asked themselves questions like, Can God deliver us? What would it hurt if we bowed down just one time? I've often thought that would have been a convenient time for them to tie their shoelaces, so they could bow down; not to worship the idol, of course, just to tie their shoes.

When we come to the crossroad of our commitment the strength of our commitment has to prove itself. The choice will not be easy, because it's all or nothing. Our security, our identity, and our popularity may be at stake. It will not be a decision we can make lightly.

CHARACTERISTICS OF THE CROSSROAD

When I'm at a crossroad of commitment in my life, *a personal decision must be made.* Other people may care; they may pray; they may offer advice; but the decision will be mine alone. I'm the one who will have to live with it and answer for it. Shadrach, Meshach, and Abed-nego stood together, but each had to make his own decision, his own commitment.

A second characteristic of a crossroad commitment is that *the decision will always cost something.* There is no such thing as a free commitment. In this situation commitment could have cost the Hebrews their lives. Your commitment may not be quite that expensive, but it will cost you something. It may cost you a friendship. It may cost you a few points in the popularity poll. But if it were free, it would also be worthless. Count on its costing.

A third thing I find at the crossroad is that *others will be influenced by it.* We never make a major decision at a crossroad without affecting other people. We may make the decision alone, and we may walk the commitment alone, but we never make an important commitment that does not affect other people. It's like the rippling effect when a stone is thrown into a pond. The whole pond is affected.

Fourth, *it's the place where God reveals Himself to us.* Note that Nebuchadnezzar asked the men, 'What god is there who can deliver you out of my hands?' Even the world realizes that our commitments are valid only because God intervenes.

A RIGHT CONCEPT OF GOD

Our concept of God in crisis situations will determine our commitment. If we think God will fail us, flee, or be fickle, we'll never make strong commitments. We would be foolish to commit ourselves to someone who is irresponsible. But if our concept of God tells us He's sure, steadfast, true, and faithful, then we can make those commitments confidently.

Shadrach, Meshach, and Abed-nego were able to make the right kind of commitment because they had the right concept of God. They said to the king, 'O Nebuchadnezzar, we do not need to give you an answer concerning this. If it be so, our God whom we serve is able to deliver us from the furnace of blazing fire; and He will deliver us out of your hand, O king' (Dan. 3:16–17). Their first concept of God was that He is able.

They went on to say, 'But even if He does not, let it be known to you, O king, that we are not going to serve your gods or worship the golden image that you have set up' (Dan. 3:18). They understood that God expects us to do right regardless of the consequences. If we have that twofold concept of God, we have the glue for a very strong bonding for our commitment.

If we can begin to see God as one who expects us to do right regardless of the consequences, we won't waver; God many times *will* bring healing and deliverance and power and anointing to our lives, but that's just the icing on the cake. Our concept of God makes a great difference.

RESULTS OF COMMITMENT

What resulted from the commitment of Shadrach, Meshach, and Abed-nego?

> *Then Nebuchadnezzar was filled with wrath, and his facial expression was altered toward Shadrach, Meshach, and Abed-nego. He answered by giving orders to heat the furnace seven times more than it was usually heated. And he commanded some valiant warriors who were in his army to tie up Shadrach, Meshach, and Abed-nego, in order to cast them into the furnace of blazing fire. Then these men were tied up in their trousers, their coats, their caps and their other clothes, and were cast into the midst of the furnace of blazing fire. For this reason, because the king's command was urgent and the furnace had been made extremely hot, the flame of fire slew those men who carried up Shadrach, Meshach, and Abed-nego. But these three men, Shadrach, Meshach, and Abed-nego, fell into the midst of the furnace of blazing fire still tied up. (Dan. 3:19–23)*

The first result of our commitment is that *we will be tried.* Bank on it: when we stand up for God, we will be tested.

The second result of our commitment is that *God will be glorified.* When we are truly committed to Him, He will receive praise.

Nebuchadnezzar looked into the fiery furnace and asked, 'Was it not three men we cast bound into the midst of the fire?' For he saw in the furnace four men 'loosed and walking about in the midst of the fire without harm, and the appearance of the fourth is like a son of the gods!' He called to Shadrach, Meshach, and Abed-nego to come out, and the three guys came out. In Daniel 3:27, we can see that the satraps, the prefects, the governors, and the king's high officials gathered around and saw that the fire had had no effect on their bodies. Their hair wasn't singed, their trousers weren't damaged, and they didn't even smell like fire. We can't even do that well if we go to a restaurant and sit in the nonsmoking section.

Nebuchadnezzar said, 'Blessed be the God of Shadrach, Meshach, and Abed-nego, who has sent His angel and delivered His servants who put their trust in Him, violating the king's command, and yielded up their bodies so as not to serve or worship any god except their own God. Therefore I make a decree that any people, nation or tongue that speaks anything offensive against the God of Shadrach, Meshach and Abed-nego shall be torn limb from limb and their houses reduced to a rubbish heap, inasmuch as there is no other god who is able to deliver in this way' (Dan. 3:28–29).

How is the world going to know about the greatness of God without committed Christians? Our problem is not a lack of display of the power of God, the miracles of God, or the anointing of God; God is ready to His part. He's just waiting for somebody to get into the furnace. He's looking for people who are totally committed, people whose purpose goes beyond their own abilities. There is a relationship between our willingness to die for God and His willingness to deliver us.

A third result of our commitment is that *God will bless our lives.* The king caused Shadrach, Meshach, and Abed-nego to prosper in the province of Babylon, according to Daniel 3:30.

Ordinary people can make an extraordinary impact on their own world. The secret lies in being totally committed to the cause of Jesus Christ. If you read the biographies of great men, you'll become convinced of a couple of things very quickly. One, all great men struggle; all great men have a fiery furnace in their lives. The second thing is that the degree of their commitment is what really made them great. They weren't smarter, they weren't faster, and they weren't better educated; they were more committed.

DEVELOPING COMMITMENT

How do we develop commitment in our lives? From the story of Shadrach, Meshach, and Abed-nego, we can pull out several principles.

Commitment usually begins in an atmosphere of struggle. Very seldom do we see strong commitment arise out of a context of prosperity. Squandered time, wasted living, and distorted values may come out of prosperity, but commitment does not. The three Jews were captives in another land, with new customs, new surroundings, new values, and different priorities. It was for them an atmosphere of struggle.

Winston Churchill really achieved greatness during the struggle of World War II. His finest hour was the hour of confrontation, the hour of challenge. After the war he became an average prime minister, but not a great one. As Churchill was anticipating the fall of France in 1940, he said, 'The battle of France is over; I expect the battle of Britain is about to begin. Upon this battle depends the survival of Christian civilization . . . Let us therefore brace ourselves to our duties and so bear ourselves that if the British Empire and its Commonwealth last for a thousand years, men will say, this was their finest hour.'

Forty-five years later, nine out of ten people would probably say that Britain's finest hour came in the days of Churchill's leadership during World War II. Commitment usually begins in dark hours.

Commitment doesn't depend on abilities or gifts. Daniel, Shadrach, Meshach, and Abed-nego were among many good-looking and intelligent youths chosen for special training, according to Daniel 1:3–4. But I like to think they weren't really chosen for those qualities. Rather, they were chosen because of their commitment.

Commitment is the result of choice; it's not a condition. People do not make great commitments because their conditions are right. People make great commitments because they choose to do right in spite of the conditions. In Daniel 1:8, it says, 'But Daniel made up his mind.'

The moment that Daniel made up his mind, the moment that Shadrach, Meshach, and Abed-nego made up their minds to serve God—that was their great moment. That's the moment God lifted them up. God blessed them because they chose commitment.

Commitment starts with the little things in our lives. No one ever made a big commitment without first making little commitments. It's a lot like learning to walk; we gain new confidence with each step. When we see that God blesses our small commitments, we begin to trust Him with bigger ones.

Don't make a commitment today to win your world for Jesus. That's idealistic and unreasonable. Make a commitment to win one person to Jesus. With the confidence you gain from winning that one, you can win two more.

Shadrach, Meshach, and Abed-nego started out on the right foot by refusing to eat the king's food. If you can't stand up and say no to the king's food, you can't stand up and say no to the king's idol. You don't all of a sudden get that kind of courage; it starts with the little things. You realize that when you said no to the king's food, God blessed you, and you prospered. If God helped you on the food issue, He can help you on the idol issue.

And step by step, we begin to build a foundation underneath us that gives us strong character for strong commitment.

This principle also works in reverse. Herein lies the danger of sinning: when you sin once, it's easier to sin twice. That's why we ought to have a healthy fear of temptation and a healthy fear of sin. Sin breaks down the walls of resistance. It causes our focus to become blurred, and all of a sudden we're doing things we shouldn't be doing. If you didn't make any strong commitments yesterday, it will catch up with you today.

Settle the issue of commitment before it arises. Don't get caught up in the emotion of the moment, because then your commitment will waver. Make your decision before the issue arises. The battle is won before the battle is begun. That's the secret behind the three Hebrews' success. They already knew what they were going to do. They didn't stand there and listen to the music and look at each other, wondering what to do. They had already settled the issue, so they didn't have to think about it.

Trust in God. In Daniel 3:28, after the Hebrews had been rescued and delivered, Nebuchadnezzar made an interesting statement. 'Blessed be the God of Shadrach, Meshach, and Abed-nego, who has sent His angel and delivered His servants who put their trust in Him.' Great commitments are built on trust in God.

Be single-minded. In Daniel 3:28, Nebuchadnezzar made another comment about these three guys. Not only did they trust in God, but he said they 'yielded up their bodies so as not to serve or worship any other god except their own God.' Single-mindedness.

In his book, *Choices*, Frederic Flach writes, 'Most people can look back over the years and identify a time and place at which their lives changed significantly. Whether by accident or design, these are the moments when, because of a readiness within us and a collaboration with events occurring around us, we are forced to seriously reappraise ourselves and the conditions under which we live to make certain choices that will affect the rest of our lives.' We are never too old for that to happen.

There are some of you reading this book today, and you're thinking, *My goodness, I've already been in this rut for twenty-five years!* Make some choices, make a commitment, take a risk—that's where the fruit is. It's never too late. Go for it! Don't allow circumstances or age or whatever to limit you. Only *you* can limit yourself.

In 1970 I read a book by Oswald Sanders, *Spiritual Leadership.* I became convinced after reading that book that the only people who are going to affect their world for God are those who become leaders and take a stand on principles that perhaps the rest of the world doesn't stand on. I can remember writing in the back of that book that regardless of the size of my congregation and regardless of the opinions of others—and I even wrote that regardless of what my father says, and my father is the greatest influence and the most important person in my life—there are some things I'm going to stand on and believe in. I'm still living off of that decision.

I was reading recently about John Wesley, a favorite hero of mine. He was writing a letter of encouragement to a fellow named George, who was leaving England to evangelize the new frontier. He wrote 'Dear George, the time has come for you to embark for America. I let you loose, George, on that great continent of America. Publish your message in the open face of the sun and do all the good that you can.' I love Wesley's liberating phrase, 'I let you loose.'

Commitment will free you and let you loose to do great things for God.

Part 2
BE A PEOPLE PERSON

14

WHAT DRAWS ME TO PEOPLE?

THE BASIS of life is people and how they relate to each other. Our success, fulfillment, and happiness depends upon our ability to relate effectively. The best way to become a person that others are drawn to is to develop qualities that we are attracted to in others.

Just as I was preparing for this chapter, I received an anonymous card from a member of my congregation. It was especially meaningful because it reflected the importance of warm, rewarding relationships:

> *When special people touch our lives then suddenly we see how beautiful and wonderful our world can really be. They show us that our special hopes and dreams can take us far by helping us look inward and believe in who we are. They bless us with their love and joy through everything they give. When special people touch our lives they teach us how to live.*

Does that reflect the kind of person you are to others? It was a humbling blessing for me to receive such a greeting card. I realized how appropriate it is to this chapter as we consider what qualities we need to develop in our lives—the qualities we enjoy in others.

This poster in a Nordstrom department store once caught my attention: 'The only difference between stores is the way they treat their customers.' That's a bold statement. Most stores would advertise the quality of their merchandise or their wide selection as what sets them apart from the rest. The difference between Nordstrom and other stores, according to an employee of the competition, is that other stores are organization-oriented; Nordstrom is people-oriented. Their employees are trained to respond quickly and kindly to customer complaints. As a result, according to writer Nancy Austin, 'Nordstrom doesn't have customers; it has fans.'

A study by TARP, Technical Assistance Research Programs, in Washington, D.C., shows that most customers won't complain to management if something goes wrong with the purchase. But TARP found out that, depending on the severity of the problem, an average customer will tell between 9 and 16 friends and acquaintances about his bad experience. Some 13 percent will tell more than 20 people! More than two out of three customers who've received poor service will never buy from that store again and, worse, management will never know why.

Every company is bound to goof now and then, but from the customer's perspective, what's important is that the company responds. This is the secret of the Nordstrom success. The TARP study also shows that 95 percent of dissatisfied customers will buy from the store again if their problems are solved *quickly*. Even better, they will each tell eight people of the situation's happy conclusion. The trick for managers and salespeople is to give customers ample time to offer feedback on the service they receive.

This chapter certainly isn't about department stores and customer satisfaction, but there are some principles from these reports that should speak to us about our relationships with others:

- Are we quick to respond to others' needs?
- Do we run from problems or face them?
- Do we talk more about bad news or good news?
- Do we give people the benefit of the doubt or do we assume the worst?

THE GOLDEN RULE

What's the key to relating to others? It's putting yourself in someone else's place instead of putting them in their place. Christ gave the perfect rule for establishing quality human relationships. We call it the Golden Rule, a name it got sometime around the seventeenth century. Near the end of the Sermon on the Mount, Christ summed up a series of profound thoughts on human conduct by saying, 'Therefore whatever you want others to do for you, do so for them' (Matt. 7:12).

In this brief command, Christ taught us a couple of things about developing relationships with others. We need to decide how we want to be treated. Then we need to begin treating others in that manner.

Recently I took my daughter Elizabeth out to a restaurant for lunch. The waitress whose job it was to take care of people, made us feel that we were really inconveniencing her. She was grumpy, negative, and unhelpful. All of her customers were aware of the fact that she was having a bad day. Elizabeth looked up at me and said, 'Dad, she's a grump, isn't she?' I could only agree with her. Everything we asked of the waitress was met with a look of disdain.

Halfway through our experience I tried to change this lady's negative attitude. Pulling out a $10 bill I said, 'Could you do me a favor? I'd like some change for this $10 bill, because I want to give you a good tip today.' She looked at me, did a double take, and then ran to the cash register. After changing the money, she spent the next fifteen minutes hovering over us. I thanked her for her service, told her how important and helpful she was, and left a good tip.

As we left, Elizabeth said, 'Daddy, did you see how that lady changed?'

Seizing this golden opportunity I said, 'Elizabeth, if you want people to act right toward you, you act right toward them. And many times you'll change them.'

Elizabeth will never forget that lesson because she had seen a noticeable change take place right before her eyes. That grumpy lady didn't deserve to be treated kindly. But when she was treated not as she was, but as I wanted her to be and believed she could become, her perspective suddenly changed.

Whatever your position in a relationship, if you are aware of a problem, it's your responsibility to make a concerted effort to create a positive change. Quit pointing your finger and making excuses, and try being a catalyst by demonstrating and initiating the appropriate behavior. Determine not to be a *reactor* but an *initiator.*

FIVE WAYS YOU WANT OTHERS TO TREAT YOU

These next five points seem too simple to even mention, but somehow we overlook them. The qualities that make relationships right aren't complicated at all. There's not a person reading this who doesn't need, like, or respond to these qualities in others.

First, you want others to encourage you. There is no better exercise for strengthening the heart than reaching down and lifting people up. Think about it; most of your best friends are those who encourage you. You don't have many strong relationships with people who put you down. You avoid these people and seek out those who believe in you and lift you up.

Several years ago Dr. Maxwell Maltz' book, *Psychocybernetics*, was one of the most popular books on the market. Dr. Maltz was a plastic surgeon who often took disfigured faces and made them more attractive. He observed that in every case, the patient's self-image rose with his or her physical improvement. In addition to being a successful surgeon, Dr. Maltz was a great psychologist who understood human nature.

A wealthy woman was greatly concerned about her son, and she came to Dr. Maltz for advice. She had hoped that the son would assume the family business following her husband's death, but when the son came of age he refused to assume that responsibility and chose to enter an entirely different field. She thought Dr. Maltz could help convince the boy that he was making a grave error. The doctor agreed to see him, and he probed into the reasons for the young man's decision.

The son explained, 'I would have loved to take over the family business, but you don't understand the relationship I had with my father. He was a driven man who came up the hard way. His objective was to teach me self-reliance, but he made a drastic mistake. He tried to teach me that principle in a negative way. He thought the best way to teach me self-reliance was to never encourage or praise me. He wanted me to be tough and independent. Every day we played catch in the yard. The object was for me to catch the ball ten straight times. I would catch that ball eight or nine times, but always on that tenth throw he would do everything possible to make me miss it. He would throw it on the ground or over my head but always so I had no chance of catching it.'

The young man paused for a moment and then said, 'He never let me catch the tenth ball—never! And I guess that's why I have to get away from his business; I want to catch that tenth ball!'

This man grew up feeling he could never measure up, never be perfect enough to please his father. I would not want to be guilty of causing emotional damage to my wife, my children, or my friends by not giving them every opportunity to succeed.

When Elizabeth and I used to play Wiffleball, I would pitch and she would swing. I told her it was my responsibility to hit the bat with the ball. Once she had swung at least twenty times without making contact with the ball. Finally in desperation and disgust she said, 'I need another pitcher; you can't hit the bat!' I was duly brought low for my failure to let her succeed. I have since done better.

The story of Eugene Lang gives us an ultimate example of encouragement. Entrepreneur Lang was *Success* magazine's 'Successful Man of the Year' in 1986. The following is part of a feature article about Lang's encouragement of others.

> *A gray-haired man stands alone in the center of the auditorium stage—a distinguished, paternal presence sporting a fine wool suit and the barest trace of a mustache. He scans the sunlit room, with its peeling paint and frayed draperies, but his gaze lingers on the people.*
>
> *They are black and Hispanic men and women who fill most of the seats in the auditorium. Though some do not speak English, their attention is fixed on the man at the podium. But his speech is not aimed at them. He has returned to this place where he once was a student to address the 61 sixth graders, dressed in blue caps and gowns, who are seated in the front rows.*
>
> *'This is your first graduation—just the perfect time to dream,' he says. 'Dream of what you want to be, the kind of life you wish to build. And believe in that dream. Be prepared to work for it. Always remember, each dream is important because it is* your *dream, it is your future. And it is worth working for.'*

'You must study,' he continues. 'You must learn. You must attend junior high school, high school, and then college. You can go to college. You must go to college. Stay in school and I'll . . .' The speaker pauses, and then, as if suddenly inspired, he blurts out: 'I will give each of you a college scholarship.'

For a second there is silence, and then a wave of emotion rolls over the crowd. All the people in the auditorium are on their feet, jumping and running, cheering and waving and hugging one another. Parents rush down the aisles to their children. 'What did he say?' one mother calls out in Spanish. 'It's money! Money for college!' her daughter yells back with delight, collapsing into her parent's arms.

The place was an elementary school in a poverty-stricken, drug-ridden, despair-plagued Harlem neighborhood. The speaker was multimillionaire entrepreneur Eugene Lang, who 53 years earlier had graduated from that very school. The date was June 25, 1981, and the big question was whether the warm and ever-confident Lang, a man who believes that 'each individual soul is of infinite worth and infinite dignity,' would fulfill his promise.

Well, he did and he still is. In fact, these kids graduated from high school and only one dropped out of high school since the sixth grade. You have to understand, in this community, 90 percent of the kids drop out of high school.

Lang began the 'I Have a Dream' foundation and now other entrepreneurs in New York City are also going into classrooms offering the same kind of scholarships. As I write there are 500–600 kids in Harlem who will receive this reward if they don't drop out of school.

People need to be encouraged. Eugene Lang believed in these kids and it made all the difference in how they lived the rest of their lives.

Lang's students speak confidently of becoming architects, computer experts, entrepreneurs of all types. Lang says 25 will go to college this year; the others will have high school diplomas, opportunities for vocational training and, eventually, jobs. 'This approach is exactly right,' observes Charles Murray of the Manhattan Institute of Policy Research, whose book Losing Ground *laments that poor people are losing their drive to climb the ladder of success.*

Ari Alvarado expressed it from the students' side: 'I have something waiting for me,' he said, 'and that's a golden feeling.' And if this program works, it may in fact become the ultimate capitalist success story—for, as George Gilder points out, the roots of capitalism lie not in greed but in giving: The true capitalist is one who invests money and energy today in hopes of a return in the uncertain future. That's what Eugene Lang has done, and it's likely that some of his dream students will follow suit. 'I want to become a doctor and do well so I can adopt a class of my own someday,' says the optimistic Alvarado. 'Just think, if all of us adopted classes . . . it could spread across the world!'

That is exactly what Eugene Lang hopes will happen: 'We have to create the opportunity to work with hope, to work with ambition, and to work with self-respect. The rewards? There is no way to describe the joy of having a young person touch your arm and smile because you have taught him new values and touched his heart and mind. The greatest experience you can have is to see that child with his new aspirations.

The happiest people are those who have invested their time in others. The unhappiest people are those who wonder how the world is going to make them happy. Karl Menninger, the great psychiatrist, was asked what a lonely, unhappy person should do. He said, 'Lock the door behind you, go across the street, find someone who is hurting, and help them.' Forget about yourself to help others.

YOU WANT OTHERS TO APPRECIATE YOU

William James said, 'The deepest principle in human nature is the craving to be appreciated.'

Have you heard the story about the young politician's first campaign speech? He was very eager to make an impression on his audience, but when he arrived at the auditorium, he found only one man sitting there. He waited, hoping more people would show up, but none did. Finally he said to the one man in the audience, 'Look, I'm just a young politician starting out. Do you think I ought to deliver this speech or dismiss the meeting?'

The man thought a moment and replied, 'Sir, I'm just a cowhand. All I know is cows. Of course, I do know that if I took a load of hay down to the pasture and only one cow came up, I'd feed it!'

Principle: We cannot underestimate the value of a single person.

With the advice from the cowhand, the politician began his speech and talked on and on for two hours as the cowhand sat expressionless. Finally he stopped and asked the cowhand if the speech was all right.

The man said, 'Sir, I am just a cowhand and all I know is cows. Of course, I do know that if I took a load of hay down to the pasture and only one cow came up, I surely wouldn't dump the whole load on him.'

Principle: Don't take advantage of people.

J.C. Staehle, after analyzing many surveys, found that the principal causes of unrest among workers were the following, listed in order of their importance:

1. Failure to give credit for suggestions.
2. Failure to correct grievances.
3. Failure to encourage.

4. Criticizing employees in front of other people.
5. Failure to ask employees their opinions.
6. Failure to inform employees of their progress.
7. Favoritism.

Notice that every single item has to do with the failure to recognize the importance of the employee. We're talking about people needing appreciation. I try to apply this principle every time I meet a person. Within the first thirty seconds of conversation, I try to say something that shows I appreciate and affirm that person. It sets the tone of the rest of our time together. Even a quick affirmation will give people a sense of value.

Treat others as you want them to treat you. Treat them as if they are important; they will respond according to the way that you perceive them. Most of us think wonderful things about people, but they never know it. Too many of us tend to be tight-fisted with our praise. It's of no value if all you do is think it; it becomes valuable when you impart it.

YOU WANT OTHERS TO FORGIVE YOU

Almost all emotional problems and stress come from unresolved conflicts, failure to have developed right relationships with people. Because of this, many people have a deep desire for total forgiveness. A forgiving spirit is the one basic, necessary ingredient for a solid relationship. Forgiveness frees us from guilt and allows us to interact positively with other people.

Earnest Hemingway, in his short story, 'The Capital of the World,' tells the story about a father and his teenage son who lived in Spain. Their relationship became strained, eventually shattered, and the son ran away from home. The father began a long journey in search of the lost and rebellious son, finally putting an ad in the Madrid newspaper as a last resort. His son's name was Paco, a very common name in Spain. The ad simply read: 'Dear Paco, meet me in front of the Madrid newspaper office tomorrow at noon. All is forgiven. I love you.' As Hemingway writes, the next day at noon in front of the newspaper office there were 800 'Pacos' all seeking forgiveness.

There are countless Pacos in the world who want more than anything else to be forgiven. The two great marks of a Christian are that they are giving and forgiving. Show me a person who walks with God, and I'll show you a person who has a giving heart and is forgiving of others.

The unfortunate truth is that many of us, instead of offering total forgiveness, pray something like this Irish Prayer:

May those who love us, love us;
And those who don't love us
May God turn their hearts;
And if He doesn't turn their hearts,
May He turn their ankles,
So we'll know them by their limping.

People who find it difficult to forgive don't see themselves realistically. They are either terribly arrogant or tremendously insecure. Though hanging onto a grudge gives some people a feeling of satisfaction, the truth is people who do not forgive are hurting themselves much more than they're hurting others. A person who possesses this characteristic and keeps score in relationships is a person who is emotionally and sometimes physically under stress. We just aren't wired to carry all the stress that goes with carrying grudges.

A few weeks ago I met with a man who came from a devastating background. His father had suffered a stroke and his mother had been in a serious accident; both are now unable to respond to him in any way. There are areas in this man's life in which he needs and wants his parents' forgiveness, but because they are physically unable to communicate, he cannot be sure that they understand him. Every day he goes to the hospital and asks their forgiveness, but he gets no response. The situation is robbing him of any joy.

This same man has an older brother that he hasn't spoken to in over two years. It is basically the older brother's fault, and my friend wants his brother to take the first step in patching up the relationship. I challenged my friend to let God cleanse his heart concerning his relationship with his parents, and to go ahead and take the first step in making the relationship with the brother right.

The following Sunday my friend approached me after the service. He didn't say a word but gave me a great big hug. I knew what had happened and said, 'You made the relationship right, didn't you?'

'Yeah, I got it taken care of,' he replied—the freedom from his burden evident in his smile.

Too often people wait too long to forgive other people. Forgiveness should be given as quickly and as totally as possible. Do it now. Don't be in the position of the young man who no longer has the opportunity to communicate with his parents. Because of his procrastination he will never experience the joy of their forgiveness and reconciliation.

One of the most striking scenes of the last decade was Hubert Humphrey's funeral. Seated next to Hubert's beloved wife was former President Richard M. Nixon, a long-time political adversary of Humphrey's, and a man disgraced by Watergate. Humphrey himself had asked Nixon to have that place of honor.

Three days before Senator Humphrey died, Jesse Jackson visited him in the hospital. Humphrey told Jackson that he had just called Nixon. The Reverend Jackson, knowing their past relationship, asked Humphrey why. Here is what Hubert Humphrey had to say, 'From this vantage point, with the sun setting in my life, all of the speeches, the political conventions, the crowds, and the great fights are behind me. At a time like this you are forced to deal with your irreducible essence, forced to grapple with that which is really important. And what I have concluded about life is that when all is said and done, we must forgive each other, redeem each other, and move on.'

Do you know how to die victoriously? Quit keeping score of the injustices that have happened to you. If you are at odds with anyone, take the first step; confront the problem and ask or offer forgiveness.

I received a letter from a pastor who, along with some of his laymen, heard me speak at a conference seven years ago. The laymen all became excited about what they had learned. The pastor put up a wall of defence, though. He wasn't excited, especially when they pushed him to put the principles into practice. Finally he left the church. Recently I received a letter from him telling me that he had been bitter toward me for the past seven years. He asked for my forgiveness. Immediately I responded, assuring him that all was forgiven.

Over my years in ministry there have been hundreds of times when I've experienced strained relationships. I have had people swear at me, tell me where to go, how to get there, and offer their assistance. But I have never knowingly let them walk out the door without telling them I love them. I don't hold any grudges or carry any resentment against anyone. I cannot stress this enough: if you don't have peace, it isn't because someone took it from you; you gave it away. You cannot always control what happens *to* you, but you can control what happens *in* you.

YOU WANT OTHERS TO LISTEN TO YOU

Recently I took a break from my work and walked across the street to the doughnut shop to get a soft drink. There was a man sitting there talking to the girl behind the counter. Recognizing me he said, 'Pastor, she's been listening to me all morning. I've been telling her my story.' I realized how important it was to him that she was listening attentively and showed interest in what he had to say. It made him feel that he had value.

My mother was the librarian where I attended college, and each time I entered the library there would be half a dozen college girls around her desk. Mom has always had an incredible counseling ministry, not because she is such a great talker, but because she is a tremendous listener. There's a difference between *hearing* people and *listening* to them. Listening is *wanting* to hear. Mom loves people and wants to hear from them; people respond to that kind of caring.

As people gain more authority, they often develop a lack of patience in listening to those under them. A deaf ear is the first indication of a closed mind. The higher people go in management and the more authority they wield, the less they are forced to listen to others. Yet their need to listen is greater than ever. The farther they get from the firing line, the more they have to depend on others for correct information. If they haven't formed the habit of listening—carefully and intelligently—they aren't going to get the facts they need, and people will resent their decisions.

I saw a television sketch which, with some variations, might seem familiar in many households. A husband is watching television and his wife is trying to engage him in conversation:

Wife: *Dear, the plumber didn't come to fix the leak behind the water heater today.*

Husband: *Uh-huh.*

Wife: *The pipe burst today and flooded the basement.*

Husband: *Quiet. It's third down and goal to go.*

Wife: *Some of the wiring got wet and almost electrocuted Fluffy.*

Husband: *Darn it! Touchdown.*

Wife: *The vet says he'll be better in a week.*

Husband: *Can you get me a Coke?*

Wife: *The plumber told me that he was happy that our pipe broke because now he can afford to go on vacation.*

Husband: *Aren't you listening? I said I could use a Coke!*

Wife: *And Stanley, I'm leaving you. The plumber and I are flying to Acapulco in the morning.*

Husband: *Can't you please stop all that yakking and get me a Coke? The trouble around here is that nobody ever listens to me.*

YOU WANT OTHERS TO UNDERSTAND YOU

How do you feel when you are misunderstood? What kinds of feelings well up inside you? Loneliness? Frustration? Disappointment? Resentment? These are common feelings when we have been misunderstood.

Peter Drucker, often called the 'Father of American Management,' claims that 60 percent of all management problems are a result of faulty communications. A leading marriage counselor says that at least half of all divorces result from faulty communications between spouses. And criminologists tell us that upwards of 90 percent of all criminals have difficulty communicating with other people. Communication is fundamental to understanding.

Let's capsulize what we've covered in these last few pages. You want others to:

✦ encourage you,

- appreciate you,
- forgive you,
- listen to you,
- understand you.

As you think about these qualities, consider how they apply to your own life. Perhaps this short course in human relations can help each of us develop qualities that we admire in others:

The least important word: I *(gets the least amount done)*

The most important word: We *(gets the most amount done)—relationships*

The two most important words: Thank You—*appreciation*

The three most important words: All is forgiven—*forgiveness*

The four most important words: What is your opinion?—*listening*

The five most important words: You did a good job—*encouragement*

The six most important words: I want to know you better—*understanding*

In life, you are either going to see people as your adversaries or as your assets. If they are adversaries, you will be continually sparring with them, trying to defend your position. If you see people as assets, you will help them see their potential, and you will become allies in making the most of each other. The happiest day of your life will be the day when you realize 'we' really is the most important word in the English language.

PUT IT TO WORK

PEOPLE PRINCIPLES

- ✦ Our success, fulfillment, and happiness depends upon our ability to relate to people effectively
- ✦ The key to relating to others is putting yourself in someone else's place instead of putting them in their place.
- ✦ Treat people the way you want to be treated:
  Encourage.
  Appreciate.
  Forgive.
  Listen.
  Understand.
- ✦ See people as assets, not adversaries.
- ✦ The word 'we' is the most important word in the English language.

PUTTING THE PRINCIPLES TO WORK:

I will apply the principles from this chapter to my relationships with people in the following ways:

1.

2.

3.

FURTHER STUDY:

Bringing Out the Best in People, Alan Loy McGinnus

The Friendship Factor, Alan Loy McGinnis

15

WHAT DRAWS OTHERS TO ME?

THE GREATEST leaders have it—that special quality which causes people to be drawn to their magnetic personalities. Extraordinary entertainers evidence this something extra. We all have the potential to develop this quality that makes the difference between personality and *personality plus.* What quality draws others to me? We can summarize it in one word: *charisma.*

Charisma can be a difficult subject to grapple with because most people think it is a mystical, elusive, undefinable quality that you either have or don't have. However, *Webster's Ninth New Collegiate Dictionary* has given several definitions to *charisma,* and this is the one we will use, 'A personal magic of leadership arousing special popular loyalty or enthusiasm.'

Each one of us has certain abilities that will increase the charisma of our personality. You don't have to make a strained effort to become something that is not comfortable with your basic nature. However, if your desire is to become a people person, then you need to develop an appealing personality that causes others to respond to you.

When we examine the personalities of some of our United States Presidents, it becomes obvious why some were more successful than others in appealing to the general public. Ronald

Reagan possessed the ability to convey humor, personal warmth, and relaxedness. He knew how to make others feel good about themselves. John F. Kennedy knew how to give others a feeling of hope. He exuded boundless energy and made many Americans feel important and needed. Our favorite leaders will always stand out because of the charisma factor.

Using the word CHARISMA as an acrostic, we can define the outstanding characteristics of charismatic people:

Concern
Help
Action
Results
Influence
Sensitivity
Motivation
Affirmation

Keep in mind that these traits are not simply inborn; they are attainable by anyone who cares about other people and wants to develop his or her relational skills. Let's look at each characteristic in CHARISMA in more depth.

CONCERN—THE ABILITY TO SHOW YOU CARE

Charismatic people have the ability to show concern for people's deepest needs and interests. That doesn't mean charismatic people are mushy or patronizing, but when you are around them, you sense their interest and care and leave them feeling that you are important.

Someone once asked Perle Mesta, the greatest Washington hostess since Dolley Madison, the secret of her success in getting so many rich and famous people to attend her parties. 'It's all in the greetings and good-byes,' she claimed. As each guest arrived she met him or her with, 'At last you're here!' As each left she expressed her regrets with, 'I'm sorry you have to leave so soon!'

At any gathering you will find two types of people—those who arrive with an attitude of 'Here I am!' and those who possess an attitude of 'There you are!' It doesn't take long to notice that people flock to the 'There you are!' people.

One of my staff members, Dan Reiland, and I were talking about charisma and why so many people have trouble getting a handle on it. He gave me a simple definition, one which makes 'charisma' easy to grasp: *Be more concerned about making others feel good about themselves than you are in making them feel good about you.* In other words, don't try to sell other people on you, try to sell them on themselves.

If you need to develop greater concern for others in your life, increase your exposure to people who are hurting. We see Jesus' sense of concern in Matthew 9:35–38 (emphasis added):

> *And Jesus was* going *about all the cities and the villages, teaching in their synagogues, and proclaiming the gospel of the kingdom, and healing every kind of disease and every kind of sickness. And* seeing *the multitudes, He* felt compassion *for them, because they were distressed and downcast like sheep without a shepherd. Then He said to His disciples, 'The harvest is plentiful, but the workers are few. Therefore beseech the Lord of the harvest to send out workers into His harvest.*

Here's the sequence: Jesus went, saw, felt, and cared. It's only when we go and expose ourselves to various situations that we will see enough to develop the concern necessary to move us to action.

It's difficult to become motivated to help people without first seeing and feeling their needs. The secret is to spend time with them. Only when you go and see will you feel and do.

HELP—THE ABILITY TO REACH OUT

Put simply, charismatic people are helpers. They are out to see others profit; they have the gift of grace. In fact, the Greek word of gift is 'charisma' meaning 'gift of grace.' God has freely bestowed upon us spiritual gifts because of His grace toward us.

In Romans 12:6 we read about this further, 'And since we have gifts that differ according to the grace given to us, let each exercise them accordingly.' And we see in Ephesians 4:11–12, 'He gave some as apostles, and some as prophets, and some as evangelists, and some as pastors and teachers, for the equipping of the saints for the work of service, to the building up of the body of Christ.'

Notice in both references the emphasis on the variety of gifts and their purpose in the kingdom. It is always for other people, never for self. There is no charisma in seclusion. You can't walk into a room and have charisma by yourself!

People have problems. Many are like the beleaguered guy who, in desperation, went to a psychiatrist for help. He told the doctor, 'Everytime I get my act together, the curtain falls down.' He needed more than mercy and concern; he needed help. You will find that if you are adept at solving problems, that will guarantee you a following forever.

My favorite cartoon character, Charlie Brown, displayed an attitude with which many of us can identify. He and Linus were talking about their problems. Linus said, 'I guess it's wrong always to be worrying about tomorrow. Maybe we should think only about today.'

Charlie Brown replied, 'No, that's giving up. I'm still hoping that yesterday will get better.'

What can you do to help people with their problems? First of all, encourage them to face their problems. Too often people would rather flee them, fight them, or forget them.

Second, encourage them to solve their problems. Use the following acrostic to teach yourself to help people with difficulties.

T Tell them it takes *time.*
E *Expose* yourself to their problems in order to relate to them.
A *Assure* them of your confidence in them.
C *Creatively* show them how to deal with their problems.
H Offer *hope* to them through the process.

I love this old story about creative problem-solving. Mr. Myrick had to go to Chicago on business and persuaded his brother to take care of his cat during his absence. Mr. Myrick's brother was not a cat-lover, but he agreed to do it as a favor. When Mr. Myrick returned from his trip he called his brother from the airport to inform him of his arrival and to check on his cat. The brother reported in a matter-of-fact tone, 'Your cat died,' and he hung up.

For days Myrick was inconsolable. Then his sadness turned to anger at his brother for being so brutally honest and insensitive. He phoned his brother. 'It was needlessly cruel and sadistic of you to tell me that bluntly that my poor cat had passed away.'

'What did you expect me to do?' demanded the brother.

'You could have broken the bad news gradually,' grumbled Myrick. 'First you could have said the cat was playing on the roof. Later you could have called to say he fell off. The next morning you could have reported he had broken his leg. Then, when I came to pick him up, you could have told me he passed away during the night. Well, it's just not your style to be civilized. Now tell me—how's Mama?'

After a long pause, a meek voice on the other end replied, 'She's playing on the roof.'

Myrick's insensitive brother had learned that there should be a process to problem-solving.

ACTION—THE ABILITY TO MAKE THINGS HAPPEN

Something exciting always seems to be happening around a person with charisma. The charismatic person has an aversion to being boring. He or she may be controversial, unusual, or entertaining, but never boring.

Be honest with yourself and evaluate how you come across to others. A young fellow in a dry church service turned to his mother and said, 'Pay the man and let's go home!' That preacher obviously lacked charisma.

When evangelist John Wesley was asked why people seemed to be drawn to him, he answered, 'Well, you see, when you set yourself on fire, people just love to come and see you burn.'

Do you want to increase your interest with other people? Develop your creativity and your confidence. Creativity is the ability to *say* things in an unusual way; confidence is the ability to *do* things in an unusual way. Charismatic people can do both. Develop these two traits and people will stand up and take notice.

As a speaker and pastor, I always want to be fresh and exciting in my presentation. I will use humor to drive home a point but never to distract from the truth. Long after the content of the message is forgotten people will remember the creative illustration and the truth that was emphasized.

RESULTS—THE ABILITY TO PRODUCE

Charismatic people want to be on the winning side of life. People like being around winners and want to play on the winning team. A boy playing chess with his grandfather says, 'Oh, no! Not again! Grandpa, you always win!'

Grandpa says, 'What do you want me to do, lose on purpose? You won't learn anything if I do that!' But the boy replies, 'I don't wanna learn anything. I just wanna win!'

Charismatic people not only want to win, they want others to win too. That creates productivity.

How does a person become productive? Find your strength and then find someone who needs your strength. Charismatic people use their strengths to help other people feel good about themselves; they are other-centered. The person who is self-centered uses his strength to dominate others.

INFLUENCE—THE ABILITY TO LEAD

Leadership is influence. If something new, exciting, and interesting is happening in your life, you will want to share it. In doing so, you will influence others and they will want to follow your lead. What happens *to* you speaks of your circumstances. What happens *in you* speaks of your character. And what happens *through you* speaks of your charisma.

Do you want to learn how to be a positive influence on others? Five factors come into play:

- ✦ Who I am—my position or title.
- ✦ Where I am—my location or job.
- ✦ Who I know—my sphere of influence. People open doors of opportunity.
- ✦ What I know—my expertise. This will keep you in a position long after who you know wears off.
- ✦ What I do—my production, character, credibility.

SENSITIVITY—THE ABILITY TO FEEL AND RESPOND

Charismatic people have the ability to be sensitive to changing situations. They are adept at taking advantage of the mood, feeling, and spirit of any situation. Most people have the ability to feel something, but they aren't sure how to react to it or express it. Charismatic people not only feel it, but they know how to react and express it.

Charismatic people find a cause; that's discernment. They also voice a concern; that's courage. And they draw a crowd; that's automatic.

In the late 1960s or early 1970s I watched a television documentary on George Wallace. At the time, he was a prominent figure in American politics, perhaps because of his 'redneck' philosophy over the civil rights issue. No one doubted where he stood as he proclaimed, 'Segregation yesterday, segregation today, and segregation forever!' It was a perfect example of a charismatic leader playing to what that crowd wanted to hear. He was masterful at taking advantage of the prevailing mood. Because he was able to forcefully express the feelings of a certain segment of society, he became the champion of their cause.

If you are to become more sensitive, you must be willing to take a risk. Take the initiative to find a need and take action. People who are overly sensitive to the point that their feelings are always hurt will withdraw from others and never take a risk.

But the charismatic person will risk getting out of his comfort zone in order to make others feel comfortable.

MOTIVATION—THE ABILITY TO GIVE HOPE

The secret of motivating others is providing them with hope. People tend to feel more positive when they are following charismatic leaders. Let's take a look at some Bible people who offered hope:

- Isaiah, speaking of God, said, 'I will do something new' (Isa. 43:19).
- Jeremiah talked about '. . . new law in their hearts' (Jer. 31:33).
- Jesus spoke about being born again (John 3:3).
- Paul called a Christian a 'new creation' (2 Cor. 5:17).
- John's vision recorded in Revelation spoke of 'a new heaven and a new earth (Rev. 21:1).

Each of these dynamic leaders constantly waved hope before their people.

Do you convey hope or despair to those around you? Learn affirmation skills, problem-solving techniques, ways to verbally encourage others, and convey belief and support in others.

AFFIRMATION—THE ABILITY TO BUILD UP

Charles Schwab, the successful businessman, said, 'I have yet to find the man, however exalted his station, who did not do better work and put forth greater effort under a spirit of approval than under a spirit of criticism.'

Everyone wants and needs to be affirmed for his accomplishments. A little boy playing darts with his father said, 'Let's play darts. I'll throw and you say, "Wonderful!"' That's what the charismatic person does for others.

We tend to become what the most important person in our life thinks we will become. Think the best, believe the best, and express the best in others. Your affirmation will not only make you more attractive to them, but you will help play an important part in their personal development.

How do we affirm others? First we need to feel good about ourselves. Then we can verbally and actively believe in others and expect them to respond positively. People are our only appreciable asset. As Christians, we cannot afford to not affirm them. If I fail to affirm a brother, we both lose.

ROADBLOCKS TO CHARISMA

Again, charisma is a trait or quality in our life that can be developed. It is not reserved for those who are extroverts and enjoy being in front of others. The potential to be charismatic lies within each of us, but first we must remove hindrances from the development of this important personality characteristic. What are some possible obstructions?

- *Pride.* A prideful person will have a tendency to look down on other people, feeling a sense of superiority. People will not follow or identify with a snobbish personality who is conscious of status and position.
- *Insecurity.* Insecure people are not willing to take a risk. They prefer to remain comfortable and probably, unexciting.
- *Moodiness.* This is an immature quality which is detrimental to personal relationships. Moody people are fickle and, thus, people who cannot be depended upon. Confidence is never built on a person who is subject to sullenness.
- *Perfectionism.* Perfectionism is an obsessive need to perform flawlessly. It stifles creativity and freedom and it turns people away. Perfectionists can rarely affirm themselves; therefore, it's very difficult for them to affirm others.
- *Oversensitivity.* Oversensitive people are constantly licking their wounds. They look inward and are not aware of the needs of others. Naturally, people don't flock around them.
- *Negativism.* By definition, negativism is the opposite of charisma. A person with a constant negative attitude is depressing to be around. Their personality says no to life in general. Others will avoid a person like that. There is no possibility of being a charismatic leader when no one wants to be around you.

Charisma begins at the cross of Jesus Christ. Let's take a look at Philippians 2:3–11 where we see Paul using the humility of Christ Himself as our pursuit (emphasis added).

> *Do nothing from selfishness or empty conceit, but with humility of mind let each of you regard one another as more important than himself; do not* merely *look out for your own personal interests, but also for the interests of others. Have this attitude in yourselves which was also in Christ Jesus, who, although He existed in the form of God, did not regard equality with God a thing to be grasped, but emptied Himself, taking the form of a bondservant,* and *being made in the likeness of men. And being found in appearance as a man, He humbled Himself by becoming obedient to the point of death, even death on a cross. Therefore also God highly exalted Him, and bestowed on Him the name which is above every name, that at the name of Jesus every knee should bow, of those who are in heaven, and on earth, and under the earth, and that every tongue should confess that Jesus Christ is Lord, to the glory of God the Father.*

There is no question that Jesus was and is highly exalted. But it began with the deepest of humility. Remember: *Charisma is being more concerned about making others feel good about themselves than you are in making them feel good about you!*

PUT IT TO WORK

PEOPLE PRINCIPLES

- The key to developing charisma: Be more concerned about making others feel good about themselves than you are in making them feel good about you.

- Traits of a person with charisma:
  CONCERN—What they show.
  HELP—What they offer.
  ACTION—What they provide.
  RESULTS—What they produce.
  INFLUENCE—What they do.
  SENSITIVITY—What they follow.
  MOTIVATION—What they give.
  AFFIRMATION—What they share.
- Charisma is a trait or quality in our life that *can* be developed! The potential lies within each one of us.

PUTTING THE PRINCIPLES TO WORK:

I will apply the principles from this chapter to my relationships with people in the following ways:

1.

2.

3.

FURTHER STUDY:

Personality Plus, Florence Littauer

Discovering Your Personality Tree, Florence Littauer

16

HOW TO BE CONFIDENT WITH PEOPLE

WHEN I'M introduced to a group of people I've never met before, it only takes a few minutes to identify those who have influence over others. What is it about them that sets them apart? Is it their sense of direction—the assurance that they know where they're going? Is it an awareness that they have certain abilities? Is it their sincerity? Their past successes? Their ability to use eye contact and body language? What do they have that everybody wants?

If there is one quality you could have that would make you successful in motivating people or convincing people to follow your lead, that trait would be confidence. And if you can combine confidence with direction, guidance, past success, or some of these other motivational mechanics, you have a powerful combination. It is quite possible for a person to know where he or she is going, yet lack the self-confidence to convince others to follow along. Self-confidence carries a conviction; it makes others believe in us.

A five-year-old boy was intently working with his crayons at the kitchen table when his mother walked in and questioned what he was doing. Her son replied, 'I'm drawing a picture of God.'

'But honey,' she responded, 'no one knows what God looks like.'

With great confidence the boy boldly stated, 'They will when I'm done.' I like that kind of positiveness.

A group of pastors were attending a conference at our church, and at the end of the first morning session they headed to the fellowship center for lunch. Several minutes later I followed, expecting that they would already be seated. Much to my surprise, all one hundred and fifty of them were lined up outside the door. Then I saw why! At the head of the line stood Joel, my then six-year-old, with both hands raised, giving orders. 'It will be a couple more minutes and then they'll be ready for you!' Joel had no clue what was going on, but he gave directions with the greatest of confidence and these pastors did as they were told. Confidence is contagious even if it's the confidence of a six-year-old.

The writer of Hebrews recognized the value of confidence: 'Therefore, do not throw away your confidence, which has a great reward' (Heb. 10:35). Confidence is not set in cement; it's possible to lose it.

Our choice of associates will have a tremendous bearing on our confidence level. Most people fall into two categories: confidence builders and confidence shakers. If you are unsure of yourself, a confidence shaker can do you in. The following story provides a great example of confidence breakdown.

A man lived by the side of the road and sold hot dogs. He was hard of hearing, so he had no radio. He had trouble with his eyes, so he read no newspapers. But he sold good hot dogs.

This man put up signs on the highway advertising his wonderful hot dogs. He stood on the side of the road and cried, 'Buy a hot dog, Mister?' And people bought his hot dogs. He increased his meat and bun orders, and he bought a bigger stove to take care of his trade. He made enough money to put his son through college.

Unfortunately, the son came home from college an educated pessimist. He said, 'Father, haven't you been listening to the radio? Haven't you been reading the newspaper? There's a big recession on. The European situation is terrible, and the domestic situation is worse.'

Whereupon the father thought, 'Well, my son's been to college. He reads the papers and he listens to the radio; he ought to know.' So the father cut down his meat and bun orders, took down his signs, and no longer bothered to stand out on the highway to sell his hot dogs.

Of course, his sales fell overnight. 'You're right, son,' the father said to the boy. 'We certainly are in the middle of a big recession.'

Confidence shakers see the negative side of everything. When they get you to buy into it, the very thing that was helping you be successful becomes your downfall.

Unfortunately, this negative process can and too often does happen in the lives of Christians. We all go through periods of testing, wondering if God really can meet our every need. With a little discouragement from a good confidence shaker, we begin to doubt His ability and our own. This can begin a downward spiral which ends in the pit of failure and frustration. Our confidence has not only been shaken but uprooted.

The positive message from Hebrews 10:35 is that our confidence has a great reward. If we keep and build on it, we will be more than recompensed. Confidence in oneself is the cornerstone to success. It is difficult for those who do not believe in themselves to have much faith in anyone else. Self-confidence breeds confidence in others, much like a boomerang which you cast out toward others only to find it comes right back to you.

WHY DO YOU NEED CONFIDENCE?

Just why do you need confidence in yourself? First of all, it will give you stability in every area of your life. Confidence equals contentment with self; contentment is knowing you have all you need for the present circumstances.

Philippians 4:11–13 provides the basis for this thought. 'Not that I speak from want; for I have learned to be content in whatever circumstances I am. I know how to get along with humble means, and I also know how to live in prosperity; in any and every circumstance I have learned the secret of being filled and going hungry, both of having abundance and suffering need. I can do all things through Him who strengthens me.'

These verses cannot be separated because there is an absolute relationship between experiencing life's lows and enjoying its highs. The Apostle Paul is resting on the assurance that his strength is in God alone. He understood that confidence and contentment gave him stability in every situation he encountered in his tumultuous life.

Contentment is taking your present situation—whatever obstacle you are facing, whatever limitation you are living with, whatever chronic condition wears you down, whatever has smashed your dreams, whatever factors and circumstances in life tend to push you under—and admitting you don't like it but never saying, 'I can't cope with it.'

You may feel distress, but you may never feel despair. You may feel pressed down, but you may never feel defeated. Paul says there are unlimited resources, and as soon as you say 'I can't cope,' you are failing to draw on these resources that Christ has readily, by His loving-kindness, made available to you. Contentment, therefore, is being confident that you measure up to any test you face because Christ has made His strength available within you.

If the first thing confidence does is to *stabilize* you, the second thing it does is to *stretch* you. The moment that I have my foundation strong and stable, I am then in position to begin stretching. Insecure people seldom stretch because they are not willing to live on the edge of life.

Helen Keller said, 'Security is mostly a superstition. It does not exist in nature, nor do the children of men as a whole experience it. Avoiding danger is no safer in the long run than outright exposure. Life is either a daring adventure or nothing.'

Think about a rubber band which is totally useless unless it is stretched. When insecurity keeps us from stretching and growing, we end up with a life that is as unexciting and useless as a limp rubber band.

CONFIDENCE HELPS YOU AS A LEADER

Confidence helps a leader to believe in other people. Don't we see others as we see ourselves? Show me a leader who believes in other people, and I will show you a leader who has a lot of confidence in his or her life.

An insecure leader, on the other hand, believes neither in himself or herself nor in others. Insecure people are afraid to risk building up others with compliments, because they are constantly in need of compliments themselves.

Here's a classic illustration of how confidence helps to build up other people. In the past I had the opportunity to help pastors develop lay ministry programs in their churches. Prior to the time of challenge and recruitment of laymen I would meet with the pastor to ask how many he thought would respond to the commitment. After a lengthy reflection he would give me a conservative number.

Each time, with great confidence, I assured him there would

be many more who would respond. I was always right and the pastor was always amazed. Each pastor gave a lower number of responses because he mentally ranked every person according to how he perceived each one's commitment level. Therefore, he assumed a low response.

The moment you place a label on someone you begin to treat him or her accordingly. Since I didn't know these people and had no preconceived labels, I assumed them all to be quality people who would eagerly respond to the challenge. They could sense my confidence in them and responded positively. Had the pastor given the challenge, his estimate probably would have been the correct one.

A leader with confidence is a leader who brings about positive change in people. A study conducted at Springfield College in Massachusetts illustrates this point. The experiment was designed to determine the effects upon school children of having to do continuous and monotonous work without any encouragement.

The children were told to draw a detailed picture of a man. When they had finished, they were asked to draw another picture of a man. This one, they were told should be better than their first. When they had finished, they were again given the same colorless order: 'Now draw another man, this time better than the last.'

No matter how poor their drawings might have been, no one was scolded or criticized for his or her performance. And no matter how well the children might have done, none of them was praised or given any encouragement. They were merely told to draw another picture.

You can probably guess the results. Some of the children got angry and displayed their resentment openly. One refused to draw any more; another said he was 'trapped' and called the instructor a 'meanie.' Most, however, just looked angry, said nothing, and continued their joyless, unrewarding toil.

Each of the drawings got worse and worse, instead of better and better, as the children had been told to make them.

People must have affirmation and praise in order to maintain a high level of performance. Withholding negative or critical comments is not nearly as important as giving positive input through compliments and praise. Again, the only people who can do this are those who feel positive about themselves. Work plus praise increases energy, but work without praise drains energy.

If you study the life of Paul, you may note he uses the word 'confidence' in three distinct but related ways. Six times Paul refers to confidence in his relationship with Christ, six times to his confidence in himself, and six times he mentions his confidence in relationships with other people. There must be a balance because all three areas are related. Without confidence in Christ we could be tempted to become egocentric and cocky. Without confidence in ourselves we are defeated, powerless Christians. Without confidence in others we are suspicious and untrusting.

Paul learned this lesson and it made him a successful motivator and servant of the Lord Jesus Christ. You cannot consistently perform in a manner that is inconsistent with the way you see yourself. The price tag the world puts on us is just about identical to the one we put on ourselves. Self-confidence is the first great requisite to great undertakings.

HOW CAN YOU BECOME CONFIDENT?

Establish your worth according to God's value system. God demonstrated our importance to Him in two great acts. First He created us in His own image, and second He—through Jesus Christ—died for our sins. God thought so much of you, believed in you, and saw you as a person of such worth, that He allowed His Son to die so that you could live. When we begin to see ourselves in the light of God's actions on our behalf, then we immediately begin to have more confidence. There is nothing more humbling than the realization that if you were the only person on this earth, Jesus would have died for you. That makes you priceless.

Another way we become confident is to *focus on God and not on our situation.* Try living according to the first three verses of Psalm 27:

> *The Lord is my light and my salvation; Whom shall I fear? The Lord is the defense of my life; Whom shall I dread? When evildoers came upon me to devour my flesh, my adversaries and my enemies, they stumbled and fell. Though a host encamp against me, my heart will not fear; Though war arise against me, in spite of this I shall be confident.*

We can make three observations from these brief verses. First, confidence is not the result of an absence of problems. It is very clear that the psalmist encountered many problems and difficulties. He mentions his enemies, evildoers who want to devour his flesh, adversaries, and a host encamping around him.

Observation number two is that confidence is a result of trusting God *in* our problems. In the midst of his difficulties, the psalmist kept focusing on God and not on his difficult situation. 'The Lord is the defense of my life.'

Third, victories yesterday give more confidence for today. In verse 2 the psalmist speaks in the past tense. 'When evildoers came upon me to devour my flesh, they stumbled and fell.' He's talking about yesterday. In verse 3, he talks about today: 'Though a host encamp against me, my heart will not fear.' Confidence today is a result of victories yesterday.

Another way to develop confidence that convinces others is to *develop friendships with confident people.* The old cliché is true: Birds of a feather *do* flock together. A big man is one who makes us feel bigger when we are with him.

Many people are doomed to suffer from the 'Charlie Brown complex.' It seems that Charlie Brown just can't do anything right. But notice that one of his problems is the fact that Lucy is always around him. Lucy does not make it any better for Charlie Brown because she is always quick to point out the error of his ways.

On one occasion Lucy puts her hands on her hips and says, 'You, Charlie Brown, are a foul ball in the line drive of life! You're in the shadow of your own goal posts! You are a miscue! You are three putts on the eighteenth green! You are a seven–ten split in the tenth frame! You are a dropped rod and reel in the lake of life! You are a missed free throw, a shanked nine iron, and a called third strike! Do you understand? Have I made myself clear?'

Do you have a Lucy around you? It's safe to say that if you surround yourself with people like her, you will have a difficult time developing a sense of confidence. Every time you start out there will be someone to remind you what you aren't, haven't been, and never will become. If we want to be confident, we must surround ourselves with confident people, people who believe in us and will be encouragers.

Another way to develop confidence is to *put a few wins under your belt.* Start with building on small successes and little by little you will tackle bigger and bigger challenges.

Recently I was listening to an interview of Jerry Coleman, the radio announcer for the San Diego Padres. He was trying to figure out why the baseball club had just blown one of their two-or-three-run leads. He commented, 'You can tell by the way they're playing they have lost confidence in themselves. They have almost set themselves up for something to go wrong.'

A few successful victories under your belt gives you the impetus to keep stretching your abilities. If you keep winning, you may see yourself as a no-limits person. Repeated failures produce the opposite effect. You begin to see yourself as a hopeless loser. The best way to develop rational, well-balanced confidence is to go after a few victories immediately following a failure. Don't allow yourself the luxury of wallowing in self-pity.

My son Joel and I like to play memorization card games. With the cards facing down the goal is to turn over a pair, so it is important to remember the positions of certain cards to obtain a match. One evening Joel beat me twice, 14 to 6. It never occurred to Joel that his choices could be wrong. Around the family room he rejoiced, declaring victory to all.

After two losses to Joel, I challenged his sister Elizabeth to a game. Elizabeth tends to be much less confident than Joel. When we started our first game she said, 'Daddy, Joel beat you two times, didn't he?'

I replied, 'Yes, he did.'

She said, 'The score was 14 to 6, wasn't it?'

Again I replied, 'Yes, it was.' And I added, 'Sissy, I bet you can beat me about 14 to 6 too.'

I arranged it so that I lost the first game 14 to 6. She was visibly eager to play another game which she won without my help. By this time *I* was beginning to develop a complex and lose confidence. So I got my wife Margaret to agree to play the next card game. I whipped her royally and retired a winner.

My father taught me the value of developing a confident attitude. Each night after dinner my older brother and I wrestled on the living room floor. One particular week Larry won each match. My father noticed my sense of defeat and discouragement and told Larry that he couldn't wrestle me for one week. Instead, Dad and I wrestled nightly, and after each struggle I beat him. Dad would raise my arm high above my head and declare me the winner.

The following week he allowed Larry and me to go back to wrestling. My brother never could pin me after that. Did I suddenly acquire extra strength? No, I had acquired confidence from having some wins under my belt.

My high school basketball coach came up with the skill-building technique which he hoped would make our team more successful. He put an extra rim on the inside of the hoop, reasoning that if we could put our foul shots through the smaller basket, we would really be good with the regulation rim in the real game. I argued with the coach over the idea I knew the guys would have difficulty sinking the ball through the smaller hoop, and the more they missed, the more discouraged they would become. I was right; they began routinely missing easy shots, because their confidence was shaken. Failure begets failure.

A great confidence booster is a personal victory list of past successes and achievements. This is a biblical concept. There are two Bible characters who practiced this: Samson, who became a total failure, and David, who became a great success.

In Judges 16:20 we see Samson's victory list: 'And she [Delilah] said, 'The Philistines are upon you, Samson!' And he awoke from his sleep and said, 'I will go out as at other times and shake myself free.' But he did not know that the Lord had departed from him.'

Now let's read about David's victory list in 1 Samuel 17:37: 'And David said, "The Lord who delivered me from the paw of the lion and from the paw of the bear, He will deliver me from the hand of this Philistine." And Saul said to David, "Go, and may the Lord be with you."'

There are two strong similarities between these two men. They both were chosen, ordained, and anointed by God, and they were both leaders of Israel at a time when Israel was battling against the Philistines. But this is where it stops; Samson and David also had three distinct differences. These differences made one a winner and one a loser.

The first thing we notice about Samson is that he wanted to please himself. He lived life in the flesh, depending on his own strength and felt no need to rely upon God, even when going into battle. He chose the road that always leads to ultimate defeat. Unlike Samson, David desired to please God. He knew that, left to his own resources, he was already defeated. So he called upon the Lord and went to battle with divine help. His weakness became God's strength and he was assured of victory.

Samson's alienation from God not only led to his defeat, it ended his leadership. For David, however, this episode with Goliath was the beginning of his leadership. It was the incident that brought him into a position where God could greatly use him. Victory lists should give us confidence, not cockiness.

Another way to increase your confidence is to *quit comparing yourself with others.* Comparisons always leave you found wanting. The following little story illustrates my point. A milk truck passes two cows grazing in a pasture. On the side of the truck are the words, 'Pasteurized, homogenized, standardized, Vitamin A added.' Noticing this, one cow says to the other, 'Makes you kind of feel inadequate, doesn't it?' I think we have all known that feeling of inadequacy when we compare what we can offer with what someone else offers.

One of the surest ways to build confidence is to *find one thing you're good at and then specialize until you are special.* It could be a sport, a task, a natural ability, or a personally developed talent.

Use that strength as much as you can to build your level of assurance and specialization. A successful leader knows that he helps his followers most by helping them discover their special giftedness, encouraging them to develop it, and then disciplining them to use it.

Also, *begin to develop a knowledge of people and product.* Remember that success is just 15 percent product knowledge and it's 85 percent people knowledge. Once you have knowledge of your product and of the people with whom you work, you have an inside edge on meeting their needs. That inevitably raises your confidence.

Here is a humorous old story which points out the importance of knowing who you're dealing with. A Baptist deacon had advertised a cow for sale. 'How much are you asking for it?' inquired a prospective purchaser.

'One hundred and fifty dollars,' said the advertiser.

'And how much milk does she give?'

'Four gallons a day,' the deacon replied.

'But how do I know that she will actually give that amount?' asked the purchaser.

'Oh, you can trust me,' reassured the advertiser. 'I'm a Baptist deacon.'

'I'll buy it,' replied the other. 'I'll take the cow home and bring you the money later. You can trust me. I'm a Presbyterian elder.'

When the deacon arrived home, he asked his wife, 'What is a Presbyterian elder?'

'Oh,' she explained, 'a Presbyterian elder is about the same as a Baptist deacon.'

'Oh dear,' groaned the deacon, 'I have lost my cow.'

The deacon had product knowledge; he knew his cow. But his lack of people knowledge defeated him.

WHAT TO DO WITH CONFIDENCE WHEN YOU HAVE IT

Now that you have all this confidence, what should you do with it? Keep refueling it! Confidence is not a constant; it fluctuates according to your success/failure ratio. We all have defeats and failures which occasionally and temporarily lower our level of confidence. If you accept the fact that you will not be outstanding in everything you attempt, you will not be devastated when your best is not good enough.

You will find that your confidence has a contagious quality. It will spread throughout your sphere of influence. The Bible provides some interesting examples of 'confidence contagion.' For instance, how many giant-killers were in Saul's army? None. When Goliath defied the armies of God, they quaked with fear (1 Sam. 17:11). David, who came to bring food to his brothers, sized up the situation, went out in faith, and killed the giant. After David the giant-killer became king, how many giant-killers arose in Israel? Quite a few. They were almost a common commodity in the army under David's leadership.

Let's take a look at 1 Chronicles 20:4–8:

> *Then Sibbecai the Hushathite killed Sippai, one of the descendants of the giants, and they were subdued. And there was war with the Philistines again, and Elhanan the son of Jair killed Lahmi the brother of Goliath the Gittite, the shaft of whose spear was like a weaver's beam. And again there was war at Gath, where there was a man of great stature who had twenty-four fingers and toes, six fingers on each hand and six toes on each foot; and he also was descended from the giants. And when he taunted Israel, Jonathan the son of Shimea, David's brother, killed him. These were descended from the giants in Gath, and they fell by the hand of David and by the hand of his servants.*

Why do you suppose there were no giant-killers in Saul's army? Surely one reason is that Saul himself was not a giant-killer. However, under David's leadership they were numerous, because David was a giant-killer. This illustrates a tremendous principle of leadership, a principle which runs throughout the Bible—it takes one to make one! When you develop confidence, those around you—friends, family, and associates—will increase in their own confidence levels. Confidence breeds confidence.

Everyone needs to be affirmed both as a person and as a coworker. It's easy to give a generic compliment such as 'You're great to work with.' But a comment that really means something to a person is specific and mentions a certain quality: 'I appreciate your efficiency in relational skills, and this is very important to the success of the group.' We don't help others by passing on empty compliments or avoiding the necessary task of sharing needed constructive criticism. Unfortunately too often we're stingy with honest praise. Build your coworkers up and encourage them by verbalizing their worth and value in front of others. Remember, praise in public and criticize in private.

Confidence can provide the momentum you need to be the person God meant you to be. It cannot substitute for character, or skill, or knowledge, but it enhances these qualities so that you can be a person who makes a difference. When you have knowledge or skill and the momentum that confidence brings, then things begin to happen in your relationships.

The largest locomotive in the New York Central system, while standing still, can be prevented from moving by a single one-inch block of wood placed in front of each of the eight drive wheels! The same locomotive, moving at 100 miles-per-hour can crash through a wall of steel-reinforced concrete five feet thick. The only difference is momentum. Confidence gives you the momentum that makes the difference.

You remember the childhood story about the train engine that did because he thought he could. Some of the larger engines were defeated when they saw the hill. Then came the little train hustling down the track repeating to himself, 'I think I can, I think I can, I think I can . . . and he began to pass all the other locomotives who were saying, "It can't be done." As he got closer to the top his speed got slower and slower, but as he reached the crest, he said, 'I thought I could, I thought I could, I thought I could . . .'

The little engine made it, but not because he had more power or more skills. The little engine made it because he *thought* he could; he had more confidence. Many times we feel like little insignificant engines. But if we hone our skills and talents, then add a good dose of confidence, we can climb hills and overcome obstacles and barriers that could have stopped us dead in our tracks. Why pull off the track and stop when we can conquer those mountains with the momentum of confidence in our engines?

PUT IT TO WORK

PEOPLE PRINCIPLES

✦ Confidence is contagious.

✦ Contentment is being confident that you measure up to any test you are facing because Christ has made His strength available to you.

✦ You cannot consistently perform in a manner that is inconsistent with the way you see yourself.

✦ Six steps to developing confidence:
Establish your worth according to God's value system.
Focus on God and not on your situation.

Develop friendships with confident people.

Put a few wins under your belt.

Find one thing you're good at and then specialize until you are special.

Begin to develop a knowledge of people and product.

- ✦ When you have knowledge or skill and the momentum that confidence brings, then things begin to happen in your relationships.
- ✦ A leader with confidence is a leader who brings about positive change in people.

PUTTING THE PRINCIPLES TO WORK:

I will apply the principles from this chapter to my relationships with people in the following ways:

1.

2.

3.

FURTHER STUDY:

How to Win Friends and Influence People, Dale Carnegie

Dropping Your Guard, Charles R. Swindoll

17

BECOMING A PERSON PEOPLE WANT TO FOLLOW

IN EVERY age there comes a time when leadership must come forth to meet the needs of the hour. Therefore, there is no potential leader who does not find his time. Tragically, there are times when no leader arises for that hour.

Why should there ever be a time when there is a lack of leadership? And if there are not enough leaders to meet the demand, what can be done about it? Michael Korda, the author of *Power!*, was asked to draw up a list of the most powerful people in America. His findings were published in an article called, 'The Gradual Decline and Total Collapse of Nearly Everyone' (*Family Weekly Magazine*, Aug. 29, 1982). Korda said, '. . . the list of movers and shakers is not at all easy to draw up. In fact, there are very few powerful figures left in American life.

'Not so long ago teachers ran their classes; generals (or sergeants) ran the Army; policemen were feared and obeyed; college presidents were respected figures, remote and awesome . . . and so on down the line. America was, in effect, ruled by authority figures.'

Unless one has been asleep, it is surely apparent that all this has changed. Korda says, 'It is the result of a long process, the consequence of our fear of power and authority. . . .' Two whole generations have turned against the very idea of power.

'Power, it was felt, had led to abuse. Therefore we could do without it . . . not only could, but must. Everything must be subject to the will of the people, expressed in open debate.'

Lack of trust in leadership has a tremendous bearing on all types of group relationships. It is conceivable that this distrust of authority figures has spread into many of our churches. In fact, it could well be the cause of much of the upheaval which has resulted in unprecedented numbers of pastors and other church staff members being asked to leave or being summarily dismissed from their positions.

When speaking at conferences I always enjoy taking time to share with lay people as well as pastors. One active layperson, speaking of a situation in his church remarked to me, 'No one seems to be in charge. No one seems to want to be accountable.' Perhaps no other statement better reflects the frustration of good churchmen. They're taught to shepherd and love, but very seldom how to lead the flock.

I teach the principle of the 'leadership umbrella.' Imagine an open umbrella held by a hand—the hand of the leader of that organization. Under the protection of that umbrella are all of the departments of the organization. The success of each department can never, will never, rise any higher than the level at which the leader holds the umbrella. Leadership sets the standard, whether the organization be a business, a church, or a family. The higher the standard, the more effective the leadership.

What is effective leadership according to effective leaders?

- British Field Marshall Bernard Montgomery: 'Leadership is the capacity and will to rally men and women to a common purpose and the character which inspires confidence.'

- ✦ President Harry Truman: 'A leader is a person who has the ability to get others to do what they don't want to do and like it.'
- ✦ An outstanding leader, Fred Smith: 'Leadership is influence.' That is simple but profound; a person may have a position of leadership, but if he is not affecting the thoughts and actions of others, he is not a leader.
- ✦ From the Bible we learn that true leadership comes from serving others. And in Matthew 15:14 we read, 'If a blind man guides a blind man, both will fall into a pit.'
- ✦ My favorite leadership proverb is this: 'He who thinketh he leadeth and hath no one following him is only taking a walk.'

Just where have all the leaders gone? They seem to have vanished. Is great leadership a commodity of the past? No, I believe that America will again produce leaders. The fact is that our country has experienced few crises in recent history. The last period of heroic leadership was during World War II, when America found itself in tremendous turmoil. Generally speaking, the emergence of leaders conforms to the law of supply and demand. Difficult times produce men and women who will rise to meet the crisis.

The complexity of our times hinders the rise of leadership. Perhaps we have become too analytical to take decisive action. We may be spending too much time studying our problems and not enough time solving them. A good case-in-point is President Jimmy Carter. When David Hartman interviewed Tip O'Neil, retired speaker for the House of Representatives, Mr. Hartman asked who, in O'Neil's opinion, was the most intelligent President. 'Unquestionably,' he answered, 'it was Jimmy Carter.' O'Neil said Carter read and studied reams of paper on technological issues that were facing our country; he had a superior understanding of the complexities of technology. But although he was an intelligent president, he was not a strong leader. Unfortunately, the perplexing and intricate issues facing America today do not produce leaders. We are being pulled in so many different directions that it's almost impossible to unite behind a leader.

Another reason there are few well-known leaders is because of the negative reaction to authority figures following the Viet Nam war years. The peace movement and the flower children sprang up because of their disdain for war and violence. A bumper sticker reflects the attitude of the times: 'Challenge Authority.' There is no longer an unquestioning loyalty to those in power. Incidents like Watergate have added fuel to the fire of mistrust. America is learning to suspect anyone with authority. Recent American history has spanned twenty to twenty-five years without producing a leadership model. Interestingly enough, however, within the last few years a new sense of pride has sprung up because of Ronald Reagan's leadership style. I believe that within the next ten to twelve years we will begin to reap more directive, visionary, strong leadership types throughout our country and in our churches.

Although you or I may never attain the height of being a renowned world leader, we each have an arena of influence. We are leaders within our homes, businesses, offices, congregations, and ministries. As such, we should strive to be the most effective leaders we can be. I believe there are five nonnegotiable characteristics that every effective leader must have: a sense of calling, an ability to communicate, creativity in problem solving, generosity, and consistency.

AN EFFECTIVE LEADER MUST FEEL A SENSE OF CALLING

True leaders feel an inner urging to take their positions; they feel a sense of responsibility. I believe that the moment a father and mother see their newborn child they experience a strong calling to be godly examples to that precious new life. For the church leader or pastor, there is a specific calling from God; a deep, innate, feeling, or desire that causes him to do what he is called to perform. For the business leader, there is an urging to rise to the challenge, to take the helm and move forward.

In Isaiah 6:1–9 we find a vivid example of a man specifically called by God. In verses 1–5, Isaiah experiences a discovery of God and a discovery of himself. He becomes overwhelmed by the grandness and glory of God Himself within the holy temple, contrasted by his own unworthiness and uncleanness. People who are called discover something bigger than themselves: a mission, a challenge, a goal, or a movement that draws them into an arena.

When a person feels set apart to lead, he should also sense a strong feeling of victory. In Isaiah 6:6–7 we read, 'Then one of the seraphim flew to me, with a burning coal in his hand which he had taken from the altar with tongs. And he touched my mouth with it and said "Behold, this has touched your lips; and your iniquity is taken away, and your sin is forgiven."' The leader experiences an assurance that he will be adequate for the work. This foretaste of victory enables them to continue on in their mission and overcome obstacles in the way.

A leader will always find his or her time. There will come times when a leader's particular gifts and talents are necessary to meet a crisis. Leaders try to use and exercise their gifts for the glory of God. They also will feel a strong desire, an urging, to be used by God. In verse 8 Isaiah is offered the opportunity: 'Whom shall I send, and who will go for Us?' And then in verse 9 he exercises the desire to be used: 'Here am I. Send me!'

This desire within the leader's heart is what I call the 'have to' feeling. Personally, I feel a sense of 'having to' declare something, point in some direction, lead others on a mission.

I do not feel a sense of choice in the matter. In fact, there are times when I would prefer to sit back and let someone else take on my challenge. But when I see or feel God doing something, that 'have to' feeling compels me to keep going. The followers of a true leader confirm his calling. He doesn't have to declare his calling, others do it for him.

What about the person who is not in Christian ministry? I believe God places each of us in areas where we can use our gifts and influence others for His sake. A man might be called to begin a business, for instance. He knows he is putting his money, his credit, even his credibility right on the line. There is something within him that drives him and compels him.

Perhaps you are wondering if a person can be a great leader without this sense of calling. I believe a person can be a good leader but not a great one. It sounds rather mystical but I believe God places His hand on those whom He calls to be great leaders. Everyone in leadership, however, can cultivate and enhance their leadership skills.

How do you sense that a leader is called? One clue is that called leaders have a lasting quality; they don't quit and couldn't if they wanted to. Also, the anointed people have the right answers; the God who called them equips them. There are many voices in the crowd, but the called leader stands out among all the others. He or she rises above the normal, the typical, the usual. The called leader tends to reproduce other called leaders; there is fruit in their ministry. Called leaders are relevant and speak to the times and issues.

AN EFFECTIVE LEADER MUST BE ABLE TO COMMUNICATE

Great leaders have the ability to visually communicate their message to people. Some time ago I watched Ronald and Nancy

Reagan on *Good Morning America.* Nancy was close to the edge of the stage and she fell off. Immediately people rushed to help her while the President watched. Knowing she was all right he looked at her and said, 'Nancy, I told you not to fall off the platform unless I wasn't getting any applause.' President Reagan was able to use an embarrassing incident as a tool to communicate. He communicated to the audience that he was in control, that he had a quick wit, and that he trusted his relationship with his wife enough to joke about her mishap.

Good communicators are able to convey a strong belief in their people; there is a very high trust factor. Again, I think Ronald Reagan demonstrated this quality as well as anyone in recent memory. Consider the following excerpt from *Fortune* magazine, September 15, 1986:

> *Picking competent people who are on his wavelength has also enabled Reagan to delegate more effectively than most presidents. Former Transportation Secretary Drew Lewis recounts an incident during the 1981 air traffic controllers' strike that set the tone for labor-management relations throughout the Reagan era. Lewis worried that Reagan's friends, whose private planes were grounded, might urge him to back down on his decision to fire the controllers, which Lewis had recommended. So the transportation chief called Reagan to test his resolve. Recalls Lewis: 'The President said: "Drew, don't worry about me. When I support someone—and you're right on this strike—I'll continue to support him, and you never have to ask that question again." From that day on, it was clear to me—whether in increasing the federal gasoline tax in 1983 or in selling Conrail—that once he said, "Fine," I never had to get back to him. I had the authority.'*
>
> *Some longtime Reagan associates speculate that his capacity to delegate stems from his Hollywood experience. Says John Sears,*

> *his former campaign manager: 'A lot of people in political and corporate life feel that delegating is an admission that there's something they can't do. But actors are surrounded by people with real authority—directors, producers, scriptwriters, cameramen, lighting engineers, and so on. Yet their authority doesn't detract from the actor's role. The star is the star. And if the show's a hit, he gets the credit.'*

Every asset that you're entrusted with—whether it's money, procedures, materials, technology—all of it is depreciating. All of it is becoming obsolete. Human assets also can depreciate in value. It's literally true that in some organizations, the people are worth less—and in some cases are worthless—compared with a year ago. But human assets can also appreciate in value. People can become worth more. Those who are powerful in leadership understand that one of the key tasks of management is to find ways to grow people.

On Edison's eightieth birthday, he was approached by an interviewer who asked him which of all his inventions was the greatest. And Edison, without a moment's hesitation, replied, 'The research laboratory.'

I doubt his answer was fully understood by Edison's own generation. People were starry-eyed over his miracle productions—the light bulb, the record player, the improvements that made radio, the telephone, and electric motors possible. He was known by his generation as the Wizard of Menlo Park. He so transformed people's dull and drudgery-oriented lives into lives that were full of entertainment and light, possibilities and alternatives, that he was respected like no other man in American industry.

But Edison understood the secret of his great success: You can't do it all yourself. If you really want to be an uncommon leader, you're going to have to find a way to get much of your vision seen, implemented, and added to by others. The leader sees the big picture, but he also sees the necessity of sharing that picture with others who can help him make it a reality.

Ronald Reagan did this exceptionally well. He established the direction for the organization but left the hands-on management to his Chief of Staff. Reagan looked to his Cabinet and White House staff to put the flesh on major initiatives and to serve up new ideas, while he focused on big issues such as tax reform or on opinion-shaping events like the summit with Soviet leader Mikhail Gorbachev. Says Harvard presidential scholar Roger Porter, who spent five years in the Reagan White House: 'He does not devote large chunks of time to peripheral issues. That is one of the keys to his success.'

More than other recent presidents and many corporate leaders, Reagan also succeeded in translating his vision into a simple agenda with clear priorities that legislators, bureaucrats, and constituents can readily understand. Lyndon Johnson had his vision of a 'Great Society,' but his legislative agenda was too cluttered. Jimmy Carter's objectives were obscured by frequent flip-flops. In contrast, Reagan's agenda of tax cuts, deregulation, a defense buildup, and a slowdown in domestic spending was set early and pursued consistently. Independent pollster Gerald Goldhaber says that nearly 70 percent of the American people can name at least one of Reagan's four priorities. By contrast, such ratings for the Johnson, Nixon, Ford, and Carter Administrations ranged from 15 percent to 45 percent.

Reagan had the ability to put the vision before the nation. How do you transfer a vision? First you must *see* it yourself very clearly; you can't transfer something that you can't see. Then you must be able to *say* it creatively so that people understand

and can grab hold of it. Finally you must be able to *show* it constantly. It must be continually placed before the followers as a reminder of the goal.

Good leaders also have self-confidence and, therefore, the confidence of others. The author of this little poem understood the value of self-confidence in leadership:

He who knows not, and knows not that he knows not, is a fool; shun him.
He who knows not, and knows that he knows not, is a child; teach him.
He who knows, and knows not that he knows, is asleep; wake him.
He who knows, and knows that he knows, is wise; follow him.

Confidence in oneself is the cornerstone. People who do not believe in themselves have trouble believing in others. Others have trouble believing in them too. Self-confidence in a leader elicits the confidence of his followers, which gives him the freedom to be a risk taker and a change agent.

AN EFFECTIVE LEADER IS CREATIVE IN HANDLING PROBLEMS

Everyone faces problems. The ability to creatively find solutions will determine the success or failure of each difficulty.

The Chinese symbol for crisis means danger. It also means opportunity. The key is to use a crisis as an opportunity for change. You'll never succeed if you throw up your hands and surrender. The Greek poet Homer understood the value of a crisis. He wrote, 'Adversity has the effect of eliciting talents which in prosperous circumstances would have lain dormant.'

Remember the story of the chicken farmer whose land was

flooded virtually every spring? Even though the floods caused him horrendous problems, he refused to move. When the waters would back up onto his land and flood his chicken coops, he would race to move his chickens to higher ground. Some years, hundreds of them drowned because he couldn't move them out in time.

One year after suffering heavy losses from a particularly bad flood, he came into the farmhouse and in a voice filled with despair, told his wife, 'I've had it, I can't afford to buy another place. I can't sell this one. I don't know what to do!'

His wife calmly replied, 'Buy ducks.'

Creativity is a trait not always admired by those who don't have it. They interpret creativity and inventiveness as stupidity and impracticality. If they see the creative person as salvageable, they will try to pull him back into the mainstream of thought. He will be told to stay busy, follow the rules, be practical, and not make a fool of himself. Traditional thinkers don't realize that creative thinkers are the geniuses of the world. Had it not been for someone's inventiveness, they might not have jobs!

Walt Disney's brother tells an amusing story about Walt's budding genius as a fifth grader. The teacher assigned the students to color a flower garden. As she walked among the rows examining the students' work she stopped by young Walt's desk. Noting that his drawing was quite unusual, she remarked, 'Walt, that's not right. Flowers don't have faces on them.'

Confidently he replied, 'Mine do!' and continued his work. And they still do; flowers at Disneyland and Disney World all have faces.

AN EFFECTIVE LEADER IS A GENEROUS CONTRIBUTOR

The measure of a leader is not the number of people who serve him but the number of people he serves. Real leaders have something to give, and they give it freely. Anthony DeMello saw a starving child shivering in the cold. Angrily he lifted his eyes to heaven and said, 'God, how could You allow such suffering? Why don't You do something?'

There was a long silence and then DeMello was startled when he heard the voice of God answer him, 'I certainly have done something—I made you.'

Consider the comments of William Arthur Ward of Texas Wesleyan College in Fort Worth, Texas:

> *If you are wise, you will forget yourself into greatness.*
> *Forget your rights, but remember your responsibilities.*
> *Forget your inconveniences, but remember your blessings.*
> *Forget your own accomplishments, but remember your debts to others.*
> *Forget your privileges, but remember your obligations.*
> *Follow the examples of Florence Nightingale, of Albert Schweitzer, of Abraham Lincoln, of Tom Dooley, and forget yourself into greatness.*
> *If you are wise, you will empty yourself into adventure.*
> *Remember the words of General Douglas MacArthur:*
> *'There is no security on this earth. There is only opportunity.'*
> *Empty your days of the search for security; fill them with a passion for service.*
> *Empty your hours of the ambition for recognition; fill them with the aspiration for achievement.*
> *Empty your moments of the need for entertainment; fill them with the quest for creativity.*

If you are wise, you will lose yourself into immortality. Lose your cynicism. Lose your doubts. Lose your fears. Lose your anxiety. Lose your unbelief.

Remember these truths: A person must soon forget himself to be long remembered. He must empty himself in order to discover a fuller self. He must lose himself to find himself. Forget yourself into greatness. Empty yourself into adventure. Lose yourself into immortality.

It sounds like Jesus, doesn't it? Great leaders are great givers.

AN EFFECTIVE LEADER ACTS CONSISTENTLY

I put this last because there are many people who are consistent but are not leaders, yet no one has ever been an effective leader over the long haul without being consistent. The moment people learn we are not dependable or responsible is the moment they will not recognize our leadership.

I recently saw a cartoon that illustrates this important principle. A young man is telling the preacher, 'Being a minister must be really hard. I mean, living for others, leading an exemplary life. That's a lot of responsibility. The pressures must be tremendous! Having to set a good example . . . people watching, waiting for one false move, one sign of human frailty they can jump on! Oh, I don't know how you handle it!'

Finally the preacher sheepishly says, 'I stay home a lot.'

Some think that the word *being* is derived from a root meaning 'to engrave.' When we speak about someone's 'being,' we are referring to all those qualities and characteristics which identify that particular individual. 'Being' may be correctly called 'the signature of our soul.' It is what we are. By our actions, though, it can be enhanced or diminished.

'The first key to greatness,' Socrates reminds us, 'is to *be* in reality what we appear to be.' Jesus expressed the same idea in the Sermon on the Mount. 'Beware of the false prophets, who come to you in sheep's clothing but inwardly are ravenous wolves' (Matt. 7:15).

A leader must be consistent in three areas: people—this builds security; principles—this provides direction; and projects—this builds morale. Leaders let people know where they're coming from. A recent study showed that people would rather follow a leader they disagree with than one they agree with if the latter is constantly changing positions.

The call to be a leader is a challenging one. The need for strong leadership has never been clearer. The price of leadership has never been higher. The temptations of leadership have never been greater. The hour for leadership has never been closer. Take the challenge! Remember, 'in every age there comes a time when leadership must come forth to meet the needs of the hour. Therefore, there is no potential leader who does not find his time. Tragically there are times when no leader arises for that hour.'

You can be the leader for your hour.

PUT IT TO WORK

PEOPLE PRINCIPLES

- ✦ Leadership is influence.
- ✦ He who thinketh he leadeth and hath no one following him is only taking a walk.
- ✦ The followers of a true leader confirm his calling. He doesn't have to declare his calling, others do it for him.
- ✦ Those who are powerful in leadership understand that one of the key tasks of management is to find ways to grow people.
- ✦ Self-confidence in a leader elicits the confidence of his followers, which gives him the freedom to be a risk-taker and a change agent.

✦ A leader must be consistent in three areas:
People—This builds security.
Principles—This provides direction.
Projects—This builds morale.

PUTTING THE PRINCIPLES TO WORK:

I will apply the principles from this chapter to my relationships with people in the following ways:

1.

2.

3.

FURTHER STUDY:

Learning to Lead, Fred Smith

Leadership, Greatness, and Servanthood, Philip Greenslade

18

MOTIVATING PEOPLE FOR THEIR BENEFIT

AT WHAT point in life does a person learn how to be persuasive? When does he learn the fine art of convincing others that what's good for him is good for them too. Have you ever been around a newborn baby who is hungry, or needs a diaper change, or just wants to be held? It doesn't take long for that baby to persuade some adult that some kind of action is being called for! Nobody enjoys being around a red-faced, crying baby for very long.

As that baby grows older, his motivational methods become more refined. He learns when to throw temper tantrums and when to take an apple to the teacher. He learns what types of behavior get him in trouble and what types get him what he wants. This ability to persuade, which is evident from the moment of birth, should become more refined and beneficial to us and those we lead as we experience life and relationships.

Just before school the other day, my son Joel wanted to go outside and see the construction workers in front of our house. He knows them all by name, and they certainly know him! He considers himself vital to the completion of the project. When I asked him if he had brushed his teeth he said he had. Well I knew he hadn't, and because he lied to me I told him he could not go outside to watch the workers and would instead have to brush his teeth. Crying, he went to his room. Shortly, he returned looking like the cat who had swallowed the canary. 'Dad,' he said, 'how about letting me go outside this morning and you can take away my television privileges for today?'

I said, 'No, I'm sorry you cannot go outside.'

He cried again and went back to his room. Two minutes later he returned with another big smile, 'How about taking my computer privileges away?'

Obviously, Joel was trying to negotiate and persuade me to change my mind. He's good at it, but in case you're wondering, he did not go outside that morning!

I heard the story of a wealthy Texan who threw a party for his daughter because she was approaching the age to marry. He wanted to find a suitable husband for her—someone who was courageous, intelligent, and highly motivated. He invited a lot of young, eligible bachelors.

After they had enjoyed a wonderful time at the party, he took the suitors to the backyard and showed them an Olympic-size swimming pool filled with poisonous snakes and alligators. He announced, 'Whoever will dive in this pool and swim the length of it can have his choice of one of three things: One, he can have a million dollars; two, ten thousand acres of my best land; or three, the hand of my daughter, who upon my death will inherit everything I own.'

No sooner had he finished when one young man splashed into the pool and reappeared on the other side in less than two seconds. The rich Texan was overwhelmed with the guy's enthusiasm. 'Man, I have never seen anyone so excited and motivated in all my life. I'd like to ask you: do you want the million dollars, 10,000 acres, or my daughter?'

The young man looked at him sheepishly, 'Sir,' he said, 'I would like to know *who* pushed me in the pool!'

The world has some misconceptions about persuasion. People have attached negative connotations to persuasion and associated it with manipulation. Actually, the Latin meaning of the word is very positive. 'Per' means 'through' and 'suasio' means 'sweetness.' So, to persuade means to use sweetness to get people to do things. Effective persuasion is a result of relating, not ruling. It speaks to the heart as well as to the head. Therefore, persuasion does not make use of force or intimidation.

Getting someone to do something without convincing them it's the right thing to do is not the result of effective motivation; it's the result of intimidation. It's like the mom who told the little kid to sit down in the grocery cart at the supermarket. He kept standing up and she kept telling him to sit down. Finally she reprimanded him firmly enough that he sat down. She heard him whisper to himself as he was scrambling down, 'I may be sitting down on the outside, but I'm standing up on the inside!'

When we succeed in getting people to sit down on the outside while they're still standing up on the inside, we are not persuading them; they are just accommodating us. We have neither convinced them nor have we met their basic needs.

ONE MAN'S PERSUASIVE ABILITY

The following incident lays the foundation for the rest of this chapter. It is a dramatic account of the persuasive ability of Emile Zola Berman as told by attorney Morton Janklo.

When Emile Zola Berman, the famous trial lawyer from New York, entered the Non-Commissioned Officers' Club at the Marine Corps boot camp at Parris Island, S.C. that hot, humid July night in 1956, the tension was immediate and palpable. The usually boisterous drill instructors were stunned into silence as Zuke Berman (as he was known to the legal world) strode into their sacred precincts as if he owned the place, went to the center of the room, climbed onto a table and, with steely-eyed gaze, stared out at the assembled noncoms.

The room grew silent. Then, with the skill of the great actor that he was, Berman spoke: My name is Emile Zola Berman. I'm a civilian. I'm a Jew, and I'm a Yankee from New York City. I've come down here to save the Marine Corps. If no one helps me, I'm going back to New York to resume my life. If you care about the Corps, and if you care about the truth, come see us in our quarters tonight and help us keep you proud to be Marines.

With that, he scrambled down off the table and strode out of the room as silently as he had entered it.

The occasion for this high drama was the most famous Marine Corps courtmartial in history. Sgt. Matthew McKeon—the embodiment of the professional Marine drill instructor—was on trial on the most serious charges stemming from the drowning deaths of six young recruits in his company during a disciplinary night-training exercise in the swamps of Ribbon Creek. Berman and I (then a young attorney with experience in the military justice system) had volunteered to defend McKeon.

The key to our defense to the most serious charges was to prove that what McKeon had done did not constitute cruelty against his troops but was, in fact, common practice among Marine Corps drill instructors training young men for combat.

When we had arrived at Parris Island a few days earlier, we had fully expected the drill instructors to cooperate with us in getting at the truth about combat training. What we met instead was a stone wall—set up, we learned, by the Marine Corps brass. Nobody would talk to us. We couldn't even get witnesses from other bases. Try as we would, we could not persuade the leadership of the Marine Corps or its drill instructors that the future and credibility of the Corps was at stake.

Berman's one-minute appearance and dramatic statement at the NCO Club was his desperate effort to break through that wall of silence. 'This will either make us or break us,' he said to me as we left the club.

Back in our quarters, Berman went to sleep, having admonished me to sit up and wait, in case, as we hoped, somebody showed up. At about 2 A.M. just as he had predicted, there was a light tap at the window. I let in an extremely frightened young drill instructor. 'I think I know why you guys are here,' he said, 'and I'm prepared to tell you what really goes on in these boot camps.' His testimony was the break in the dam. Before we were finished, dozens of drill instructors had come forward to testify that, indeed, the march in the swamp was common practice to discipline troops and that there was nothing 'cruel or unusual' about this behavior.

Zuke Berman had persuaded a group of the toughest men in the world to do what was right in the face of fear. I have taken Attorney Janklo's account of Berman's motivational ability and pinpointed the seven principles of persuasion which follow.

KNOW PRECISELY WHAT YOU ARE TRYING TO ACCOMPLISH

Before you can persuade others on any issue, you need to know just exactly what it is you want to accomplish. Zuke Berman was specific in his purposes and goals. Businessman H.L. Hunt also understood the importance of goals; he identified three steps that we must take to reach a goal. First, we must decide what we want, then decide what we are willing to give up, and, finally, go for it.

In working with pastors one of the first things I suggest is that they develop a statement of purpose in order to help them determine where they want to go. You can't accomplish anything that counts until you know where you're going. When I first formed our statement of purpose at Skyline, I asked the church board members to assist me. I posed the question: what is the purpose of this church? Twenty-two members gave me sixteen different answers. I realized that if our lay leaders didn't agree on our purpose, we would accomplish nothing great for God. We first needed to develop one statement of purpose. So we worked together, clarified our thinking, and agreed on our common purpose for the church.

There is an inspiring plaque in the Smithsonian Museum of Science. It is a statement John Fitzgerald Kennedy made in the early 1960s: 'This nation should commit itself to achieving the goal, before this decade is out, of landing a man on the moon.' We know what happened in July 1969; we all watched it on television. Because the president stated a definite, achievable goal, the nation enthusiastically got behind it.

In commenting on the success of the historic moonflight, Albert Siepert, Deputy Director of Kennedy Space Center, stated in 1969: 'The reason that NASA has succeeded is because NASA had a clear-cut goal and expressed it. By doing this, we attracted the best of men to our goal, and we got the support of every phase of government to reach our goal.' A goal is a dream with a deadline.

To give yourself a handle on establishing and accomplishing goals, keep in mind these 'Five C's.'

- *Consideration.* What is the needed response? That's what Mr. Berman asked himself when he asked those tough Marine drill sergeants for help.
- *Credibility.* What must I do to get the needed response?

- *Content.* What must I say to get the needed response?
- *Conviction.* How must I say it?
- *Conclusion.* What steps do I need to take to get the needed response? Now that I have said, felt, and determined to do something, what action will I take?

A lot of organizations remind me of the little girl who was riding on a bus with her father and was unsure of her destination. She asked, 'Daddy, where will we be when we get to where we are going?' Better we should know where we're headed *before* we get on the bus!

PLACE YOURSELF IN THE OTHER PERSON'S SHOES

We persuade, not from our own perspective, but from getting the perspective of others. Mr. Berman did this in his statement, 'I've come down here to save the Marine Corps.' He did not say, 'I have an exceptional record, and I'm here to prove it to you.' He immediately identified with the pride of the Marines and he therefore had their attention as well as their respect.

Be aware of the specific reasons why the other person requires persuasion and perhaps has resisted it. What is there about your goals that he resists or resents? What need or priority of his is threatened by your goals? How can you alleviate that fear? These Marines were worried that if they came forward in defiance of their superiors' policy to keep the story quiet, they might get into trouble.

Berman did not attempt to mislead the Marines by telling them there was no risk; the risk was obvious. He chose, instead, to appeal to their pride as men and as Marines. He put himself on their side and made them realize that his objective was one they shared, namely to save the Marine Corps. By putting yourself in the other fellow's shoes, you develop a sensitivity to that person's needs and can better address the issues that concern him or her. It is not always easy to do, but it's usually necessary if you're to be successful.

Recently I joined Dr. Carl George and Dr. C. Peter Wagner for a conference called 'How to Break the 200 Barrier.' When they assigned me that topic I knew it was a 'hot button' because most churches in America are below that number. I recalled that stage in my own ministry in Hillham, Indiana. I had to be able to identify with the pastors of small churches before I could encourage them. There were three questions that I had to answer before I could put myself in their shoes. These are generic questions which you, too, can use.

First, *what do they know?* With what kinds of experiences have they dealt? If all you have is a hammer, everything looks like a nail. Have they been using one kind of tool? Ask people questions about what is important to them. Find out what is unique in their lives.

Second, *what do they feel?* Effective persuasion takes into account a person's emotions. Once the emotion is identified, steps can be taken to form a plan of action.

Bob Conklin, in *How to Get People to Do Things,* recalled the story of Ralph Waldo Emerson and his son struggling with a female calf and trying to wrestle her into the barn. Drenched with sweat, the great sage was on the brink of losing his self-control when an Irish servant girl came by. She smiled sweetly at Emerson as she thrust a finger into the animal's mouth. Lured by this maternal gesture, the calf peacefully followed the girl into the barn.

'People are like the calf,' says Conklin. 'You can poke them, prod them, push them, and they don't move. But give them a good reason—one of *their* reasons—a way in which they will benefit, and they will follow gently along. People do things for *their* reasons. Not *your* reasons. And those reasons are emotional, aroused by the ways they feel.'

The story is told that when Michael Faraday invented the first electric motor, he wanted the interest and backing of the British Prime Minister, William Gladstone. So Faraday took the crude model—a little wire revolving around a magnet—and showed it to the statesman. Gladstone was obviously not interested.

'What good is it?' he asked Faraday.

'Someday, you will be able to tax it,' replied the great scientist.

He won his point and the endorsement of his efforts by appealing to the interests of the Prime Minister. Here was an invention that represented Faraday's sweat, toil, and genius, but to win Gladstone's approval, it had to represent the British pound sterling.

The third question is, *what do they want?* People have certain needs and expectations. If they can see that what you want can also give them what they want, they will be much more open and receptive. That great motivational speaker, Zig Ziglar, frequently says, 'You can get everything in life you want, if you help enough people get what they want.' If we hit the 'hot buttons,' then people will be willing to pay the price.

Tom Hopkins writes in *How to Master the Art of Selling*, 'You have to close through your eyes.' He gives the example of a blind real-estate salesman who attributed his great success to the fact that he could not see the properties he sold and therefore, had to sell through the eyes of his prospects. 'You must see the benefits, and features, and limitations of your product or service from your potential buyer's viewpoint,' Hopkins says. 'You must weigh them on his scale of values, not your own. You must close on the benefits that are of value to him.' Your perspective determines your actions and reactions.

When the other fellow takes a long time, he's slow.
When I take a long time, I'm thorough.
When the other fellow doesn't do it, he's lazy.
When I don't do it, I'm busy.
When the other fellow does something without being told, he's overstepping his bounds.
But when I do it, that's initiative.
When the other fellow overlooks a rule of etiquette, he's rude.
But when I skip a few rules, I'm original.
When the other fellow pleases the boss, he's an apple polisher.
But when I please the boss, that's cooperation.
When the other fellow gets ahead, he's getting the breaks.
But when I manage to get ahead, that's just the reward for hard work.

Sydney J. Harris, the columnist, wrote: 'Thomas Aquinas, who knew more about education and persuasion than almost anybody who ever lived, once said that when you want to convert someone to your view, you go over to where he is standing, take him by the hand (mentally speaking), and guide him. You don't stand across the room and shout at him; you don't call him a dummy; you don't order him to come over to where you are. You start where he is, and work from that position. That's the only way to get him to budge.'

EXPOSE THE PROBLEMS IMMEDIATELY

One of the classic parts of the speech by Zuke Berman is his opening statement: 'My name is Emile Zola Berman. I'm a civilian. I'm a Jew, and I'm a Yankee from New York City.' To be a civilian, to be a New Yorker, and to be Jewish were really not the ideal qualifications for a defense counsel in South Carolina in a prominent Marine courtmartial in July of 1956. But by laying all of his cards on the table at the beginning,

Mr. Berman knew that these possible stumbling blocks would be behind him, not down the road ahead.

When you face the potential problems at the start and get the emotions out, then you can get to the important issues. Otherwise, issues are never heard and all that is dealt with are the 'yes, but's . . .' I rely heavily on this principle in leading my church. For example, just before a congregational business meeting, I send out a letter addressing all the potential problems that the church is facing at that time. The fact that the congregation knows the leader is already aware of the problems gives them confidence and peace of mind.

Always deal with the problem issues up front. This establishes a base of trust, which is necessary in any relationship. Failure to recognize and handle problems allows them to color the issues and create barriers and negative feelings. It creates a credibility gap. Count on having to deal with problems at some point. Better it be at the start, before they have the chance to fester and become insurmountable.

BE PREPARED TO TAKE A RISK

You might have to stick your neck out and make commitments that may cost you something. Mr. Berman stuck his neck out when he declared, 'If no one helps me I'm going back to New York to resume my life.'

Whenever you are attempting to change an opinion—whether of a jury in a homicide trial or of a friend, spouse, or parent—you're going to meet strong levels of resistance. There will come a moment when you've made your best case and you must be prepared to stand by it and take the consequences. Most people, when attempting to advance a point of view persuasively, become fearful that they will fail, and that fear is conveyed to the person they are trying to persuade.

Fear is the surest cause of failure. If you can work up your courage, as Zuke Berman did, present all aspects of your case, and walk away prepared for possible loss, you will most often be a winner. People have enormous respect for someone who says, 'This is my case. I've been as honest as I know in explaining my position, and I hope that you will agree with me.'

Leaders have two important characteristics: They are going somewhere, and they are able to persuade other people to go with them. Effective risk-taking leadership takes place when I sense *conviction* (the cause is right), and when I sense *confidence* (I can do it and others will help me do it).

APPEAL TO THE HIGHER VISION

Most people are inherently decent and fair and they want to 'do the right thing.' They're not always sure, however, what fairness or rightness is, and they are often full of anxiety when forced to say yes or no. It is your job, as the persuader, to make them understand the human values represented by your position. They must be made to feel empathy for what you are trying to do so that emotionally they want to give you the response you seek. Zuke Berman did this when he said, 'I've come down here to save the Marine Corps.' Those drill instructors understood that and admired his courage in taking them on.

The civil rights movement enjoyed its ultimate victory over bigotry when network news showed the dogs being loosed on the marchers in Selma, Alabama and the police crashing into the crowds with their clubs. Suddenly, people all across America understood the real effects of unfair and inhumane policies. Their emotions were aroused in a positive way, and it wasn't long before the President and the Congress felt that the public would support a strong Voting Rights Acts.

People don't buy newspapers. They buy news. It isn't glasses that are purchased; it's better vision. Women who spend big bucks for cosmetics are really trying to buy good looks. Millions of drills have been sold; yet not a single person wanted one. They were buying holes. Diet books are not sold by publicizing the evils and risks of being overweight; they're sold by ads depicting how attractive one can become by shedding a few pounds. Athletes do not go through the agony of practice and training to avoid losing; they do it to make the team and be a winner. Appealing to a higher vision is simply helping others become not only what they are capable of becoming but what they really want to become.

This method of motivation is not new. It was described profoundly by the philosopher Lao-tse 2,500 years ago, 'A leader is best when people barely know he exists, not so good, when people obey and acclaim him, worse when they despise him. But of a good leader, who talks little, when his work is done, his aim fulfilled, they will say, "We did it ourselves."'

In the early part of the twentieth century, the same philosophy was echoed by Harry Gordon Selfridge, developer of one of the largest department stores in London. Selfridge, who achieved success by being a leader rather than a boss, said this of the two types of executives:

The boss drives people; the leader coaches them.
The boss depends upon authority; the leader, on good will.
The boss says 'I'; the leader, 'We.'
The boss fixes the blame for the breakdown; the leader fixes the breakdown.
The boss knows how it is done; the leader shows how.
The boss says 'Go!'; the leader, 'Let's go!'

KNOW WHEN TO STOP

The number-one reason most people lose arguments is not because they're wrong; it's because they don't know when to quit. There is a moment when you have marshalled all of the factual and emotional issues in your favor and have expressed them as best you can. If you continue to hammer away, you do nothing but build resentment in the person you are trying to persuade.

Zuke Berman could have said a lot more that night in the NCO Club. He could have talked about the attitudes of the brass, enumerated the issues in the case, talked about the suspicions that every man in the room had committed the same acts as did the defendant, or taken questions from the audience. In fact, he did none of these things because he knew, intuitively and brilliantly, that to belabor his point would weaken his position.

There is great dignity in simplicity. Most of the immortal works of literature not only have the brilliance of brevity but also the dignity of simplicity. The Lord's Prayer consists of only fifty-seven words, none more than three syllables. The Declaration of Independence, which revolutionized the thinking of the New World, can be read by a fourth-grader in less than five minutes. Simplicity is eloquent; it speaks loud and clear without insulting the intelligence of the listener.

COVER YOUR TOPIC WITH ENTHUSIASM

Occasionally there will be times when you're dealing with an issue about which you know you're right, but none of your techniques of persuasion can budge your opposition. Be enthusiastic! Columbia Law School professor, Jerome Michael, teaches his students this technique: 'If you have the facts on your side, hammer the facts. If you have the law on your side, hammer the law. If you have neither the facts nor the law, hammer the table.'

A speech without enthusiasm is like a landscape painted entirely in shades of grey—there is form but no color. Enthusiasm alone will many times give you the edge you need.

In England there is a monument to the sport of rugby, the forerunner of America's football. The statue depicts an eager boy leaning down to pick up a ball. At the base of the statue is this inscription: With a fine disregard for the rules, he picked up the ball and ran.

The statue and inscription tell a true story. An important game of rugby was taking place between two English schools. During the closing minutes of the contest, a boy more gifted with enthusiasm and school spirit than with experience was sent into the game for the first time. Forgetting all the rules, particularly the one that says a player does not touch the ball with his hands, and conscious only of the fact that the ball had to be at the goal line within seconds if his school were to be victorious, the boy picked up the ball and, to the amazement of everyone, started the sprint of his life to the goal line.

The confused officials and players remained frozen where they stood. But the spectators were so moved by the boy's spirit and entertained by his performance, that they stood up and applauded long and loudly. This incident totally eclipsed the rest of the game's action. As a result, a new sport was born: Football. It wasn't because of carefully worded arguments and rule changes; it was because of one boy's enthusiastic mistake!

PUT IT TO WORK

PEOPLE PRINCIPLES

✦ To 'persuade' means to use sweetness to get people to do things.

- A goal is a dream with a deadline.
- Five 'Cs' in Motivating People:

  Consideration—What is the needed response?

  Credibility—What must I do to get it?

  Content—What must I say to get it?

  Conviction—How must I say it?

  Conclusion—What steps do I need to take?
- We motivate best from the other person's perspective.
- You can get everything in life you want if you help enough people get what they want.

PUTTING THE PRINCIPLES TO WORK:

I will apply the principles from this chapter to my relationships with people in the following ways:

1.

2.

3.

FURTHER STUDY:

Be a Motivational Leader, LeRoy Eims

See You at the Top, Zig Ziglar

19

HOW TO BE A PERSON PEOPLE RESPECT

THE HEADLINE on the front cover of *Time*'s May 25, 1987 issue contains simply two words: 'What's Wrong?' I want to share a couple of paragraphs from that issue's lead article, because it gives us a shocking glimpse of the moral fiber of America today.

> *Hypocrisy, betrayal and greed unsettle the nation's soul. Once again it is morning in America. But this morning Wall Street financiers are nervously scanning the papers to see if their names have been linked to the insider-trading scandals. Presidential candidates are peeking through drawn curtains to make sure that reporters are not staking out their private lives. A congressional witness, deeply involved in the Reagan Administration's secret foreign policy, is huddling with his lawyers before facing inquisitors. A Washington lobbyist who once breakfasted regularly in the White House mess is brooding over his investigation by an independent counsel. In Quantico, Virginia, the Marines are preparing to court-martial one of their own. In Palm Springs, California, a husband-and-wife televangelist team, once the adored cynosures of 500,000 faithful, are beginning another day of seclusion.*

Such are the scenes of morning in the scandal-scarred spring of 1987. Lamentation is in the air, and clay feet litter the ground . . . Oliver North, Robert McFarlane, Michael Deaver, Ivan Boesky, Gary Hart, Clayton Lonetree, Jim and Tammy Bakker . . . Their transgressions—some grievous and some petty—run the gamut of human failings, from weakness of will to moral laxity to hypocrisy to uncontrolled avarice. But taken collectively, the heedless lack of restraint in their behavior reveals something disturbing about the national character. America, which took such back-thumping pride in its spiritual renewal, finds itself wallowing in a moral morass. Ethics, often dismissed as a prissy Sunday School word, is now at the center of a new national debate. Put bluntly, has the mindless materialism of the '80s left in its wake a values vacuum?

What is amazing about this article, which does not even mention more recent moral disappointments, is that it appeared in a secular magazine, not a Christian periodical. The world is calling attention to what I consider the biggest problem in our community today: the lack of morality and ethics. The Christian community faces an incredible credibility problem among leaders. If we don't get hold of this situation and turn it around, it will cause more damage to the church than anything else in this century.

One of the two or three life-changing books that I have read in the last ten years is *The Man Who Could Do No Wrong* by Dr. Charles Blair, a good friend, a wonderful Christian man, and the pastor of Calvary Temple in Denver, Colorado. I attended a conference in which Dr. Blair shared the story which was later revealed in his book.

He was a highly trusted pastor, a man with tremendous vision, who wanted to do something great for God. Unfortunately, and unknowingly, he hired fund raisers who did not share his ethics. As a result, he eventually found himself indicted and convicted of fraud.

Dr. Blair took total responsibility for the problem because he was the one who hired these men and trusted their methods. What makes this book so gripping is that this man, an outstanding Christian leader, straightforwardly admitted his wrong. The cover is gripping in itself as it reads, 'Alarm bells should have rung when they called me the man who could do no wrong.'

Dr. Blair talks about the fact that he was loved by his people, respected by the community, and had developed a sense of invulnerability. Everything he did and said just turned out right; he had the 'Midas Touch.' After hearing him speak and then reading his book, I was moved to understand the importance of credibility. I had an opportunity to ask him about this situation and he said, 'John, I literally set myself up for a fall by bringing people around me and trusting them implicitly without checking on them.'

Alarm bells should have rung, but Dr. Blair had felt no need to be on the alert. Not one of us is in a position where we can do no wrong. We should always be alert to alarm bells ringing to warn us that we may be on the edge of a potential disastrous problem.

LEADERS AND CREDIBILITY

As surely as every leader has his strengths, he also has his weaknesses. On a visit to Canterbury Cathedral, I had to laugh at a line of graffiti scrawled on one of the walls: 'The Archbishop cheats at Scrabble.' Even the Archbishop has a crack in his armour! But don't we all? The important thing is that we discover where our cracks are so we can deal with them.

Leaders are on the frontline of spiritual battle and are very susceptible to Satan's attacks. Often they are among his first victims. Leaders are exposed to pressures and temptations beyond the usual run of testing. Pitfalls face the unwary and traps abound even for the experienced. Satan knows that if he can get leader to fall, many followers will go scrambling after.

Leaders are to live a higher standard than followers. It is a biblical principle which must be honored consistently. Leaders will be judged differently because their gifts and responsibilities are different.

Note the following triangle. It shows that followers have many options in how they live, how they spend their time, and choices they make. However, the farther up you go on that triangle, the more leadership you assume, the fewer options you have. At the top you basically have no options because you are a servant-leader. The options decrease as the responsibility increases.

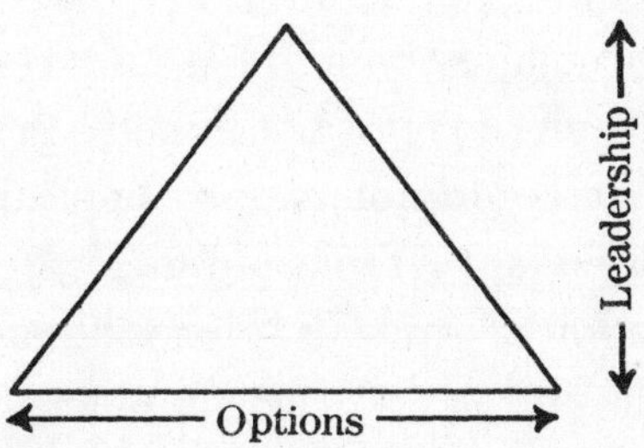

Most people do not understand this precept. Many leaders live on the principle that the more influence they have, the more options and choices they have. They begin to live as though they are above the law. James 3:1 highlights this truth: 'Not many of you should presume to be teachers, my brothers, because you know that we who teach will be judged more strictly' (NIV). And

Jesus in Luke 12:48 also states the same principle: 'And from everyone who has been given much shall much be required; and to whom they entrusted much, of him they will ask all the more.'

As leaders, we must remember that God has given us much, but He also requires much in return. We are not judged by the same standards as the world. We may sin as the world does, and we can certainly be forgiven as the world is, but it's not that easy to return to our position of leadership once we have lost credibility with others.

Some fallen Christian leaders do not seem to understand or to want to understand God's Word as it applies to forgiveness and restoration. Their attitude is that since they have asked God's forgiveness, they have every right to return to their position and privilege. Everything is *not* as it was.

When we fall, we must go through a period of proving ourselves and regaining that precious ground of credibility. Leadership is not a position which one is given but a position which one earns by proving faithful.

Possibilities for failure abound, but mistakes can be avoided if the leader will listen for the 'alarm bells' in his or her life. I am convinced that we do not have to step into the pitfalls. If we're looking for them, we can avoid them. Herein lies the key to success: Listen for 'alarm bells.' The following questions may trigger alarm bells in your own life. Consider them carefully.

IS MY PERSONAL WALK WITH GOD UP TO DATE?

That question should prompt a quick and positive answer. If not, you are getting too close to the edge, too close to trouble. My friend Bill Klassen asks me each time we meet, 'Do you have a word from the Lord that is up to date?' or 'What have you been learning recently from the Lord?' Bill isn't asking me for a history lesson; he wants to know what God is teaching me today.

You will find that leaders who are effective are leaders who are disciplined in their daily lives. A disciplined daily walk is the best protection to keep us from falling into sin.

Why is this so essential to your personal credibility? Because the Word of God convicts our hearts. Psalm 119:11 says, 'Thy word have I treasured in my heart that I may not sin against Thee.' It also helps us think like God. The things that we think on are the things that we become. If we are not spending time with God, we're spending that time with whatever it is that has become more important to us. When this happens we quickly become insensitive to His Spirit and therefore, we no longer have the strength to resist temptation and do spiritual battle. It boils down to a simple fact: sin will keep us from the Word or the Word will keep us from sin.

A person of integrity is one who has established a system of values against which all life is judged. That system of values is determined by a person's walk with God. I once heard Billy Graham tell this story about a family from South Carolina who went to New York City for a vacation. They told all their friends they would attend the Broadway play, *My Fair Lady*. Unfortunately it was sold out and they couldn't obtain tickets. They were disappointed and embarrassed to have to go back home and tell their friends they missed the highlight of their trip, so they decided to do the next best thing. They picked up discarded tickets, purchased a program, and bought the musical tapes. In their motel room they learned all the songs and reviewed the program. Back home they sang and whistled the tunes to all of *My Fair Lady*'s hits hoping no one would suspect they never saw it.

When we, as Christians and leaders, begin to put on a facade, we're in trouble. When we attempt to 'talk the talk' without 'walking the walk,' we are destined to failure. We can avoid this pitfall by keeping our walk with God close and consistent.

AM I KEEPING MY PRIORITIES STRAIGHT?

Priorities have a tendency to sneak out of position when we're not paying attention. Countless numbers of Christian leaders have become 'successful' only to discover the tragic price for their success was a broken marriage or loss of health. At some point along the road to success, their priorities shifted.

The first priority of any Christian should be his or her relationship with God. That means growing closer to Him, worshiping and loving Him, and being obedient to Him. The careful maintenance of this relationship is the surest safeguard against failure. One of my favorite passages is John 21:15 where Jesus asks of Peter, 'Peter, do you love Me more than these?' The question the Chief Shepherd most wants His under-shepherds to answer is not, 'How much do you know about Me?' or even, 'How much are you telling the world about Me?' It is, 'How much do you love Me?'

Our second priority should be our family responsibilities and our third concern should be our ministry or career commitments. Paul tells us in 1 Timothy 5:8, 'But if any one does not provide for his own, and especially for those of his household, he has denied the faith, and is worse than an unbeliever.'

Scripture provides two illustrations of leaders who did great damage to the cause of the kingdom because they didn't keep their families in order. Both of them were judges—Eli and Samuel. I have always felt that since Eli and Samuel had a mentor-student relationship, Eli's chief weakness also became Samuel's chief weakness. That is discipleship in a negative sense.

Let's take a look at 1 Samuel 3:11–13. 'And the Lord said to Samuel, "Behold, I am about to do a thing in Israel at which both ears of everyone who hears it will tingle. In that day I will carry out against Eli all that I have spoken concerning his house, from beginning to end. For I have told him that I am about to judge his house forever for the iniquity which he knew, because his sons brought a curse on themselves and he did not rebuke them."'

Now Samuel was a very successful judge. In 1 Samuel 3:19–20 it is said of him, 'The Lord was with Samuel as he grew up, and he let none of His words fall to the ground. And all Israel from Dan to Beersheba recognized that Samuel was attested as a prophet of the Lord' (NIV).

Yet, Samuel watched the nation that he loved and led turn from the purposes of God. As God's chosen people, the Israelites were never meant to have a king; God was to be their king. But because Samuel failed to rear his sons in the fear of the Lord, Israel rejected the rule of God over them. In 1 Samuel 8:1–5 we read:

> *And it came about when Samuel was old that he appointed his sons judges over Israel. Now the name of his first-born was Joel, and the name of his second, Abijah; they were judging in Beersheba.*
>
> *His sons, however, did not walk in his ways, but turned aside after dishonest gain and took bribes and perverted justice. Then all the elders of Israel gathered together and came to Samuel at Ramah; and they said to him, 'Behold, you have grown old, and your sons do not walk in your ways. Now appoint a king for us to judge us like all the nations.'*

Such sober warnings in the Word of God should impress upon us the importance of keeping our priorities straight: God first, family second, ministry or career third. Only when a leader's relationship to God is right, and only when responsibilities as a family member are being properly met, can the leader be fully faithful in exercising the ministry God has given him or her.

AM I ASKING MYSELF THE DIFFICULT QUESTIONS?

What are the critical questions? The first one is, *Why am I doing this?* Why am I spending time on this project or with these people? What are my motives? If you're doing the right job for the wrong reasons, don't count on God to bless your project.

The second question is, *How should it be done?* This deals with presumption. The danger of presumption is ever-present, especially for people called to an adventurous ministry of faith. Moses strikes the rock to produce water on one occasion and then presumes quite wrongly that this is to be God's method on a later occasion.

The third critical question is, *When should I do it?* This question deals with timing. When does God want His task accomplished? Again, aggressive leaders have a tendency to run ahead as Abraham did when he tried to speed up God's promise to Ishmael. We have a tendency to want short-term success at the expense of God's long-term will.

AM I ACCOUNTABLE TO SOMEONE IN AUTHORITY OVER MY LIFE?

In 1 Thessalonians 5:12–13 we read, 'But we request of you, brethren, that you appreciate those who diligently labor among you, and have charge over you in the Lord and give you instruction, and that you esteem them very highly in love because of their work. Live in peace with one another.'

You are at peace among yourselves when you are accountable to someone in authority. This is one reason why I believe in the local church. Every Christian should be a member of a local congregation and should submit to those in authority. It is very unhealthy for Christian organizations to have members on the board who are not tied in to a local church. I would be very frightened to follow someone who was not responsible to anyone. Only God Himself can handle that kind of power and authority.

My friend Ron Jenson provided me with a great idea: Stop here for a minute and write down the name of the person to whom you are accountable.

Now write out 'five questions I hope no one ever asks me' on a sheet of paper. List four questions that will address your weaknesses, and then enlist the help of a Christian brother or sister who will keep you accountable in these areas. The fifth question you should seek to answer is this: Have I lied about any of the previous four questions or have I intentionally left out anything?

I believe that much of the problem of credibility in the Christian community is caused by people with power, who struggle with the same tough moral issues as the rest of the world, yet are often not accountable to anyone. Authority minus accountability equals a very dangerous situation.

AM I SENSITIVE TO WHAT GOD IS SAYING TO THE BODY OF CHRIST?

Are you sensitive to the fact that God speaks to others too? If you can't answer an unqualified yes, you're skating on thin ice. In the checks and balances of Christian integrity, the Spirit speaks to others in the body who compliment us and make up for our weaknesses.

Paul beautifully portrays this principle in 1 Corinthians 12 when he speaks about how one member of the body is not to despise another; rather, we are to complement each other. Not one of us has a corner on God's gift. Ask yourself this question: 'Am I a listening leader or am I a lording leader?' 1 Peter 5:2–3 instructs us not to lord it over others. When we're more interested in telling people what to do than in listening to what they are presently doing, we are off balance.

AM I OVERLY CONCERNED WITH IMAGE BUILDING?

I am bothered by the amount of professionalism and role-playing within the ministry. Too many of us have become more interested in image-building than in kingdom-building. Pretense has replaced passion in our preaching. How we deal with the following four areas will reveal our authenticity, both in the church and outside of it.

- *Character.* Do I make decisions based on what is right or what is most easily accepted? Am I a leader or a follower?
- *Change.* Do I change my personality, speech, or actions according to the people I am with?
- *Credit.* When I do something for the Lord, do people see me or do they see my God? And do I care who receives the credit?
- *Channel.* Does God work through my life to touch others? If other lives are not changing as a result of mine, this is a good indication that the image I'm building is my own, not God's. Only if you are open, honest, transparent, and vulnerable with others can God use you to change others.

AM I OVERLY IMPRESSED BY SIGNS AND WONDERS?

We all seek to experience revival. But more than seeking revival, we need to seek God. Then we certainly will experience revival, healings, and miracles. But if we pursue revival for revival's sake, we're seeking after secondary results.

Luke 10:17–20 speaks to this. 'The seventy returned with joy, saying, "Lord, even the demons are subject to us in Your name." And He said to them, "I was watching Satan fall from heaven like lightning. Behold, I have given you authority to tread upon serpents and scorpions, and over all the power of the enemy, and nothing shall injure you. Nevertheless, do not rejoice in this, that the spirits are subject to you, but rejoice that your names are recorded in heaven."'

God is not in the entertainment business. When He works miracles it is for one purpose only—the ultimate good of His Kingdom. A wise old minister once said to a younger one, 'God can work miracles through anybody. If He made Balaam's donkey speak by a miracle, don't get puffed up if He decides to work a few through you.'

When God does a great work through you, does it humble you or does it feed your ego? The appreciation and fascination for God's moving should never dim or replace our desire for holy living and righteous character.

AM I A LONER IN MY SERVICE TO THE LORD?

Hebrews 10:23–25 admonishes us, 'Let us hold fast the confession of our hope without wavering, for He who promised is faithful; and let us consider how to stimulate one another to love and good deeds, not forsaking our own assembling together, as is the habit of some, but encouraging one another; and all the more, as you see the day drawing near.'

It is never healthy to be a 'Lone Ranger' in service or ministry. Bring your family and your colleagues along with you. Not only is it more fun to share the joy with others, but being part of a team can provide a system of accountability. I'll never forget the first time I heard Reverend Paul Y. Cho. He stood up before more than a thousand pastors in New York and introduced one of his friends and staff members. Then he looked at his audience and said, 'I bring my friend with me because I find I am susceptible to sexual temptations and he is my safeguard.' The air was still and silent but we all knew what he meant. He takes someone with him so he won't mess up morally. He draws strength from a brother.

When we design our lives after the Lone Ranger concept, we are sure to suffer some unfavorable consequences. We develop a distorted perception of ourselves, our ministries, and other people. We are imbalanced and incomplete without the other members of the body of Christ and their spiritual gifts. We become irrelevant because we don't live where other people live. There is a sense of exclusiveness and an inability to relate to the real world.

AM I AWARE OF MY WEAKNESSES?

To be forewarned is to be forearmed! Perhaps we should ask an even more important question: *Am I honest about my weaknesses?* Most of us know our deficiencies, but we have a tendency to try to cover them.

Take a moment now and consider areas of weakness that could cause you to become sidetracked in your life. Realize that these are the very areas in which you will be tempted. Are you tempted by opportunities simply because they may be ego-gratifying? Do you expect too much of others or not enough of yourself? Do you get your feelings hurt easily?

Besides having a weakness for chocolate, I have difficulty in keeping my schedule within the bounds of human endurance. When I allow myself to become overextended, it has a negative effect on those around me. Realizing that this is an area of personal weakness, I have set standards to help me maintain my priorities. First, each outside activity has to meet certain qualifications which I have imposed. And second, I have established a committee of three to review my schedule. Remember, though, that the first step in overcoming this weakness was to admit to myself that there was a problem.

IS MY COMMITMENT CONSTANTLY BEFORE ME?

This is supremely important if God has called you into a position of Christian leadership.

Paul says in 1 Corinthians 7:24, 'Brethren, let each man remain with God in that condition in which he was called.' Remember when Paul stood before King Agrippa and said, 'I was not disobedient to the heavenly vision.' Paul could have been tempted to give up, take other options, or yield to the persecution, but the thing that kept him on track was the vision before him.

The world continually thrusts opportunities at us which would distract us from God's call. There is nothing more tragic than when a Christian leader loses God's anointing on his life by allowing himself to become sidetracked. There is no higher violation of God's trust. For when a leader stumbles, others fall.

There have been many times when God has helped me resist temptations because I stopped and considered the harm it would do to others if I yielded.

I grew up in a church where the pastor was building a great work for God but he fell morally. Twenty years later the church is still staggering under the effects of that moral fall. That man no doubt experienced God's forgiveness, but he will spend the rest of his life wondering what he could have accomplished for God if he had not messed up. It's better not to do it than to do it and regret it.

I once heard Cavett Roberts, a great motivational speaker, say, 'If my people understand me, I'll get their attention. But if my people trust me, I'll get their action.' People respond quickest and most ably when the leader has credibility. If God can maintain His faith in you, so will others.

PUT IT TO WORK

PEOPLE PRINCIPLES

- ✦ Leaders are to live a higher standard than followers.
- ✦ Leadership is not a position which one is given. It is a position which one earns by proving faithful.
- ✦ A person of integrity is one who has a system of values against which all life is judged.
- ✦ Authority minus accountability equals a very dangerous situation.
- ✦ When we design our lives after the Lone Ranger ideal, we are sure to suffer some unfavorable consequences.
- ✦ When a leader stumbles, others fall.

PUTTING THE PRINCIPLES TO WORK:

I will apply the principles from this chapter to my relationships with people in the following ways:

1.

2.

3.

FURTHER STUDY:

The Other Side of Leadership, Eugene B. Habecker

The Man Who Could Do No Wrong, Charles Blair

20

YOU CAN BE AN ENCOURAGER

THE KEY to encouragement is in knowing what gives people courage; what spurs them on to action. Too many of us take pleasure in discouraging people by pointing out their mistakes and getting excited about their failures rather than focusing on their strengths and getting excited about their possibilities.

In this chapter I want to focus particularly on 'on the job' relationships. In the work force, successful managers have learned the tremendous value of encouragement. It's the greatest management principle. Why? Because you get the kind of behavior you reward. You don't get what you hope for, ask for, wish for, or beg for. You get what you reward.

It's a fact of life that people spend the most time doing what they believe will benefit them most. If they do not benefit in some way for doing the right things, they will seek other avenues of self-fulfillment. This can lead to self-destructive behavior. It's a simple thing to offer encouragement, but it can have a tremendous effect on someone's life.

When we think of organizational success, we often think in terms of dollars, cents, statistics, facts, and figures. But data and charts are nothing more than mere symbols that represent the collective behavior of human beings. Reward people for the right behavior, and you get the right results; fail to reward the right behavior and you're likely to get the wrong results.

People are encouraged to continue that behavior which brings them rewards. At home one summer we tried this principle with the kids. We set up ways for the kids to earn merit points which could be turned into money. They earned points for positive activities such as reading the Bible, Bible memory, general reading, piano practice, maintaining a clean room, and so on. Some tasks earned more points than others.

One evening I opened the front door and Joel ran to me with the news that so far he had earned 113 points. He didn't say 'How are you, Dad?' 'How was your day?' 'It's great to see you.' His greeting let me know that he was excited about success.

Behavior that is rewarded is behavior that will continue. This concept is transferable for the mom in the home, the pastor in a church, or the leader of an organization. Polls taken in the work force reveal that American workers are not giving their all; they're giving half-hearted effort to their jobs. Yet the American work ethic is still alive. If American workers deeply believe in the value and importance of hard work then why aren't they willing to give their best? The answer may be found in the reward system. Are they being encouraged by the right incentives? I believe that people withhold their best efforts when they see little or no relationship between what they do and how they are rewarded.

REWARDS IN ACTION

One Father's Day our family went to a restaurant for dinner. Unfortunately, all of San Diego chose to be at this restaurant on this particular day. Though we had a reservation there was an incredible line of people waiting to be seated. At the reservation desk stood three hostesses surrounded by a mob of unhappy people. Their stomachs were growling with hunger and it was reflected in their unsmiling faces.

After observing the scene for a few minutes I approached the desk and said, 'Ladies, I have a reservation, but I see there are a lot of people here and you're under pressure. I have a large group with me today, but we want to help you. You tell me, what can I do to make your job easier? Do you want us to divide our group and go in different sections?' A hostess looked up, and smiled, and agreed that it would help for us to divide. Then I added, 'I'm not going to stand here at the desk because you already have so many people pressing you. We're going to stand off to the side here and whenever you need anything just wave at me.'

Every time the hostess walked by I asked her how she was doing and if there was any way we could help. Within twenty minutes we had our table. We rewarded the person who helped us. At the end of the our meal I again talked to the three ladies and said, 'I know what's going to happen. Your manager is going to get a lot of complaints because I heard a lot of unhappy people.' I gave them my name and telephone number and instructed them to have the manager call me if they did receive complaints. I assured them I would tell him what a terrific job they did. They smiled and were relieved. They had been rewarded for a job well done.

Once we understand the principle, we have to determine what kind of behavior deserves reward and encouragement. Look for solid solutions to problems; short-term quick fixes won't endure. Reward long-term people and programs that have been productive. At a conference I once asked the audience what success meant to them. One fellow said simply, 'Success is lasting.' He had a good point. Consider what will work and last over the long haul. Also identify the main factors that are most important to the long-range success of your team and communicate these to them.

In a conference at our church Josh McDowell said, 'The longer I'm in the ministry and the more that I travel and see things happening, the more I have respect and appreciation for things that are long-term.' That's tremendous insight. Go for quality and not quick fixes.

QUALITIES THAT SHOULD BE REWARDED

As the senior pastor over a multiple staff I look for and reward several qualities that I feel are very important for my staff members to exhibit. I expect these things from everyone, whether they are a pastor, a secretary, a custodian, or an intern. A *positive attitude* is at the top of the list. No matter how smart or gifted a person is, if his or her attitude is not what it should be, it affects the entire team. *Loyalty* to the church, the pastor, and to one another is another crucial quality. Staff members are also rewarded for their *personal growth* because as they grow so grows their ministry. Each member of the pastoral staff is expected to reproduce his or her life into another person who could also be trained for leadership. *Creativity* is another quality that is rewarded. We want staff members who can ask the right questions and can also find creative answers and solutions.

Another behavior that I encourage is *risk-taking* instead of risk-avoiding. 'Safety first' may be the motto of the masses, but it's not the watchword of leaders. No gain is ever made without the possibility of a loss. Steven Jobs, cofounder of the brilliantly successful Apple Computer, was asked how he managed to create such a flourishing new company. His reply: 'We hire great people, and we create an environment where people can make mistakes and grow.'

Leaders need to encourage *applied creativity* instead of mindless conformity. An organization's most important asset is not its buildings, land, or holdings. It is the creative minds within that organization. To illustrate: An employee of a company complained about the working style of a fellow worker. He said that when the guy wasn't casually walking around, he could be found sitting in his office, feet on the desk, gazing out the window. He saw his coworker's laid-back behavior as a waste of the company's money. The manager replied to his concern with: 'His last idea was worth two million dollars to the company. If he only comes up with one idea like that each year, he's worth his salary.'

Now I'm not advocating slothfulness, but sometimes the creative mind is misunderstood and criticized. However, if everyone is encouraged to develop their creativity within pre-approved reasonableness, the organization will benefit. Success is held in the hands of those who provide the solutions.

Determine to encourage what I call *decisive action* instead of paralysis by analysis. One pastor wanted to end a dying ministry in his church but was concerned about a small group of people who wanted to keep it going. A friend suggested, 'Take it to committee. That'll kill it for sure.' The purpose of any organization is to get results and that takes action, not endless introspection and meetings. Once the consulting has taken place and the reports have been delivered, it's time for a decision.

One executive summed up the importance of decisiveness beautifully: 'To look is one thing. To see what you look at is another. To understand what you see is a third. To learn from what you understand is still something else. But to act on what you learn is all that really matters.'

Encourage your people to work smarter, not harder. If your priorities are right—if you're working smart—your results will be fruitful. Success is not determined by how many hours you spend, but how you spend your hours. Comedian Woody Allen once remarked that showing up is 80 percent of life. Many employees behave as if showing up and being busy is 100 percent of work. Unfortunately, most of us aren't rewarded for achieving specific goals that contribute to output.

The key to working smarter is knowing the difference between motion and direction. In the final analysis, *results* are what matter; attendance and activity don't.

Encourage simplification instead of needless complication. Find and eliminate the unnecessary. Cutting the fat will produce increased efficiency which, in turn, will crease production.

Learn to ignore the 'squeaking joints' and encourage the quiet, effective producers. Many times we manage by the squeaky wheel principle. The one who yells the loudest and longest is the one who gets the attention. What we need to do is look for and encourage the person who is quietly and effectively accomplishing something. You will be amazed at how fast the 'squeaky wheels' catch on.

Consider this skeletal anatomy of an organization:

The wishbones *wish somebody else would do the work.*
The jawbones *talk a lot but do little else.*
The knucklebones *knock what everyone else does.*
The backbones *actually do the work!*

Encourage and reward quality work instead of fast work that is mediocre. The product needs to be something the organization can be proud of and that reflects the quality of the organization. There really are greater payoffs for quality work such as lower cost, higher output, and worker pride. Did you realize that the American car has a built-in cost factor of 25 percent because of work that needs to be redone in production due to ineffective work the first time?

Personal charisma should not be allowed to substitute for steadfastness in performance. Consistency should be recognized and rewarded. Again, look at the person who is dependable and accountable over the long haul. There are many who can make us smile and laugh but never really come through with the goods. Know the difference and encourage the producer.

Recognize and reward those who work well together. This is a key in management because none of us is as smart as all of us. There is value in creative teamwork.

TOP TEN REWARDS

Let's take a look at the ten best ways to reward good work. When we reward people with something that is meaningful to them, we are encouraging them as well as increasing their personal value and worth.

1. *Money.* Money does talk; it tells an individual how valuable he is to whoever pays his salary. Pay for leadership and you get leaders. Pay peanuts and you get monkeys. Did you hear about the clothing manager who turned out thousands of sweat shirts with 'Money isn't everything' printed on them? He went bankrupt!

'How can I ever show my appreciation?' a woman asked Clarence Darrow, after he rescued her from legal woes.

'My dear lady,' responded Darrow, 'ever since the Phoenicians invented money there has been only one answer to that question.'

No, money isn't the only way to show appreciation for a job well done, but it's one of the best ways.

2. *Recognition.* People need continual affirmation so they know they are meeting a need and doing it well. Lawrence Peter says

there are two kinds of egotists: those who admit it and the rest of us.

3. *Time off.* If someone has worked extended hours on a special project, give them an afternoon or day off with a hearty thanks on the way out.

4. *A piece of the action.* Not all of us have the opportunity of profit sharing within a company, but we can pass on additional responsibility for work well done.

5. *Favorite work.* Reward good work by assigning people tasks they enjoy doing. Find out what they like to do best and give it to them.

6. *Advancement.* Allow only your producers to advance and move forward, not your workers. This is a biblical principle we see modeled in the Parable of the Five Talents.

7. *Freedom.* Give producers the autonomy to do their jobs in the way they feel most comfortable. Don't stifle them by trying to fit them into your own mold.

8. *Personal growth opportunities.* Reward your people with the opportunity of further career education. Provide books, conference attendance, tapes, and speakers that will enhance them.

9. *Special time together.* If you are the leader, boss, or pastor, take time to socialize over a meal in order to affirm someone's productivity.

10. *Gifts.* Your thoughtfulness in taking time to select a gift that would be meaningful shows a productive person that you appreciate him or her.

Money and recognition are the two most powerful rewards. Almost everybody responds to praises and raises!

In the final analysis, encouragement is your key to helping other people succeed. The ability to encourage is and always will be much more of an art than a science; your success depends both on your sensitivity and your skill. To use an analogy, I can only supply you with a canvas, brush, easel, pallet of colors, and a few lessons. Producing the masterpiece is up to you. You have to know how to compose the picture and blend the colors to bring about the desired effect. The same is true with people. If you are a leader you may bring together a group of highly skilled people, but that alone won't insure success. You need to know how to improve their shortcomings and build their assets by the skillful use of simple encouragement.

PUT IT TO WORK

PEOPLE PRINCIPLES

- Encouragement is your key to helping other people succeed. The ability to encourage is and always will be much more of an art than a science; your success depends both on your sensitivity and your skill.
- The key to encouragement is in knowing what gives people courage; what spurs them on to action.
- It's a fact of life that people spend the most time doing what they believe will benefit them most.
- Reward people for the right behavior and you get the right results. Fail to reward the right behavior and you're likely to get the wrong results.
- People withhold their best efforts when they see little or no relationship between what they do and how they are rewarded.

PUTTING THE PRINCIPLES TO WORK:

I will apply the principles from this chapter to my relationships with people in the following ways:

1.

2.

3.

FURTHER STUDY:

Encouraging People, Donald Bubna
Top Performance, Zig Ziglar

21

LOVING DIFFICULT PEOPLE

ARE YOU aware of the tremendous advantage frogs have over humans? They can eat anything that bugs them! Wouldn't it be great if we could consume our relational problems rather than letting them consume us! What 'bugs' you the most about people? Is it inconsistency? Inflexibility? Inability to give and take? I am most bugged by people who—you guessed it—have bad attitudes. I can handle disagreements or differences of opinion, but negative attitudes really get to me.

I find that many Christian people suffer from guilt in their relationships with others. Christians are often taught that we should be full of grace. Just what does that mean? Does God expect us to get along peaceably with *everybody*? Are we the ones who must always 'turn the other cheek?' Are we supposed to simply overlook other people's faults and idiosyncracies? Right relationships with difficult people can seem like an impossible standard to reach. Just what are we supposed to do?

The Apostle Paul offers this practical advice, 'If possible, so far as it depends upon you, be at peace with all men' (Rom. 18). I would like to paraphrase that verse: Do the best you can to get along with everyone. Yet realize that once in a while you are going to have a relationship with a difficult person that may fall short of the ideal.

Right now, picture in your mind someone with whom you do not have an ideal relationship. As you continue reading, I want you to constantly call to mind this particular person. I trust you will then read about some characteristics and solutions that will help you creatively deal with the situation and be able to rise above it.

A personal inventory of the 'Three P's' will help you determine your part in a difficult relationship or association.

- *Perspective.* How do I see myself? How do I see others? How do others see me? Our perspective determines how far our relationships will develop.
- *Process.* Do I understand the stages of a relationship? Do I realize there are some stages in a relationship that are more crucial than others?
- *Problems.* When facing difficulties in a relationship, how do I handle them?

Show me a person who sees himself or herself in a negative light and I will show you a person who sees others in a negative way. The opposite is true too. A person who sees himself positively also looks for the good in others. It's all in one's perspective.

Some people see a relationship as a series of isolated incidents, and one bad incident can break the relationship. People who think this way never develop deep relationships. Their friendships are precarious, on-again-off-again types of associations. These people run every time a difficult situation arises. They seldom, if ever, develop longstanding relationships.

PERSPECTIVE AND RELATIONSHIPS

Let's take a look at *perspective* first. I act as I see myself. In fact, it is impossible to consistently behave in a manner that is inconsistent with the way we see ourselves. Understandably, this is the cause of many marital problems. Just the other day I met with an unhappy man and his irate wife. I listened as she relentlessly spewed out bitterness and animosity toward her husband. When I confronted her with her anger and unforgiving spirit, she frantically pointed her finger at her husband and said, 'I'm not the one who is angry and bitter, he is!' She transferred her negative emotions to him. She saw her husband as she herself was.

Only when we view ourselves with 20/20 vision will we be able to see other people clearly. Perspective is crucial. That's why Jesus spoke about judging others: 'Why do you look at the speck in your brother's eye but do not notice the log that is in your own eye? . . . first take the log out of your own eye' (Matt. 7:4–5). He is telling us we need to deal with our own attitudes before we criticize another person.

In Matthew 22:39 we read Jesus' command to 'love your neighbor as yourself.' He knew that if we truly loved ourselves, we would also love our neighbor. He also knew that before we could really love our neighbor, we would need to love ourselves—not a selfish, self-serving type of love, but a deep appreciation of who we are in Christ. Most of the time our relational problems stem from the fact that we ourselves have problems or issues that haven't been resolved. It is not possible to treat another person's hurt until we have first discovered the cure and accepted the treatment ourselves.

The story of the Good Samaritan in Luke 10:30–37 illustrates this principle. The robbers who beat up the traveler used people. They stole from the traveler and saw him as a victim to exploit. The priest and the Levite were legalistic and withdrawn. They saw the beaten, robbed victim as a problem to be avoided, because they believed if they touched a dead man they would be unclean according to the Law. The Good Samaritan was a social outcast—despised, ignored, and rejected by society. He knew what it was like to be passed by and uncared for, but he also had experienced the cure. When he saw this victim, he was able to empathize with him. He looked upon him as a person who needed to be loved, identifying with the traveler's problem and sharing in the solution.

Recently I read an interesting article by Jacques Weisel about self-made millionaires. One hundred entrepreneurs were interviewed in a search for the common denominator that bound them together. The interviews revealed these highly successful men and women could only see the good in people. They were people builders, rather than critics. Again, it is perspective that helps build relationships.

When you realize that people treat you according to how they see themselves rather than how you really are, you are less likely to be affected by their behavior. Your self-image will reflect who you are, not how you're treated by others. You will not be riding an emotional roller coaster. This type of stability will have a tremendous effect on how you feel toward and deal with others.

The key to successful relationships really gets down to responsibility. I am responsible for how I treat others. I may not be responsible for how they treat me; but I am responsible for my reaction to those who are difficult. I can't choose how you'll treat me, but I can choose how I will respond to you.

UNDERSTANDING PERSONALITY TYPES

There are several types of difficult people, and it's helpful to identify their common traits in order to learn how to deal with them effectively. As we review these traits remember that you *can* choose how to react to them. The effect of difficult relationships—whether they make us or break us—is determined, not by the treatment we receive but by how we respond to it.

Take a look at the 'Sherman Tank' personality. This label may bring to mind a person who runs over everything and anything that is in the way. These people have a tendency to intimidate others because of their 'I'm-right-and-you're-wrong' attitude. They intimidate through sheer force and power; their behavior is aggressive and even hostile. Because of the Sherman Tanks' insensitivity, people tend to battle with them. It is difficult to sit down and reason or rationalize with 'tanks.'

Don't lose hope; there is a strategy for dealing with the Sherman Tanks of life. First consider this person's influence as well as the issue at stake. How important is the point being fought over, and how many people are being influenced by the 'tank?' If the issue could have a direct, negative effect on others within the organization, it probably will be worth fighting over. But if it is an insignificant issue or a matter of pride, it's not worth the battle. When crucial issues arise, however, you must stand up to this personality. True, there is no easy way around these people. Be direct, because they probably don't understand tactfulness. Look at them face to face and confront the specific issues at hand. Unfortunately these people cause more pain than any of the other difficult personality types because they feel little pain themselves. As a result, they can afford to be unreasonable. What adds to the burden of dealing with these people is that, with their power to intimidate, they can pull together many allies.

Another difficult personality with whom we all come in contact is the 'Space Cadet.' These people live in their own worlds, walking to the beat of a different drummer. They usually do not respond to normal motivation techniques. Frustration is the overwhelming feeling I get when working with this type of person. I have learned that when working with or speaking to a large group of people, I should not be greatly influenced by this person's feedback. Probably the people you know who fall into this category, you have labeled 'weird.'

Consider these guidelines when working with a Space Cadet:

- ✦ Don't evaluate your leadership by the Space Cadet's response. In fact, don't even ask his or her opinion about something because you'll get an off-the-wall answer. Space Cadets aren't good sounding boards.
- ✦ It's not a good idea to place a Space Cadet in a 'team ministry' position. When you need a group of individuals to pull together to accomplish a goal, the Space Cadet has difficulty pulling with other people in the same direction.
- ✦ Don't place Space Cadets in positions of leadership, because they won't be able to determine the heartbeat of others.
- ✦ Don't write your Space Cadet friend off as a lost cause, though. Search for the key to his or her uniqueness and seek to develop it. Many Space Cadets are extremely brilliant and creative; they have much to offer if you put them in the right spot. They work best when they work alone, so find an area in which they're interested and give them space to dream and create.

The 'Volcano' is an explosive, unpredictable type of person who tends to be unapproachable. How do we treat them? Should we walk around them softly, or test the waters to see what kind of day they are having? It's difficult to relax around them because we don't know when the heat is about to rise. Just as the Space Cadet causes frustration, the Volcano causes tension. Those who have to work with this person can never relax; they never know what might set him or her off.

How should we handle Volcanoes when they blow up? Calmness is the key. Remove them from the crowd and remain calm yourself. They don't need an audience, and you'll be better off to keep your blood pressure down. Once you have them alone, let them vent steam. Allow them to blow as hard and as long as necessary; let them get it all out. Don't try to interrupt because they won't be hearing you. In the attempt to get the story straight, you may need to go back and ask them to repeat some details. Minimize any exaggeration and remove any hearsay that has mingled in so you can deal only with the facts and not the emotion. Then provide a soft, clear answer concerning the situation. Finally, hold these people accountable for the things they say and the people they harm.

Another person who is difficult to deal with is the 'Thumb Sucker.' Thumb Suckers tend to pout, are full of self-pity, and try to get people to cater to their own desires. This pouting is used as leverage to manipulate others. If things are not going their way, they can create a heavy atmosphere that is as oppressive as a rain cloud. They can do this very cleverly. Often they employ the silent treatment to get what they want.

Here's a strategy in dealing with this individual. First, make the Thumb Sucker aware of the fact that moodiness is a *choice*. This is essential. People become moody to manipulate people and gain control. They are very seldom moody by themselves. Teach them that they are responsible for the atmosphere they create, especially if they are in a position of leadership. Everybody in the world has problems; the thumb sucker has no right to add his or her personal petty grievances to the load. As a pastor, I feel responsible for creating an 'up' mood for the many volunteers who work in the church, being encouraging, motivating, and positive. If you choose to lead, then you also need to choose to be even-tempered.

Sometimes it is helpful to expose the Thumb Suckers to people who have *real* problems. Perhaps it will cause them to see themselves in a different light and to have a more grateful heart and positive attitude. I knew a man who exhibited a thumb-sucking attitude, constantly feeling sorry for himself because his work was not appreciated. He was a church custodian and a perfectionist at it. The sanctuary was always spotless and the grounds were beautiful. Unfortunately this orderliness became overly important to him. It upset him when the children and adults walked across his polished floors, dropped papers on the lawn, and spilled water from the sinks. He focused his attention on himself and his clean church and lost sight of the big picture. The people coming to church to learn about Jesus should have been more important. To help him reestablish his priorities, I took him to the cancer ward at the local hospital, pointing out that these people were so sick they probably would never be well enough to come to church, and many of them probably would die without knowing Jesus. My little exercise worked; the following week there was a marked change in his attitude. He began to quit feeling sorry for himself and be grateful that he had a part in sharing Jesus.

It is important to never reward or give attention to moody people. Giving them an opportunity to publicly exhibit their negative attitudes gives them a sense of recognition. The best method of attack is to praise this person's positive ideas and actions and ignore him when he's sucking his thumb.

Thumb Suckers are subject to mood swings; they're negative only part of the time. The 'Wet Blanket,' on the other hand, is constantly down and negative. He is the classic impossibility thinker who sees a problem in every solution. He is afflicted with the dreaded disease of Excusitis—finding problems and making excuses.

The most difficult thing about working with a person like this is that he or she usually takes no responsibility for his or her negative attitude and behavior. It's either 'the other guy's fault' or it's 'Just the way I am,'—a way of blaming God. Again, don't reinforce the Wet Blanket's behavior by providing a platform from which to make excuses. Kindly but firmly point out that you have confidence in this person, but his or her present attitude is hindering progress. He needs to choose whether or not he's going to risk being positive and responsible. If he chooses to change his behavior, he'll have a cheering section. If he chooses to not change, though, your best move will be away from him.

The 'Garbage Collector' is locked even deeper into the mire of negativity than the Thumb Sucker and the Wet Blanket. Garbage Collectors have surrendered the leadership of their lives to negative emotions. Oh, how they love to rehearse and replay the injuries they have suffered at the hands of other people. They nurse their wounds and hold onto their wounded ill spirits. Briefly and concisely, they stink! The fact that there is garbage in life is depressing enough, but to collect it and haul it around town in a dump truck for public viewing is downright sick.

How do you deal with these people? First confront them about the way they try to represent other people. I never allow a person to tell me 'there are many others who feel this way also.' I won't hear them out unless they give me names. That single requirement takes a lot of the 'stink' out of their garbage because it usually boils down to just one or two individuals who have an affinity for garbage too. I challenge their statements by pinning them down when they make generalizations and exaggerations. If they have created a serious enough situation, it may become necessary to destroy their credibility by exposing them to a decision-making group. In my case, this would be the church board or the pastoral staff.

'The User' is the person who manipulates others for his or her own personal gain. Users avoid responsibility for themselves, while demanding time and energy from others to benefit their own situations. They often use guilt to get what they want. They put on a weak front in order to get people to feel sorry for them and help them out.

How do you work with Users? First, set predetermined limits on how far you will go to help them. Otherwise, they will push your guilt button and you will weaken. Remember that these people will not only take you the second and third mile, they'll take you to the cleaners if you allow them. Require responsibility from the user. Even if you feel disposed to help him, make sure he is responsible for some part of the job. Otherwise, you will wind up carrying the load while he goes on his merry way—more than likely looking for another gullible soul.

Last, don't feel obligated to users, and don't feel guilty for not feeling obligated. Most of the time a simple, firm no is the best medicine.

Perhaps you have recognized someone you know in each of these caricatures. Or maybe you're dealing with a person so difficult, he is in a category all by himself. Take heart; there are certain general rules which you can put into practice that will enable you to work more effectively with problem people.

1. Love them unconditionally.
2. Ask God for wisdom in working with them.
3. Stay emotionally healthy yourself.
4. Do not elevate people to positions of leadership in order to rescue them.
5. Be honest with God, yourself, and them.

THE PROCESS OF RELATIONSHIPS

It's important to understand the process of relationships; specifically the stages of a relational breakdown. Let's take a look at them one by one.

- *The honeymoon stage* is the one we begin with. We usually have an unrealistic view of the relationship at this point. Obviously, what attracts people to each other, whether it be a business relationship, a friendship, or a romance, are their positive qualities. The excitement of finding someone who meets some need in our lives tends to temporarily blind us to their negative traits.

- *Specific irritation* is the stage where we begin to open our eyes and see things we don't like. Here we develop a memory bank of these negative traits. But then we also see the relationship in a more realistic light. If you look back at the early weeks of your marriage or of a new job, you will probably recall the first incident that shook you into reality—the time you realized the honeymoon was over.
- *General discomfort* should cause us to deal with the specific irritations that have piled up in our memory banks. We become more open, honest, and transparent about telling someone why they're making us uncomfortable.
- *Try harder* is a stage of development where we raise our energy level to make a success of the relationship. Unfortunately, sometimes it's very hard to separate the problem from the person.
- *Exhaustion* often becomes a serious problem in a relationship because we are too tired to try any longer. We tend to throw up our hands and quit at this crucial point.
- *Separation* is the final stage. By this time the relationship has usually been terminated with little hope of restoration. Usually, by the time this happens we are too numb to even care or hurt.

This series of stages does not have to be completed; the cycle can be broken. Most often, if the process is reversed, it happens during the stage of general discomfort. At that point it is still possible to make the decision to accept what you don't like about a person and to love that person unconditionally. As you try harder to overlook a person's faults, it becomes easier to again focus your attention on his or her positive traits.

PROBLEMS IN RELATIONSHIPS

In most relationships it is inevitable that at some point a confrontation will take place. At this crisis point it's very important to approach the offending party prepared with the right attitude. If a confrontation is handled correctly, it can actually strengthen the relationship. If not, it can bring an abrupt, unhappy end to the relationship. In order for this not to happen, follow these six guidelines:

1. *Bring in principal persons involved in the conflict.* Experience has taught me that unless all persons involved come together, the whole story will never be pieced together accurately.

2. *Line up the facts.* Relying on hearsay evidence or 'general impressions' will only invite emotion-laden rebuttals and, possibly, resentful counterattacks.

3. *Never reprimand while angry.* Make sure you are in control of your emotions. The angrier you are, the less objective you'll be—and the less effective your reprimand. It's prudent to delay a confrontation until you've coolly asked yourself two questions: Could I have contributed to the problem? Were there mitigating circumstances I'm overlooking?

4. *Be precise about the offense.* Let the person know exactly what the charge is. Don't try to soften the blow by hemming and hawing or refusing to cough up the details.

5. *Get the other person's side of the story.* Always give the offender the chance to explain what happened and why they behaved as they did. There may be extenuating circumstances. (Sometimes, you may even be part of them.)

6. *Be sure you keep comprehensive records.* The better your documentation—how the mistake came about, when it happened, who was involved, etc.—the more even-tempered and productive the reprimanding session will be.

7. *Don't harbor a grudge.* Once you've handed out the

reprimand and administered any sanctions, don't carry around hostilities. Let that person know you consider the problem a closed book and act accordingly.

Do you remember the episode of Amos and Andy in which Andy kept slapping Amos on the chest, until one day Amos decided he had endured enough? He decided to fix Andy once and for all. Showing Kingfish some explosives tied to his chest underneath his jacket, he proudly said, 'the next time Andy slaps me on the chest, he's going to blow his hand off.' Poor Amos hadn't thought through the consequences of his retaliation. It never pays to hold a grudge to the point of explosion; it will do more damage to you than to the offending party.

Our ultimate goal in dealing with problems should be to present the truth in such a way as to build the relationship, not destroy it. Unfortunately, this cannot always be accomplished. If a relationship cannot stand an honest face-to-face encounter, then it probably is not a healthy relationship. In some cases, ending the relationship is the only solution, but this should be the last choice.

PUT IT TO WORK

PEOPLE PRINCIPLES

- ✦ Show me a person who sees himself negatively and I will show you a person who sees others in a negative way.
- ✦ Most of the time our relational problems stem from the fact that we ourselves have problems or issues that haven't been resolved. It is not possible to treat another person's hurt until we have first discovered the cure and accepted the treatment ourselves.
- ✦ When you realize that people treat you according to how they

see themselves rather than how you really are, you are less likely to take personally their behavior toward you.

- ✦ The key to successful relationships really gets down to responsibility: I am responsible for how I treat others. I may not be responsible for how they treat me; however, I am responsible for my reaction to those who are difficult. I can't choose how you'll treat me but I can choose how I will respond to you.

PUTTING THE PRINCIPLES TO WORK:

I will apply the principles from this chapter to my relationships with people in the following ways:

1.

2.

3.

FURTHER STUDY:

The Fine Art of Getting Along With Others, Dale E. Galloway
Untwisting Twisted Relationships, William Backus

22

HOW TO BE A PERSON WHO CAN HANDLE CRITICISM

OUR ABILITY to take criticism can make us or break us. No one is indifferent to criticism; it causes us to respond either positively or negatively. Just yesterday I spoke to a woman whose husband has been traumatized by destructive criticism. He has become bitter; his personality and outlook on life have turned negative.

Learning how to handle criticism was one of the most difficult lessons I ever had. I grew up in a church where the surest sign of success was a unanimous pastoral vote. At annual conference the hottest topic of discussion was the vote at the various churches. Heaven help the pastor who received negative votes! It seemed that little importance was placed on whether or not the church was experiencing growth and maturity or people were growing in their relationships with Christ. If the pastor received a unanimous vote, that was the pinnacle of his career and he was highly esteemed. It also meant that the church was spiritually in tune.

Coming from that background, I went to my first pastorate in Hillham, Indiana. At the end of the first year we had thirty-three members; the vote was thirty-one 'yes,' one 'no,' and one 'abstain.' That put me in a panic. I immediately called my father and asked if he thought I should resign the church. He couldn't imagine why I was so upset and laughed hysterically. Little did I realize that would be the best vote I'd ever receive in my career as a pastor! Knowing there was just one person, possibly two, who did not like what I was doing was very difficult for me to handle. Since then I've learned that if you want to do great things for God, there will always be someone who doesn't want to participate.

TAKING A POSITIVE APPROACH

I heard a story about a critical, negative barber who never had a pleasant thing to say. A salesman came in for a haircut and mentioned that he was about to make a trip to Rome, Italy. 'What airline are you taking and at what hotel will you be staying?' asked the barber.

When the salesman told him, the barber criticized the airline for being undependable and the hotel for having horrible service. 'You'd be better off to stay home,' he advised.

'But I expect to close a big deal. Then I'm going to see the Pope,' said the salesman.

'You'll be disappointed trying to do business in Italy,' said the barber, 'and don't count on seeing the Pope. He only grants audiences to very important people.'

Two months later the salesman returned to the barber shop. 'And how was your trip?' asked the barber.

'Wonderful!' replied the salesman. 'The flight was perfect, the service at the hotel was excellent; I made a big sale, and I got to see the Pope.'

'You got to see the Pope? What happened?'

The salesman replied, 'I bent down and kissed his ring.'

'No kidding! What did he say?'

'Well, he placed his hand on my head and then he said to me, "My son, where did you ever get such a lousy haircut?"'

There's a saying that 'what goes around comes around.' This is especially true in the area of attitudes. If you are a critical, negative person, life will treat you badly. On the other hand, if you have a positive, joyous outlook, the joy you share will be returned to you.

There are two kinds of people who are highly subject to criticism. The first group are the leaders. Aristotle said it well, 'Criticism is something you can avoid easily by saying nothing, doing nothing, and being nothing.' Yes, one of the costs of leadership is criticism. If you're willing to stand apart from the crowd, you're putting yourself in a vulnerable position, so count on some degree of criticism.

Once after speaking about negative attitudes at a conference, I received a note that I have kept: 'Realize that the guys who criticize will minimize the guys whose enterprise rise above the guys who criticize and minimize.' That's what a leader does—he rises above. When you are willing to stick your neck out, someone will want to chop it off.

Don't let that threat keep you from being all you can be. Rise above it, as did the late Adolph Rupp, the former University of Kentucky basketball coach. Throughout Rupp's coaching career he experienced an uphill struggle against those who were critical of his methods. There were many who took issue with Rupp—he was difficult and sanctimonious—but it is difficult to fault the trapper with the skins on the wall. By the end of his career he had 874 victories and was the winningest coach in college basketball history.

Besides leaders the other group of individuals who are prone to criticism are the 'leapers,' people who leap into public eye because they are change agents. They bring unwelcome and uncomfortable change into people's lives even though it usually is for their benefit. Many years ago the medical community strongly opposed the idea of vaccinating children against disease because it was new and unknown. People who make discoveries and create inventions find it takes time for people to accept their ideas because people fear change.

In the closing years of John Wesley's life he became a friend of William Wilberforce. Wilberforce was a great champion of freedom for slaves before the Civil War. He was subjected to a vicious campaign by slave traders and others whose powerful commercial interests were threatened. Rumors were spread that he was a wife-beater. His character, morals, and motives were repeatedly smeared during some twenty years of pitched battles.

From his deathbed, John Wesley wrote to Wilberforce, 'Unless God has raised you up for this very thing, you will be worn out by the opposition of men and devils; but if God be for you, who can be against you? Are all of them together stronger than God? Be not weary in well-doing.' William Wilberforce never forgot those words of John Wesley. They kept him going even when all the forces of hell were arrayed against him.

The question for leaders and leapers is not 'Will I be confronted with criticism?' but 'How can I handle and learn from criticism and confrontation?' It is possible to learn how to take criticism successfully, and the following ten suggestions can help you help yourself.

TEN TIPS FOR TAKING CRITICISM

1. *Understand the difference between constructive and destructive criticism.* You need to learn how to interpret criticism. Is it positive criticism to build you up or negative to tear you down? Someone once said that constructive criticism is when I criticize you; destructive criticism is when you criticize me.

To determine the motive behind the confrontation, ask yourself some questions. First, in what spirit is it given? Look beyond the words and determine the motives. Is the critic projecting a gentle attitude or a judgmental attitude? If your critic's attitude is kind, you can rest assured that the criticism is meant to be constructive.

Second, when is the criticism given? Times of confrontation must be shared privately, not within public view or hearing. If a person criticizes someone publicly, you can be sure his or her intentions are not the best. They are out to destroy and not to build.

Third, why is the criticism given? This question deals with the attitude of the critic. Is it for personal benefit and growth, or is it given from personal hurt? Sometimes the person who has experienced difficulties and problems will deal with others in a negative, critical way.

2. *Don't take yourself too seriously.* If you can develop the ability to laugh at yourself, you will be much more relaxed when given or giving criticism. Face it, we all do some stupid and silly things. Blessed is he who can enjoy his blunders. We are approved by God; we don't have to win the approval of others and look good in their eyes. We are not perfect people. Too many of us take ourselves too seriously and God not seriously enough.

'Life at St. Bashan's' cartoon strip portrayed a pastor who was forced to learn how to handle criticism. A parishioner approaches the pastor after the service and says, 'Reverend, I want you to know that wasn't one of your better sermons.'

Openly the pastor responds with, 'And Bill, I want you to know I'm grateful for constructive criticism.' In the next frame the pastor walks into the study, locks the door, and then falls to his knees with a cry, 'Augggghhh!'

We've done that, haven't we? Outwardly we appear to appreciate the words, but in private we fall apart emotionally, becoming angry, vindictive, or deeply hurt.

3. *Look beyond the criticism and see the critic.* When someone comes to me with news about another person, I am more interested in the person who said it than what was said. In fact, that's one of my first questions: *Who* said it? *Who* told you that? When I find out who the perpetrator is, I know whether or not to listen. I will either straighten up and take it seriously or I will think to myself, 'There they go again.'

Keep in mind certain considerations regarding your critic: First, is it someone whose character you respect? Adverse criticism from a wise man is more to be desired than the enthusiastic approval of a fool. Second, is this person frequently critical? Is criticism a pattern? If so, don't place too much value in what they say. Possibly it's a way to get attention. Criticism from a positive person, on the other hand, probably deserves your attention.

There is a story about a twelve-year-old boy who in all of his twelve years had never spoken. After being served oatmeal for breakfast several times in a row a miracle happened! To everyone's shock, he yelled, 'Yuck, I hate oatmeal.'

His mother was overwhelmed. She ran across the room and threw her arms around his neck. 'For twelve long years your father and I were convinced you couldn't talk!' she cried. 'Why haven't you ever spoken to us?'

Bluntly the boy explained, 'Up till now, everything's been OK.' I'm not sure if she kept serving him oatmeal to keep him complaining, but this boy knew how to be heard.

Finally, ask yourself this question: Does the critic sincerely want to help me? Is he or she on your team, believing the best in you, desiring to help? Remember that people who are busy rowing seldom have time to rock the boat.

4. *Watch your own attitude toward the critic.* A negative attitude toward criticism can be more destructive than the criticism itself.

Remember, a chip on the shoulder indicates wood higher up! The late Herman Hickman, great football coach at Tennessee, Army, and Yale, said, 'When you are being run out of town, get to the head of the line and look as though you are leading the parade.

1 Peter 2:21–23 provides the right attitude toward criticism:

> *For you have been called for this purpose, since Christ also suffered for you, leaving you an example for you to follow in His steps, who committed no sin, nor was any deceit found in His mouth; and while being reviled, He did not revile in return; while suffering, He uttered no threats, but kept entrusting Himself to Him who judges righteously.*

Could it be that a poor attitude reveals the fact that we have trusted in ourselves, rather than in God who knows the entire situation? If we are trusting Him and are obedient, we can expect some criticism. He often calls us to take an unpopular stand. He has also called us to love those who are critical of us.

5. *Realize that good people get criticized.* Jesus, whose motives were pure and character was spotless, was called a glutton (Matt. 11: 19); a winebibber (Luke 7:34); a Samaritan (John 8:48); and a friend of sinners (Matt. 11:19 and Mark 2:16). If our lives are Christlike we can expect criticism. In fact, there are times when we should see criticism from the world as verification that our lives have been changed. A person whose mind is polluted and whose vision is not clear cannot understand or interpret behavior based on obedience to God. So if you're living on a higher plane than the world, expect some criticism.

6. *Keep physically and spiritually in shape.* Physical exhaustion has a tremendous effect on the way we act and react; it distorts the way we see and handle life. Recently Margaret and I were

returning home from a long trip, and after being up many hours and hassling with several airline connections, we were both physically wiped out. Realizing that any attempts to communicate could put us over the edge, Margaret proposed that we each bury our face in a book. It worked. By the time the plane landed in San Diego, we were not exactly alert but we were still friends. It's a simple fact of life: These minds and bodies need rest.

Elijah succumbed to opposition when he was in a state of weariness. Jezebel was a firecracker, and her opposition sapped the preacher's strength. Elijah complained, 'It is enough, now, O Lord, take away my life; for I am no better than my fathers' (1 Kings 19:4). Elijah was completely shaken. Watch weariness because Satan will take advantage. When we become overly tired, we become overly critical, and at the same time we are less able to handle criticism from others.

7. *Don't just see the critic; see if there's a crowd.* The following story illustrates this point.

Mrs. Jones had invited a great and well-known violinist to entertain at her afternoon tea. When it was all over, everyone crowded around the musician.

'I've got to be honest with you,' said one of the guests, 'I think your performance was absolutely terrible.'

Hearing his criticism, the hostess interposed: 'Don't pay any attention to him. He doesn't know what he's talking about. He only repeats what he hears everyone else say.'

I'm suggesting that you expand your vision; go beyond the critic and see if he has a cheering section. Consider the possibility that you are hearing the same criticism from several people. If this is the case, and the critics are reliable, you need to realize that you have a challenge to work on. If, on the other hand, you're dealing with a pocket group of negative people, your challenge is to not be affected by them.

George Bernard Shaw, the Irish playwright, certainly had his critics, but he knew how to handle them. After one opening, a critic voiced his displeasure. He said, 'It's rotten! It's rotten!' To which Shaw replied, 'I agree with you perfectly, but what are we two against so many!'

8. *Wait for time to prove them wrong.* Time is your best ally; it allows you to prove yourself right. Often, as events unfold, the cause for criticism is eliminated and you will be vindicated. You may be thinking, 'Easy for you to say, Maxwell, you're not where I am.' But I've been there many times. If you know your action or decision was right, hang in there. Time will prove you out.

Abraham Lincoln, the most loved president of the United States, was also the most criticized president. Probably no politician in history had worse things said about him. Here's how the *Chicago Times* in 1865 evaluated Lincoln's Gettysburg Address the day after he delivered it: 'The cheek of every American must tingle with shame as he reads the silly, flat, and dish-watery utterances of a man who has been pointed out to intelligent foreigners as President of the United States.' Time, of course, has proved this scathing criticism wrong.

9. *Surround yourself with positive people.* When you have optional time, spend it with people who will build you up. Enough quality time with positive people will minimize the effect of negative criticism. It will also discourage you from being critical. When a hawk is attacked by crows, he does not counterattack. Instead, he soars higher and higher in ever widening circles until the pests leave him alone. Circle above your adversaries rather than battle with them. If your positive attitude has any effect on negative people, it will be because of your example, not your defensiveness. So rise above them. It really is hard to soar like an eagle if you identify with turkeys!

10. *Concentrate on your mission—change your mistakes.* Most

people do exactly the opposite—they change their mission and concentrate on their mistakes. If you run from your task each time you make a mistake, you will never accomplish anything. You will always be in a state of frustration and defeat. The only real mistakes in life are the mistakes from which we learn nothing. So instead of dwelling on them, count on making them, learning from them, and moving on to finish the job. There's an Arabian proverb that says if you stop every time a dog barks, your road will never end. Don't let your mistakes become roadblocks; make them building blocks.

In order to build strong relationships you need to know how to take criticism gracefully, but there are also times when you will have to be the critic. It is possible to confront without ruining a relationship, but use caution, because careless confrontation can be devastating. Before you confront, check yourself in the following areas.

TEN TIPS FOR GIVING CRITICISM

1. *Check your motive.* The goal of confrontation should be to help, not to humiliate. Three key questions will help expose your true motives. First, ask yourself, *Would I criticize this if it were not a personal matter?* Sometimes we react differently when we are emotionally or personally involved. Here's what I mean:

Sluggo:	'That new kid in school is a big fat-head!'
Nancy:	'You shouldn't call people names like that. I never call people names.'
Sluggo:	'Well, I just got mad when he said you were silly looking.'
Nancy:	'What else did that big fat-head say?'

Second, ask yourself, *Will criticism make me look better?* Cutting someone down to boost yourself up is the lowest form of ego gratification. It's the sign of a very insecure person. Remember that it isn't necessary to blow out another person's light to let your own shine.

Third, ask yourself, *Does this criticism bring pain or pleasure to me?* When it is painful for you to criticize others, you're probably safe in doing it. If you get the slightest bit of pleasure out of doing it, you should hold your tongue.

2. *Make sure the issue is worthy of criticism.* To whom does it really matter? Sometimes our pride causes us to engage in skirmishes that need never happen. Continual, petty criticism is the mark of a small mind; you have to be little to belittle. The secret to not letting yourself be distracted and needled by insignificant issues is to keep your head up and your eyes on the goal.

3. *Be specific.* When you confront you must be tactfully explicit. Say exactly what you mean and provide examples to back yourself up.

I once had a staff person who had great difficulty confronting; he hated to make people face up to areas in which they needed to change. On one particular occasion I coached him. He rehearsed with me everything he was going to say to the individuals in question. After the confrontation I asked him how it went. He assured me everything went smoothly and there were no problems; in fact, he said the people did not even question him. At that moment I knew something had gone wrong. Total acquiescence is not a normal reaction to honest confrontation. Two days later the truth came out. One of the individuals said to me, 'The other day we spent thirty minutes with Pastor So-and-so, but we have no idea what he was trying to tell us.' The pastor had spent half an hour dancing around the issue without ever addressing it. He would have been better off to have left it alone.

If you can't be specific, don't confront. People can usually tell when you're skirting an issue and will not respect you for it.

4. *Don't undermine the person's self-confidence.* Try to find at least

one area in which you can praise the person before you expose the problem. Stay away from all-inclusive statements like, 'You always . . .' or 'You never . . .' Assure them that you have confidence in them and their ability to handle the situation correctly.

5. *Don't compare one person with another.* Deal with people on an individual basis. Comparisons always cause resentment and resentment causes hostility. There's no need to create a bigger problem than the one you already have, so why arouse heated emotions? If you stick to the facts, you'll be less likely to put the person on the defensive.

6. *Be creative or don't confront.* Will Rogers said, 'There is nothing as easy as denouncing. It doesn't take much to see something is wrong, but it does take some eyesight to see what will put it right again.'

Look beyond the problem and see if you can help find some solutions. For most of us it's much easier to be critical than to be creative. But unless you're willing to help to some degree in turning the situation around, you're not ready to comment on the problem.

7. *Attack the problem not the person.* Deal with the issue at hand. When a confrontation becomes a personal attack, you destroy your own credibility and find yourself in a no-win situation. The expected outcome of a confrontation should be that the offender leave with a clear understanding of the problem and the hope that he can turn it around.

8. *Confront when the time is right.* The right time is just as soon as you know something is wrong. When you've completed your homework then you're prepared. Sometimes people tell me about their relationship problems and ask me for advice. The scenario is always the same and so is my advice: You cannot escape the need to talk to the person. When you wait too long you lose the opportune moment and the issue becomes history.

When you confront the person in a timely fashion you are better able to keep the facts straight and use the incident as an opportunity to help the person grow.

9. *Look at yourself before looking at others.* Instead of putting others in their place, put yourself in their place. Have you successfully done what you're accusing the other guy of failing to do? Look at things from his point of view. You may see that you're the one who needs to make changes.

10. *End confrontation with encouragement.* Always give confrontation the 'sandwich treatment.' Sandwich the criticism between praise at the beginning and encouragement at the end. To leave a discouraged person without hope is cruel and vindictive. Goethe, the German poet said, 'Correction does much, but encouragement does more. Encouragement after censure is as the sun after a shower.'

In my effort to simplify things as much as possible, I have come up with one-word descriptions of the various ways people will respond to confrontation:

BYE. The 'bye' people never profit from confrontation; they don't hang around long enough. Their egos are too fragile.

SPY. Spies become suspicious of everyone. They begin an investigation to find out who in the organization is out to get them. Often they will avoid risking a failure again.

FRY. Some people will simply get mad and either fly off at the handle or do a slow burn.

LIE. The liar has an excuse for every mistake. Therefore he never faces up to the reality of his situation.

CRY. Cry babies are overly sensitive and become hurt by confrontation. Unlike the 'bye' people, criers hang around in hopes that people will see how mistreated they are and sympathize with them. They have a martyr complex.

SIGH. These people have a 'That's-too-bad,-but-there's-nothing-I-can-do-about-it' attitude. They don't accept any responsibility for making right the wrong.

FLY. This category of people takes criticism and flies with it. They learn from it and become better because of it.

Which category has fit you in the past? Are there changes you need to make before you can take criticism and fly with it? I challenge you to start today.

PUT IT TO WORK

PEOPLE PRINCIPLES

- ✦ If you're willing to stand apart from the crowd, you're putting yourself in a vulnerable position. Count on some degree of criticism.
- ✦ When you are willing to stick your neck out, someone will want to chop it off. Don't let that threat keep you from being all you can be. Rise above it.
- ✦ The question is not 'Will I be confronted with criticism?' but 'How can I handle and learn from criticism and confrontation?'
- ✦ If you develop the ability to laugh at yourself, you will be much more relaxed when given or giving criticism.
- ✦ A negative attitude toward criticism can be more destructive than the criticism itself. A chip on the shoulder indicates wood higher up.

✦ In order to build strong relationships we need to know how to take criticism gracefully, but there are also times when we will have to be the critic. It is possible to confront without ruining a relationship.

PUTTING THE PRINCIPLES TO WORK:

I will apply the principles from this chapter to my relationships with people in the following ways:

1.

2.

3.

FURTHER STUDY:

Your Attitude: Key to Success, John C. Maxwell
Helping Those Who Don't Want Help, Marshall Shelley

23

BEING A PERSON PEOPLE TRUST

TRUST IS crucial in any type of relationship, whether it be within a family, a business, a church congregation, or in a friendship. When this important foundation exists, strong, positive relationships are built and fed by encouragement and consistency. People who receive a high level of trust have developed their character and have earned the right to be trusted.

Twenty-five years ago I read a book by W. Curry Mavis, *Advancing the Smaller Church*, in which he said something that I still buy today. He said the greatest problem in most local churches is low morale. If you can get the people's spirits lifted, then things can happen. High morale is the result of the leader's confidence and trust in the people he leads. Morale is conveyed through a sense of common purpose and it produces a state of psychological and emotional well-being based on such factors as principle, conduct, confidence, and teaching.

Trust depends very little upon a person's name, his station in life, how much money he has in the bank, or his position. The key to consistent and dependable trust lies in the *character* of the person who leads. Whether we lead in our homes, businesses, or churches we are responsible for being trustworthy. We have to prove by example that we are as good as our word. There is absolutely no other way to establish a reputation for being trustworthy except to be trustable.

Charlie Brown has an incredible trust in human nature. Every once in a while cartoonist Charles Schultz shows us Lucy holding a football for Charlie Brown to kick. With an assuring smile on her face, Lucy insists that she can be trusted; she vows that she will not cause him the pain and humiliation of falling on his backside by removing the ball just before he kicks. Charlie Brown always takes a running charge at the ball and Lucy always pulls back the football, causing him to kick at the air and hit the ground. But he continues to make the attempt, confident that one day Lucy will demonstrate trustworthiness.

Most of us are not as naive as Charlie Brown. Before we are willing to put our trust in someone, we want to see that they are reliable. We're not willing to give too many second chances where lack of trust is a factor.

You can help develop trust in people by applying the key principles which follow.

DEMONSTRATE WHAT YOU WANT TO INSTILL

People need to see what they ought to be. A cartoon punch line read, 'No matter what you teach the child, he insists on behaving like his parents.' That's certainly a humbling truth for all parents.

Dennis the Menace often reinforces this truth. On one occasion, while holding the remnants of a tricycle which has been smashed to smithereens, Dennis the Menace asks his dad, 'What are some of those words you say when you hit a bad golf shot?' He had learned that there was a certain way to behave when you're frustrated.

When I disciple others it is important to me to *be* what I teach or ask others to do. This is a crucial truth: We teach what we *know*, but we reproduce what we *are*. To teach others to do right is wonderful. To do right is even more wonderful! It may be a harder way to teach, but it's a much easier way to learn.

Dr. James Dobson, psychologist and author, tells us that kids begin to buy in to your spiritual guidance and direction in the area of values at about five years of age! During the early years of your child's life you are the primary role model, the most significant person in his or her life. If what you say is different from what you do, your child will choose to imitate what you do every time. In the words of Zig Ziglar, 'Your children pay more attention to what you do than what you say.' So the most valuable gift you can give your little ones is the example of a clear, consistent, disciplined approach to faith in God. It is most important that they see this beginning in their earliest years. What they learn and establish in their lives during these years can go a long way in getting them through the tumult of adolescence.

ENCOURAGEMENT CAUSES GROWTH

Encouragement has the effect of a gentle rain; it causes steady growth. The secret of Andrew Carnegie's genius for developing others was his ability to encourage good qualities, while holding faultfinding to a minimum. Confidence withers under faultfinding, as the following story about a singer illustrates.

She made her debut at the age of five in a church cantata. The choir director told her parents that someday she would be a great singer. The entire congregation had fallen in love with the little girl in pigtails—her voice, her poise, her instinctive stage presence.

She continued to sing and after college went to study music in Chicago. One of her instructors was a man named Fritz. Though he was old enough to be her father she fell in love with him and they were married. Wherever she sang Fritz would be there. Afterward he would point out all of her mistakes, constantly urging her toward perfection. In their apartment he set alarm clocks telling her it was time for practice. His trained ear caught the slightest imperfection.

Gradually her singing got worse instead of better. Musical directors stopped hiring her. Under the constant barrage of criticism, her spirit was breaking, she was losing her assurance, her naturalness.

While her career was plummeting, the husband died. Even after he was gone, she sang little, haunted by his familiar voice pointing out her errors. A couple of years later she happened to meet a jolly, carefree salesman named Roger. He knew little about music, but liked her voice and encouraged her to take up singing again. In a few months they were married.

Friends noticed that she seemed to be regaining her self-assurance, and that the strident quality had left her voice. It was pure and joyous, as it had been when she was a child. Now musical directors eagerly sought her out.

The woman's first husband, though well-intentioned, had broken both her spirit and her voice by constant faultfinding. The second man, by contrast, gave her the encouragement she needed by stressing only the good in her.

I have yet to find the person, whatever his or her station in life, who did not perform better under a spirit of approval than under criticism. There are enough critics in the world; what we need are more cheerleaders!

You can learn to be an encourager by practicing the following procedures.

1. *Appreciate people for who they are.* This truth is dramatically played out in the lives of children. They have a way of mirroring what they hear about themselves. Recently I watched a talk show

which was devoted to the subject of teenage suicide. More and more teenagers are attempting suicide as an escape from the demands of life. They feel they can never measure up to the standards of performance expected by parents and others. They feel appreciated only when they've done well, not because they're unique and priceless individuals. As a result, many kids see life as a no-win situation.

2. *Anticipate they will do their best.* When working with people I always try to look at them not as they are, but as what they can be. By anticipating that the vision will become real, it's easy for me to encourage them as they stretch. Raise your anticipation level and you raise their achievement level.

3. *Admire their accomplishments.* Thank them and praise them for what they have done. Remember, man does not live by bread alone; sometimes he needs a little buttering up. Remember the effect of praise on the singer.

4. *Accept your personal responsibility.* If you oversee people you are responsible to take the heat at times. I developed a tremendous admiration for Coach Bear Bryant when I heard him say:

> *I'm just a plowhand from Arkansas, but I have learned how to hold a team together—how to lift some men up, how to calm down others, until finally they've got one heartbeat together, a team. There's just three things I'd ever say: If anything goes bad, I did it. If anything goes semi-good, then we did it. If anything goes real good, then you did it. That's all it takes to get people to win football games for you.*

Again, let me emphasize the importance of character in developing trust. Bishop Abel Muzore tells of a critical period in his life when he had been asked by his people to lead the African National Council. He knew that all previous leaders in Rhodesia who had been critical of unjust government policies toward Black Rhodesians had been either deported from the country, put in a restricted camp, or killed.

He struggled with his decision and prayed as he had never prayed before. He did not want to be killed, or deported, or placed in a restricted camp, yet his people were calling him to lead them. During the time he was struggling with his decision, a friend handed him this poem:

People are unreasonable, illogical, and self-centered—love them anyway!
If you do good, people will accuse you of selfish ulterior motives—do good anyway!
If you are successful you will win false friends and true enemies—succeed anyway!
The good you do today will be forgotten tomorrow—do good anyway!
Honesty and frankness make you vulnerable—be honest and frank anyway!
The biggest people with the biggest ideas can be shot down by the smallest people with the smallest minds—think big anyway!
People favor underdogs but follow only top dogs—fight for some underdog anyway!
What you spend years building may be destroyed overnight—build anyway!
Give the world the best you've got and you'll get kicked in the teeth—give the world the best you've got anyway!

BELIEVE THE BEST

Develop a person's expectation level by believing the best in him or her. When you look up to people they begin to look up to their dreams. A few weeks ago I spoke to some salespeople about their expectation level of those they oversee. I explained that how we view a person is reflected by how we treat a person. If we have a high expectation level and believe in people, we will encourage them. Again, it is the principle of seeing people not as they are but as they can be.

The business manager at our church placed his house on the market. One Saturday he and his wife posted signs all over the neighborhood announcing an open house. As they prepared for the day, Ken told his wife Mary Lynn, 'We're going to have all kinds of people come in and out of the house today, most with absolutely no resources or intention of buying. But we're going to treat them all the same—as if they were our guests.'

Sure enough they had dozens of people come through just to look. One young couple in their early twenties asked to see the house. They announced that they were newly married, she had no job, and he was just starting a new job. After the tour they extended their thanks and left. Ken and Mary Lynn announced to each other, 'Well, we'll never see them again.' But in just thirty minutes they saw a very expensive car drive up and park in front of the house. The same young couple returned—this time with mom and dad. The father shook Ken's hand and said, 'The kids sure liked your home. This will be a cash sale; how short can we make the escrow?'

I'm certain that Ken and Mary Lynn's high level of anticipation filtered through to each person who crossed the threshold of their home. They had no idea what benefits that positive attitude would bring.

Many people, unfortunately, have a low personal expectation level. We need to know how to develop a dream for others and then share it with them. Begin by seeing it for them. We can all learn a lesson from the 'four-eyed fish.' These odd-looking creatures are native to the equatorial waters of the western Atlantic region. The technical name of this genus of fish is anableps, meaning 'those that look upward,' because of their unusual eye structure. Unique among vertebrates, the anableps have two-tiered eyes, with the upper and lower halves of each eyeball operating independently and having separate cornea and irises. The upper eyes protrude above the surface of the water and enable the anableps to search for food and to spot enemies in the air. The lower eyes remain focused in the water, functioning in the usual fishlike fashion. Thus, in rather ordinary ways these four-eyed fish navigate with ease in the waters of their environment. But, in addition, the anableps enjoy a remarkable capacity to sustain life by participating in the 'higher' world above their primary environment. They see in both worlds.

If we can develop four eyes, two for seeing what is and two for seeing what might be, we can help others dream. Everyone needs to be exposed to a vision. Unfortunately, not everyone will go for it. Pursue it with those who are ready to stretch.

HELP OTHERS BE SUCCESSFUL

Develop confidence in others by helping them experience success. We've all heard the slogan, 'It doesn't matter whether you win or lose'—until you lose! Winning increases our self-image, our outlook on life, and lifts our expectation level. It gives us the confidence that we can succeed again. How can you help make another person successful? It's fairly simple. Make sure their gifts and abilities match their tasks. Otherwise you set them up for sure failure. Discern their gifts and desires and match them to the opportunities available. When you have the ability to suit them to a job at which they can succeed, an incredible bond of trust and respect develops.

Everyone enjoys the glory of the spotlight and the opportunity to shine. But it's a sign of a mature person who will afford another that prized position of recognition. For example, I have shared my faith in Christ effectively for many years but I also train others to develop their witnessing skills. If I sense a prospect is extremely open and receptive to making a commitment to Christ, I allow the trainee the opportunity of leading the person to Christ. Likewise, if the trainee is struggling, I will jump in to assist. Success for the leader is a single victory. However, when the protege experiences success, it becomes a double win.

EQUIP PEOPLE FOR FUTURE GROWTH

'Give a man a fish and he eats for a day. Teach a man to fish and he eats for a lifetime.' In other words, if you want to help him, don't give him a fish, give him a fishing rod. This principle applies to personal growth. You and I can't grow another person, but we can give him the equipment to develop himself. We do this by first showing him that the growth is beneficial; we whet his appetite for growth. Then we expose him to people like himself who have moved out and become successful; we prove that it can be done. And finally, we provide an opportunity for him to use his new equipment. And we stand back and encourage.

In the late 1800s a salesman from the East arrived at a frontier town somewhere on the Great Plains. As he was talking with the owner of the general store, a rancher came in. The owner excused himself to take care of the customer. The salesman couldn't help overhearing the conversation. It seems the rancher wanted credit for the things he needed.

'Are you doing any fencing this spring, Josh?' asked the storekeeper.

'Sure am, Will,' said the rancher.

'Fencing in or fencing out?'

'Fencing in. Taking in another 360 acres across the creek.'

'Good to hear it, Josh. You got the credit. Just tell Harry out back what you need.'

The salesman couldn't make much sense of this. 'I've seen all kinds of credit systems,' he said, 'but never one like that. How does it work?'

'Well,' said the storekeeper, 'it's like this. If a man's fencing out, that means he's running scared with what he's got. But if he's fencing in, he's growing and getting bigger. He's got hope. I always give credit to a man who's fencing in!'

Give people the encouragement they need to fence in. Provide the encouragement and the know-how for them to expand their horizons. The rewards will not only come back to them, they will come back to you. By believing in people and helping them trust in themselves, you have established a relationship in which everyone involved is a winner.

PUT IT TO WORK

PEOPLE PRINCIPLES

- People who receive a high level of trust have developed their character and have earned the right to be trusted. When this important foundation exists, strong, positive relationships are built and are fed by encouragement and consistency.
- Trust depends very little on a person's name, his station in life, how much money he has in the bank, or his position. The key to consistent and dependable trust lies in the character of the person who leads.
- Keys to being a trustable person:
  Demonstrate what you want to instill.
  Be an encourager.

Believe the best in others.
Help others experience success.
Equip people for future growth.

PUTTING THE PRINCIPLES TO WORK:

I will apply the principles from this chapter to my relationships with people in the following ways:

1.

2.

3.

FURTHER STUDY:

How to Have a Better Relationship with Anybody, James Hitt
How to Get Along with People in the Church, A. Donald Bell

24

DEVELOPING A WINNING TEAM

ONE NIGHT after working quite late, I grabbed a copy of *Sports Illustrated*, hoping its pages would lull me to sleep. It had the opposite effect, though. On the back cover of this issue was an advertisement that caught my eye and got my mental juices flowing. It featured a picture of John Wooden, the coach who led the U.C.L.A. Bruins for many years.

The caption said: 'The guy who puts the ball through the hoop has ten hands.' They called John Wooden the wizard of Westwood. In a span of twelve seasons he brought ten national basketball championships to U.C.L.A. Two back-to-back championships are almost unheard of in the competitive sports world, but he led the Bruins to seven titles in a row! It took a consistently high level of superior play; it took good coaching and hard practice. But the key to the Bruin's success was Coach Wooden's unyielding concept of teamwork.

This ad was exciting because it said so much about teamwork. When a basketball player becomes a high scorer, we make him a hero. But could he have done it had he been facing the opposition alone? I doubt it. It took eight other hands to prepare the way for his successful baskets. It was a team effort all the way.

In Genesis 11:1–6 we can read a biblical account of team

effort: the building of the Tower of Babel. In this account we find some key concepts that can help you build an effective team (emphasis added).

> *Now the whole earth used the* same language *and the* same words. *And it came about as they journeyed east, that they found a plain in the land of Shinar and settled there. And* they said to one another, 'Come let us *make bricks and burn them thoroughly.' And they used brick for stone, and they used tar for mortar. And* they said, 'Come let us *build for ourselves a city, and a tower whose top will reach into heaven, and let us make for ourselves a name; lest we be scattered abroad over the face of the whole earth.' And the Lord came down to see the city and the tower which the sons of men had built. And the Lord said, 'Behold,* they are one people, *and* they all have the same language. *And this is what they began to do, and* now nothing which they purpose to do will be impossible for them.

I'll stop here long enough to point out that their efforts were for a wrong cause. But God saw here the incredible power of a group of people coming together. In verses one through six we see how to develop a successful team. There are only two essential ingredients: first, a common goal, and second, the ability to communicate that goal. 'Come let us build for ourselves . . . a tower' expresses both a desire to work together and a goal.

That phrase also expressed a motive—'for ourselves.' God didn't like what he saw because it was for an evil purpose; therefore, in verse seven we read that He decides to stop the team. Nevertheless, this account provides an excellent example of the importance of good teamwork.

It's easy to understand a sports team. Their goal is clear

because lights and numbers flash when they have reached it. You know they are a team because they wear identical uniforms. Their purpose and focus is clear because all eyes and attention are centered on the ball, and all motion swiftly moves toward it.

But there are other kinds of teams that are harder to analyze. Wearing the same uniform, whether it be a baseball cap or a clerical collar, working in the same office, or being paid by the same organization does not make a team. Uniformity is not the key to successful teamwork. The glue that holds a team together is unity of purpose.

I was taught something about teamwork early in high school when I played basketball. We had some talented guys, and all but two were big enough to stuff the ball in the basket. We were expected to be third or fourth in the state, but our team had a problem. There was a tremendous division between the juniors and seniors. On the starting lineup we had two juniors and three seniors and instead of throwing the ball to the most open man, we threw it to the fellow who was in our same grade. Our team was divided; we had fights in the locker room as well as on the court. Because of the lack of teamwork we did not achieve what we could have with all the talent represented on that team. Our goals were not shared.

WINNING TEAMS PLAY TO WIN

There are four major attributes which characterize a winning team. First of all, a winning team plays to win. Team members realize that wins and losses are often determined by attitude alone. The difference between playing to win and playing not to lose is often the difference between success and mediocrity.

Remember when the Olympics were held in Los Angeles a few years ago? There was an interesting article about the best of the best who competed in those games. The bottom line was that the difference between a gold-medal-winner and a silver-medal-winner is not skill, it's attitude.

When I moved to the West Coast, the only thing I left my heart tied to was Ohio State football. I continued to follow the team and catch Ohio State games on television whenever possible. Their trips to the Rose Bowl were especially exciting for me. But anybody who knows anything about college football knows that when any of the Big Ten comes to the West Coast to play, it's usually a West Coast victory. Though the eastern teams often had superior talent, they often did not take a risk. I think the Big Ten teams play not to lose—not a winning strategy.

WINNING TEAMS TAKE RISKS

The second characteristic of winning teams is that they are risk-takers. My philosophy of life is to throw the ball and go for it! Don't move three yards and huddle together and hope. Take a risk and let what happens happen. It will make the difference between a successful team and a mediocre one. On my office wall hangs a plaque that says, 'I don't have to survive.' I want my team to perform above the level of mediocrity. It's far better to try and fail than to fail to try.

The following poem appeared in Ann Landers' column. Each line contains a truth and a test:

To laugh is to risk appearing a fool.
To weep is to risk appearing sentimental.
To reach out for another is to risk involvement.
To expose feelings is to risk rejection.
To place your dreams before the crowd is to risk ridicule.
To love is to risk not being loved in return.
To go forward in the face of overwhelming odds is to risk failure.

But risks must be taken because the greatest hazard in life is to risk nothing.
The person who risks nothing does nothing, has nothing, is nothing.
He may avoid suffering and sorrow, but he cannot learn, feel, change, grow, or love.
Chained by his certitudes, he is a slave. Only a person who takes risks is free.

I love the story about the old farmer, ragged and barefooted, who sat on the steps of his tumbledown shack, chewing on a stem of grass. A passerby stopped and asked if he might have a drink of water. Wishing to be sociable, the stranger engaged the farmer in some conversation.

'How is your cotton crop this year?'

'Ain't got none,' replied the farmer.

'Didn't you plant any cotton?' asked the passerby.

'Nope,' said the farmer, ' 'fraid of boll weevils.'

'Well,' asked the newcomer, 'how's your corn doing?'

'Didn't plant none,' replied the farmer, ' 'fraid there wasn't going to be enough rain.'

'Well,' asked the inquisitive stranger, 'what did you plant?'

'Nothing,' said the farmer, 'I just played it safe.'

A lot of well-intentioned people live by the philosophy of this farmer, and never risk upsetting the apple cart. They would prefer to 'play it safe.' These people will never know the thrill of victory, because to win a victory one must risk a failure.

C.T. Studd made a great statement about risk-taking: 'Are gamblers for gold so many and gamblers for God so few?' This is the same great missionary who, when cautioned against returning to Africa because of the possibility of his martyrdom, replied, 'Praise God, I've just been looking for a chance to die for Jesus.' How can a guy like that fail? He has everything to win and nothing to lose.

WINNING TEAMS KEEP IMPROVING

The third characteristic of winning teams is they continue to try harder. They realize that when they're through improving, they're through. It's interesting to note that during the 1980s no team playing professional basketball, baseball, or football won a World Series or national championship for two years in a row. It's hard to stay on top. Once you get there, you tend to try to maintain the situation and hang onto the glory. This is a big mistake, because there's always someone below who is hungry for victory. They'll make the necessary sacrifices and take the risks to get the top. It's easier to win when you've got nothing to lose. It never pays to rest on your laurels; you must be willing to give them up if you want to keep winning.

Lon Woodrum, a dear friend of mine in his late 80s, continues to be an outstanding speaker, writer, and poet. He has set a goal for himself to read a book a day. I questioned him about that, thinking that at his age he should be taking life a little easier. He said, 'John, I have a tendency to get lazy. I want my 86-year-old mind to keep growing and learning. I want to die with a book in my hand.' Lon is going to live until he dies. I know a lot of people who are breathing, but who are already dead!

Art Linkletter put it this way.

I never want to be
What I want to be,
Because there's always something out there
Yet for me.
I get a kick out of living
In the here and now,

But I never want to feel
I know the best way how.
There's always one hill higher,
With a better view,
Something waiting to be learned
That I never knew.
Till my days are over,
Never fully fill my cup;
Let me go on
Growing up.

The highest reward for man's improvement is not what he gets for it; it's what he becomes as a result of it. Ask yourself why you are trying to improve. Is it to receive something for it? If so, that's the wrong motive. Try to improve because it makes you a better person.

WINNING TEAM MEMBERS CARE ABOUT EACH OTHER

The fourth characteristic of a winning team is that each member cares about the success of every other member. They enhance each other. Andrew Carnegie realized that before he could be successful, he needed to make his employees successful. He once said, 'It marks a big step in your development when you realize that other people can help you do a better job than you could do alone.' In the business world he was known for his outstanding development of people. Once he had thirty millionaires working for him. That's when a million dollars was a million dollars. Someone asked Carnegie how he induced that many millionaires to work for him. He replied that they weren't millionaires when he hired them; they made it while they were with him.

'How did you find such men?' people inquired.

Carnegie answered, 'It's like mining for gold. When you start, you may have to move tons of dirt to find a gold nugget . . . but when you start mining for gold, you overlook the dirt.'

Charles Brower said, 'Few people are successful unless a lot of other people want them to be.'

Do you recall when Edmond Hillary and his guide, Tenzing, made their historic climb of Mt. Everest? Coming down from the peak Hillary suddenly lost his footing. Tenzing held the line taut and kept them both from falling by digging his ax into the ice. Later Tenzing refused any special credit for saving Hillary's life; he considered it a routine part of the job. As he put it: 'Mountain climbers always help each other.'

If you're an old enough sports fan, you'll remember the days of the Boston Celtics and Red Auerbach. When he knew they had won the game, he always lit up his cigar. That was his trademark. Whenever he lit his cigar he sent out smoke signals to the other team—it's our win! When I can tell that my team, the Skyline staff, is working together on a winning project, I mentally light a cigar!

Just how do we develop a winning team? Three key areas together determine the success of the team: hiring, firing, and inspiring. Let's consider each one in turn.

HIRING RIGHT

The most important feature of any organization is the quality of the staff. Great athletic coaches know it takes more than inspiration to win; they must have talent. Therefore coaches take a major hand in the hiring. After all, staffs that just happen get happenstance results!

Most pastors of large churches tell me that staffing is their number-one frustration. A few years ago I was in a forum with pastors of some of the largest churches across the country. Our agenda included a variety of topics for discussion. The very first item was the question, 'What things frustrate you the most in ministry?' It is no exaggeration to say that 80 percent of the next two and one half days were spent discussing staff and staff-related problems. Rather than moving with their staffs toward mutual goals, many of these senior pastors were preoccupied with staff-related problems.

Perhaps you may be reading this and feeling that because you have a smaller church with only one other staff member, this section is not relevant to your situation. Don't make the mistake of thinking you can get by with inferior staff members because you are small. The opposite is true. In a business of 100 employees, if one is inferior, the loss is only 1 percent. But if a church has a payroll of two, and one is inferior, the loss is 50 percent.

Kurt Einstein in *Success* magazine said that hiring the wrong person is an extremely costly mistake. If that employee is fired within six months, it costs the company at least two years salary. You can see the damaging financial effect of not hiring correctly.

There are three hindrances to hiring outstanding staff, especially in Christian circles. *The first is in getting references from previous employers.* Honest references are almost always sabotaged by tolerance, because no one wants to blow the whistle on a poor worker. It is my Christian responsibility to be as objective as I can when giving a reference. To do otherwise would be deceitful. An employer does an employee no favors by recommending him for a job for which he is not suited.

Another hindrance to hiring top-quality staff is the fact that you are probably a small organization and *smaller organizations have less to offer than larger organizations.* But take my advice: Don't let the size of your church or organization determine the quality of your staff. Go for the winner and offer him or her your vision for the future. Don't offer your present situation unless you plan to camp there permanently. Hire a person who can grasp your dream. If they understand that you have the ability to make that dream a reality, they may be willing to leave a comfortable situation to move into an exciting one.

Rick Warren, pastor of the Saddleback Valley Community Church in Southern California, showed this type of entrepreneurial spirit when he responded to God's call to plant a church. As the assistant pastor of a church with more than 3,000 members he became the interim pastor when the senior pastor left. The congregation approached Rick with the possibility of taking the leadership of that church. He turned them down. Captured by his vision of planting a new church, he gave up what was in his hand.

The third hindrance in hiring outstanding staff is not knowing what qualities to look for in prospective staff members. Perhaps you know what job needs to be done but are not sure of the qualities a person needs to do the job best. Here's a hiring formula that will help you *RATE* an individual:

Relationship + **A**ttitude × **T**alent + **E**xpectation = **P**roduction

Let's consider the importance of each of these words.

RELATIONSHIPS

Kurt Einstein of *Success* magazine says of this important characteristic in a work-related situation: '87 percent of all people fail, not because of capability but because of personality.' People usually don't fail because they can't do the job, but because they can't get along with their coworkers.

If you work only for yourself, you may not need too many relational skills. However, if you work with people, you must have (or seek to develop) the ability to interact positively with them. Can you talk to people easily? Do you listen to them? Do you have a sense of humor and the ability to laugh at yourself without being sensitive and defensive? Do you enjoy people and working with them? Are you warm and approachable?

The leader of any group must exemplify certain relational essentials. First, he must respect his staff. They will not only absorb his respect, they will reflect it back to him. He also needs to provide open and honest two-way communication of all issues. Open communication establishes an atmosphere of trust which is essential if a group of people is to function as a team.

Some leaders have a great deal of insecurity and are, therefore, fearful of trusting those with whom they work. This type of leader looks at others with a suspicious mind, dwelling on possible underlying motives: Is a staff member out to take over their position? Determine if your fears are real or not. If they are not, dispel them and trust your people.

A leader will be hurt in one of two ways. He can be nontrusting and hold his people at a distance, never sharing or being open with them. Though his feelings may not be hurt because he won't allow anyone to get close to him, he will be hurt in other ways because no one will ever help him. His will be a lonely trip with no one to hug, love, or share the joy of ministry. On the other hand a leader can choose to be open and transparent and chance the possibility of being hurt by one who takes advantage of that trust. That is a risk worth taking. I would hate to think of the rich, deep friendships I would never have developed had I not risked trusting people.

ATTITUDES

This is the tiebreaker for hiring a team member. If I have interviewed two people who are on equal footing, their attitudes will always determine my decision. It doesn't matter how capable a person is, if he has a negative mind-set, he will be destructive to the team. A negative mind-set manifests itself in a critical spirit and nonsupport of other team members. If I ever sense that this is a problem with a staff member, that person will soon be looking for a new job. I can help a person improve his abilities, but only he can change his attitude.

TALENT

Businessman Jim Cafcart looks for three things in helping people become productive:

- *Talent.* What are they good at?
- *Interests.* What are they fascinated by?
- *Values.* What do they believe in?

Interests and values pretty much determine how and to what extent one uses his talents. It is a fact that we are not equal in dislikes. The Parable of the Talents in the Gospel of Matthew certainly underlines this truth. The ability of the employer to discern the gifts and abilities of potential employees is essential for the success of the team.

EXPECTATIONS

A leader needs to know what his staff members expect of him and the staff needs to know what's expected of them. Here are some of my expectations of staff members:

- *Growth.* I expect continual personal growth and departmental growth. Each staff member should be stretching to his or her utmost and the results should be visible. As this happens, each area of leadership will feel the positive effect.
- *Teamwork.* The whole is more important than its parts. Though each member of the team should be producing

results in his or her own department, this growth is subordinate to the health and growth of the body as a whole.

- *Leadership.* They must learn how to influence people and develop people. This generally happens as staff members stretch and grow themselves.

In *Leadership* magazine I once saw a cartoon of a pastor sitting at his desk talking on the telephone. The caption read, 'Well then, will you take two secretaries and one choir director for one assistant pastor and a singles man?' This leads me to the next aspect of staffing, firing staff members.

FIRING A WORKER

Being released from one's responsibilities can have a devastating effect on a person. It is not an action to be taken on a whim but only after careful, prayerful consideration. The following questions can help in making the decision. First, *has the church outgrown the pastor or has the pastor outgrown the church?* It is not uncommon for either to happen. I know what it is like to realize that the challenge is gone and it is time to move on to other possibilities. I have also known churches to forge ahead while the pastor sat wringing his hands, wondering what to do with a situation beyond his control.

Before letting a staff member go, another question to ask is, *who believes this person needs to be replaced?* If I, as the pastor or leader, am the only one who believes a change needs to be made, then I should tread carefully. Perhaps there is a personality conflict that needs attention and resolution. When it's time for a change to be made, more than one person should be sensing that need. Other staff, members of the church board, other key associations, and even the staff member in question, will feel the need for this change. To guard against personal prejudices and unfair evaluations I yearly ask the church board to participate in an anonymous review of all the staff members. This provides a wide spectrum of the effectiveness of each staff member.

The third question to be answered: *What is the basis for the dismissal?* What grounds are serious enough to let someone go? By far the most important thing to review is moral integrity. When there is a basic character problem—lying, moral compromise, deceitfulness—a quick removal is in order. I am convinced that when a person has lost trust, his or her ministry and service is over within the Christian community. I certainly believe in forgiveness, rehabilitation, and restoration into fellowship, but not restoration to a position.

Other possible grounds for dismissal would include serious relational problems. If a person is chronically at odds with other members of the team, there is need for removal. Or when a staff member shows an obvious negative attitude toward the church or organization, it's time to let that person go. Negative thinking can spread like a cancer. Finally, if a staff member reveals a serious lack of ability that cannot be corrected, he or she should be released.

As the pastor, it is my responsibility to have the best person possible in each position. The church board holds me accountable for this. If I neglect to do this, then I am not keeping the church's highest potential as a priority. The board holds me accountable just as it does my staff. My own job is on the line if there is someone else who can better lead and serve.

If firing is necessary, just how do we make the transition a little smoother? Assume we have worked through the tough questions. We have tried to balance mercy with stewardship and forgiveness with accountability. The decision becomes clear; the person must be removed from ministry or work responsibility. Then what?

First of all, we do it personally. A letter or memo is too cruel and impersonal, allowing feelings of desertion to be magnified and bitterness to be cultivated. A personal encounter allows for tears, anger, and other emotions that accompany such a blow. It also gives opportunity for the person to raise questions. Obviously, the news should be delivered promptly and directly before some grapevine has a chance to reach the worker being terminated.

Do it gently. There is no need to write a twelve-page list of the person's shortcomings. In fact, that person should have had that twelve-page list several weeks prior and been given a probation period to work on his or her problems. When the dismissal is given the person may become angry or defensive and that is the time for a 'soft answer.' Gentleness, however, does not require dishonesty. If the person is ill-equipped for ministry or leadership, it is more harmful to pretend otherwise. Remember that *how* and *when* these messages are given can soften the blow.

Do it without bitterness or malice. Those who deliver the message of dismissal must be under the Holy Spirit's control. Emotional outbursts or attacks on the person's character are counterproductive to the goal of the person's growth and eventual healing.

Close off responsibilities quickly. The longer a lame duck has to drag on in the job, the lower his or her productivity and the more he depresses the zeal of others. A drawn-out firing process opens the door to lobbying for a reversal and excuses for poor performance. Also, it is possible for the leader to lose his objectivity when he starts getting pressure from pocket groups. He will then begin second-guessing his decision to fire.

Be discriminating. 'All the facts' do not need to be divulged to those whose interest is to slander or gossip. The details of a moral failure may serve to titillate warped appetites for scandal more than to promote healing in the body of Christ. Choose your words cautiously. Do not make matters worse than they are and needlessly jeopardize the person's future.

Anticipate the person's reactions and be prepared with your answers. Also consider the effect on those who are close to the person. How might you help those who may be hurt or offended in this change. Do you need to be involved in some emotional healing? Finally, consider where that person might go if possible, and try to help them in that transition.

INSPIRING YOUR PEOPLE

Harold S. Geneen, former Director, President and CEO of IT and T said, 'The essence of leadership is the ability to inspire others to work together as a team—to stretch for a common objective.'

The leader needs to pave the way for those following by exemplifying a positive, hopeful attitude. A leader motivates his team toward the end result by continually reminding team members of the overall vision and the importance of accomplishing the goal. When the leader communicates clear expectations, he also gives his people a freedom to create. Most importantly, a leader expresses the most profound inspiration when he believes in his people—when they feel and know that he thinks they are the best and his total confidence is in them.

E.E. Kenyon of *American Weekly* shared this story of a surefire way to inspire the team (though not one I would recommend). The normally sourfaced boss smiled genially at the salesmen he had called together for a meeting. 'Well, gentlemen,' he said, 'I've called you in to announce a big sales contest which I am starting immediately and which I will personally supervise.'

There was an excited murmur from the assembled salesmen, and an eager voice from the rear called out: 'What does the winner get, Mr. Smithson?'

'He gets,' announced the boss, 'to keep his job.'

PUT IT TO WORK

PEOPLE PRINCIPLES

- ✦ Uniformity is not the key to successful teamwork. The glue that holds a team together is unity of purpose.
- ✦ Characteristics of winning teams:

  They play to win.

  They take risks.

  They keep improving.

  They care about each other.
- ✦ People who prefer to 'play it safe' will never know the thrill of victory. To win a victory, one must risk failure.
- ✦ The highest reward for man's improvement is not what he gets for it, it's what he becomes as a result of it.
- ✦ It marks a big step in your development when you realize that other people can help you do a better job than you could do alone.
- ✦ Relationships + Attitude × Talent + Expectation = Production
- ✦ The essence of leadership is the ability to inspire others to work together as a team—to stretch for a common objective.

PUTTING THE PRINCIPLES TO WORK:

I will apply the principles from this chapter to my relationships with people in the following ways:

1.

2.

3.

FURTHER STUDY:

People Power, John R. Noe

You and Your Network, Fred Smith